Central Issues in Contemporary Economic Theory and Policy

General Editor: **Gustavo Piga**, *Managing Editor, Rivista di Politica Economica, Rome, Italy*

Published titles include:

Mario Baldassarri, John McCallum and Robert A. Mundell (*editors*)
DEBT, DEFICIT AND ECONOMIC PERFORMANCE

Mario Baldassarri (*editor*)
HOW TO REDUCE UNEMPLOYMENT IN EUROPE

Mario Baldassarri (*editor*)
THE NEW WELFARE
Unemployment and Social Security in Europe

Mario Baldassarri, Michele Bagella and Luigi Paganetto (*editors*)
FINANCIAL MARKETS
Imperfect Information and Risk Management

Mario Baldassarri and Bruno Chiarini (*editors*)
STUDIES IN LABOUR MARKETS AND INDUSTRIAL RELATIONS

Mario Baldassarri and Pierluigi Ciocca (*editors*)
ROOTS OF THE ITALIAN SCHOOL OF ECONOMICS AND FINANCE
From Ferrara (1857) to Einaudi (1944) (three volumes)

Mario Baldassarri, Cesare Imbriani and Dominick Salvatore (*editors*)
THE INTERNATIONAL SYSTEM BETWEEN NEW INTEGRATION AND NEO-PROTECTIONISM

Mario Baldassarri and Luca Lambertini (*editors*)
ANTITRUST, REGULATION AND COMPETITION

Mario Baldassarri, Luigi Paganetto and Edmund S. Phelps (*editors*)
EQUITY, EFFICIENCY AND GROWTH
The Future of the Welfare State

Mario Baldassarri, Luigi Paganetto and Edmund S. Phelps (*editors*)
THE 1990s SLUMP
Causes and Cures

Mario Baldassarri, Luigi Paganetto and Edmund S. Phelps (*editors*)
INTERNATIONAL DIFFERENCES IN GROWTH RATES
Market Globalization and Economic Areas

Geoffrey Brennan (*editor*)
COERCIVE POWER AND ITS ALLOCATION IN THE EMERGENT EUROPE

Laura Castellucci and Anil Markandya
ENVIRONMENTAL TAXES AND FISCAL REFORM

Bruno Chiarini and Paolo Malanima
FROM MALTHUS' STAGNATION TO SUSTAINED GROWTH

Guido Cozzi and Roberto Cellini (*editors*)
INTELLECTUAL PROPERTY, COMPETITION, AND GROWTH

Debora Di Gioacchino, Sergio Ginebri and Laura Sabani (*editors*)
THE ROLE OF ORGANIZED INTEREST GROUPS IN POLICY MAKING

Luca Lambertini (*editor*)
FIRMS' OBJECTIVES AND INTERNAL ORGANISATION IN A GLOBAL ECONOMY
Positive and Normative Analysis

Riccardo Leoni and Giuseppe Usai (*editors*)
ORGANIZATIONS TODAY

Marco Malgarini and Gustavo Piga (*editors*)
CAPITAL ACCUMULATION, PRODUCTIVITY AND GROWTH
Monitoring Italy 2005

Gustavo Piga and Khi V. Thai
THE ECONOMICS OF PUBLIC PROCUREMENT

Central Issues in Contemporary Economic Theory and Policy
Series Standing Order ISBN 978–0–333–71464–5
(*outside North America only*)

You can receive future titles in this series as they are published by placing a standing order. Please contact your bookseller or, in case of difficulty, write to us at the address below with your name and address, the title of the series and the ISBN quoted above.

Customer Services Department, Macmillan Distribution Ltd, Houndmills, Basingstoke, Hampshire RG21 6XS, England

From Malthus' Stagnation to Sustained Growth

Social, Demographic and Economic Factors

Edited by

Bruno Chiarini
University of Napoli 'Parthenope', Italy

and

Paolo Malanima
Institute of Studies on Mediterranean Societies, National Research Council (ISSM-CNR), Naples, Italy

palgrave
macmillan

Softcover reprint of the hardcover 1st edition 2013 978-0-230-39248-9

First published 2013 by
PALGRAVE MACMILLAN

Palgrave Macmillan in the UK is an imprint of Macmillan Publishers Limited, registered in England, company number 785998, of Houndmills, Basingstoke, Hampshire RG21 6XS.

Palgrave Macmillan in the US is a division of St Martin's Press LLC, 175 Fifth Avenue, New York, NY 10010.

Palgrave Macmillan is the global academic imprint of the above companies and has companies and representatives throughout the world.

Palgrave® and Macmillan® are registered trademarks in the United States, the United Kingdom, Europe and other countries.

ISBN 978-1-349-35197-8 ISBN 978-0-230-39249-6 (eBook)
DOI 10.1057/9780230392496

This book is printed on paper suitable for recycling and made from fully managed and sustained forest sources. Logging, pulping and manufacturing processes are expected to conform to the environmental regulations of the country of origin.

A catalogue record for this book is available from the British Library.

Library of Congress Cataloging-in-Publication Data

From Malthus' stagnation to sustained growth : social, demographic and economic factors / edited by Bruno Chiarini, Paolo Malanima.
p. cm.

1. Malthusianism. 2. Population. 3. Economic development. 4. Economics.
I. Chiarini, Bruno. II. Malanima, Paolo.

HB863.F76 2012
304.6—dc23 2012022994

10 9 8 7 6 5 4 3 2 1
22 21 20 19 18 17 16 15 14 13

Contents*

*These chapters were originally published as articles in the journal *Rivista di Politica Economica* and have been reproduced exactly and in their entirety, including any minor typographic errors or omissions which may have been present in the original.

Demographic Dynamics and Economic Changes in Europe before the 19th Century: Interpretative Schemes

Bruno Chiarini
University of Naples "Parthenope"

Paolo Malanima[*]
ISSM-CNR, Naples

The growing interest in economic growth in the very long run has promoted a rich literature and theoretical models which try to explain pre-industrial stagnation and modern economic growth in a unified framework. The transition from Malthusian stagnation to modern growth has also been the subject of intense research. According to Malthus, preventive-positive checks lead the size of the population to a self-equilibrating pattern. Discoveries and innovations, introducing a break to this framework without changing the functioning of the mechanism, actually do not affect the fate of population. Any technological improvement can only produce a temporary rise in living standards.

These predictions are consistent with the evolution of population, technology and output *per capita* for most of human history in Europe. For thousand of years, the standard of living was roughly constant and did not differ greatly across countries. Angus Maddison estimates that the growth rate of GDP *per capita* in Europe between 500 and 1500 was zero. Furthermore, Ronald D. Lee reports that the real wage in England was roughly the same in 1800 as it had been in 1300. A Mathusian approach to long-term economic history has been recently put forward by Gregory Clark in his debated book *A Farewell to Alms*. A similar picture may be drawn using the data reconstruction of Paolo Malanima for Italy. The phenomenon of sustained growth in living standards is only a few centuries old. Similarly, the pattern of population growth is consistent with the predictions of the Malthusian model. Fluctuations in population and wages also bear out the

* *<chiarini@uniparthenope.it>*; *<paolo.malanima@issm.cnr.it>*.

predictions of the Malthusian model. Several studies on the pre-industrial epoch and for a wide range of countries report positive income elasticities of fertility and negative income elasticities of mortality and a strong positive correlation between real wages and marriage rates. Negative shocks to population, such as the Black Death, were reflected in higher real wages and faster population growth. Finally, the prediction of the Malthusian model that differences in technology should be reflected in population density, but not in standards of living, is also borne out.

However, the empirical implications of the Malthusian model are more complex than simply a tendency of real wage to revert to its long-run equilibrium level together with very slow population growth. Many factors have impinged on the fertility and mortality rates. A most striking feature of the preindustrial epoch is the simultaneous effect of contradictory forces. Pushing simultaneously towards growth and poverty, these forces have often been intertwined, leading, from time to time, to emphasize some implications instead of others.

Thus, studying hypotheses and the observed patterns in pre-industrial populations is still important for several reasons. Firstly, it is still not clear whether the Malthusian model is a good tool to understand demographic dynamics and economic changes in Europe before the 19th century. Secondly, even if we admit that there is some consensus in the theoretical and empirical literature (both for historians and economists) in defining the pre-industrial period as "Malthusian", most of the models and schemes make an arbitrary selection of which elements of the Malthusian model are considered relevant for the analysis.

A reconstruction of the European economy from the Middle Age to the modern growth must inevitably consider the many contradictory forces that have characterized the evolution of the economy. In this volume we present just some of the elements and ideas to enrich the discussion:

Mortality and fertility: In this paper Bruno Chiarini and Massimo Giannini stress as large drops in population were caused by the Black Death which, along with wars (armies raised death rates through the epidemics that followed in their wake), the rise of urbanization (cities were death traps) and the development of trade (another vehicle to spread epidemics) created a new mortality regime with higher death rates, but also with a change in the birth schedules. These shocks were so large that population growth was curbed for centuries and the implication for the wage-population relationship is not so intuitive as the Malthus one.

Demographic-technology relationship: Guido Alfani emphasizes as in macro-demographic theoretical framework used for interpreting the preindustrial epoch, there are two crucial determinant: the Malthusian one, that population equilibrates with resources at some level with the intermediation of technology and a conventional standard of living; and the Boserupian one, that technological change is itself spurred by increases in population. Obviously, the implication may be somewhat different.

Finite natural resources: a paper of Giovanni Scarano deals with the relation between economic growth and the earth's carrying capacity for mankind. Economists have almost totally neglected the relation between population and economic growth in a truly Malthusian perspective, that is, focusing on the problem of the population pressure on finite natural resources. Many endogenous growth models have dealt with human capital accumulation, but this is a topic which, even though partially related to such demographic dynamics as that of fertility, concerns above all the supply side of the models and the technical change it entails.

Poverty trap and consumption behaviour: Edgardo Bucciarelli and Gianfranco Giulioni focus on building a single economic model which could explain the dynamics both of income per worker and of population in order to interpret the transition from the Malthusian stagnation to sustained modern growth. The paper relies on the recent idea put forward by Charles Karelis in his book, *The Persistence of Poverty*, according to which the marginal utility is increasing at low levels of consumption. Karelis' main result is that under increasing marginal utility of consumption, the choice of making no effort to improve the standard of living is rational. This provides a potential explanation for poverty traps. By using insights from the solution of the agents' utility maximization problem, the paper shows how the model can generate different types of dynamics: the Malthusian trap, a high standard of living situation where the growth rate of income per worker fades out, and one where the latter variable increases.

The role of energy: an element that is central to the analysis of the preindustrial period and in the transition is the role of the energy. Silvana Bartoletto shows that the introduction of new energy carriers and engines, able to convert energy into mechanical work, are the main factors at the origin of the sudden surge in growth rates of output *per capita*. In a further paper, Paolo Malanima explains the transition to modern growth as a discontinuity founded on the increase in productive capacity, due to the introduction of new energy carriers and engines able to transform energy into mechanical work. This change, on the other hand, will be correlated to the pressure of population on the agrarian system and the ensuing increase in prices both of the traditional energy sources and of labour.

The importance of the historian report: written documents from the past may seem valuable to the economic historian. To this end, a paper of Patrice Bouche tries to summarise a selection of intellectual responses formulated at the time of the unfolding in Britain of what we now call the Post-Malthusian period of rapid population increase. By analysing, as it were, some insiders' views of the said stage of demographic evolution, the aim is to provide researchers in economic history with a different vantage point, a decentralised point of view from which to look at the range of possible causes and consequences.

Oded Galor stresses as the inconsistency of the predominant theories of economic growth with some of the most fundamental characteristics of the growth process, and their limited ability to shed light on the origins of the vast global disparity in living standards, have led to the development of a unified theory of economic growth that captures the growth process in its entirety. The Unified Growth Theory explores the fundamental factors that have contributed to the remarkable transition from stagnation to growth and examines their significance for the understanding of the contemporary growth process of developed and less developed economies. The approach unveils the factors that have generated the Malthusian trap and uncovers the forces that triggered the take-off from stagnation to growth. Further, Unified Growth Theory sheds new light on the origins of the perplexing divergence in income *per capita* across developed and less developed regions in the past two centuries.

Unified Growth Theory and Comparative Development

Oded Galor*
Brown University, Providence

Unified Growth Theory explores the fundamental factors that have contributed to the remarkable transition from stagnation to growth and examines their significance for the understanding of the contemporary growth process of developed and less developed economies. Moreover, it sheds light on the role of historical and pre-historical characteristics in the divergence of income per capita *across regions of the world in the past two centuries.*
[JEL Classification: O10, J10].

Keywords: united growth theory, demographic transition, comparative development, malthusian epoch, genetic diversity.

* <*Oded_Galor@brown.edu*>.

1. Introduction

The transition from an epoch of stagnation to an era of sustained economic growth has marked the onset of one of the most remarkable transformations in the course of human history. While living standards in the world economy stagnated during the millennia preceding the Industrial Revolution, income *per capita* has undergone an unprecedented tenfold increase over the past two centuries, profoundly altering the level and distribution of education, health and wealth across the globe. The rise in the standard of living has not been universally shared among individuals and societies. Variation in the timing of the take-off from stagnation to growth has led to a vast worldwide divergence in income *per capita.* Inequality, which had been modest until the nineteenth century, has widened considerably, and the *ratio* of income *per capita* between the richest and the poorest regions of the world has been magnified from a moderate 3:1 *ratio* in 1820 to a staggering 18:1 *ratio* in 2000 (Graph 1).

An equally striking development has emerged in the world distribution of population. The decline in population growth in Europe and North America toward the end of the nineteenth century and the long delay in the onset of a corresponding demographic transition in less developed regions, well into the second half of the twentieth century, have generated significant bifurcation in the global distribution of population. The share of world population that resides in the prosperous region of Europe has declined by nearly one-half over the past century, whereas the fraction of the human population that lives in the impoverished regions of Africa and Latin America has doubled.

Throughout most of human existence, the process of development was marked by Malthusian stagnation: resources generated by technological progress and land expansion were channeled primarily toward an increase in the size of the population, providing only a glacial contribution to the level of income *per capita* in the long run. While cross-country variations in technology and land productivity were reflected in differing population densities, their effect on variation in living standards was merely transitory.

In contrast, over the past two centuries, various regions of the world have departed from the Malthusian trap and have witnessed a considerable increase in growth rates of income *per capita*. The decline in population growth over the course of the demographic transition has liberated productivity gains from the counterbalancing effect of population growth and enabled technological progress and human capital formation to pave the way for the emergence of an era of sustained economic growth.

GRAPH 1

THE EVOLUTION OF REGIONAL INCOME *PER CAPITA* OVER THE PAST TWO THOUSAND YEARS

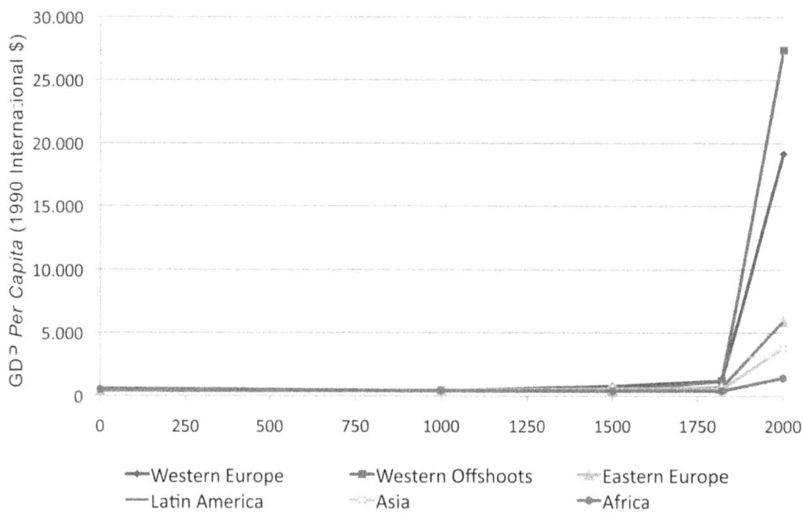

Source: MADDISON A. (2001).

The transition from an epoch of Malthusian stagnation to an era of sustained economic growth and the corresponding divergence in income *per capita* across the globe have been the center of intensive research during the past decade. The inconsistency of the predominant theories of economic growth with some of the most fundamental characteristics of the growth process and their limited ability to shed light on the origins of the vast global disparity in living standards have led to the development of a unified theory of economic growth that captures the growth process in its entirety.

Unified Growth Theory explores the fundamental factors that have contributed to the remarkable transition from stagnation to growth and examines their significance for the understanding of the contemporary growth process of developed and less developed economies. First, it unveils the factors that have generated the Malthusian trap. What accounts for the epoch of stagnation that has characterized most of human history? Why did episodes of technological progress in the pre-industrial era fail to generate sustained economic growth? Why has population growth counterbalanced the expansion of resources *per capita* that could have been generated by technological progress?

Moreover, the theory uncovers the forces that triggered the take-off from stagnation to growth. What is the origin of the sudden spurt in the growth rates of income *per capita* and population during the course of industrialization? What was the source of the striking reversal in the positive relationship between income *per capita* and population growth that existed throughout most of human history? Would the transition to the modern state of sustained economic growth have been feasible without the decline in population growth? What are the hurdles faced by less developed economies in their attempts to transition to a sustained-growth regime?

Further, Unified Growth Theory sheds new light on the origins of the perplexing divergence in income *per capita* across developed and less developed regions in the past two centuries. What accounts for the sudden take-off from stagnation to growth among some countries in the world and the persistent stagnation in others? Why has the positive link between income *per capita* and population growth reversed its course in some economies but not in others? Has the transition to a state of sustained economic growth in advanced economies adversely affected the process of development in poorer ones? Have variations in prehistorical biogeographical factors had a persistent effect on the composition of human capital and economic development across the world?

2. - Toward a Unified Theory of Economic Growth

Nonunified theories of economic growth have been instrumental in advancing the understanding of the role that technological progress and the accumulation of factors of production have played in the modern era of economic growth. Nevertheless, they are inconsistent with the qualitative aspects of the growth process over most of human existence and they fail to identify the forces that triggered the take-off from stagnation to sustained economic growth-insights that are instrumental for understanding the contemporary growth process and the origins of the great divergence in income *per capita* over the past two centuries.

The preoccupation of non-unified theories of economic growth with the growth process of developed economies in the past century and of less developed economies in the past few decades has become harder to justify in light of the disparity between the main features of the modern growth era and those that have characterized the growth process over most of human existence. It has become evident that as long as growth theory rests on distinct and disjoint theories to characterize the process of development during the Malthusian Epoch and the Modern Growth Regime, the understanding of the contemporary growth process will be limited and distorted.[1] «It is as though an artist were to gather the hands, feet, head and other members for his images from diverse models, each part perfectly drawn, but not related to a single body, and since they in no way match each other, the result would be monster rather than man». (Copernicus, Quoted by Kuhn, 1957).

The advancement of Unified Growth Theory has been fueled by the conviction that the understanding of global variation in economic development would be fragile and incomplete unless the prevailing theory of economic growth reflects the principal driving forces behind the entire process of development and captures the central role that historical factors have played in bringing about the current disparities in living standards.[2] Moreover, it has been fostered by the realization that a comprehensive understanding of the hurdles faced by less developed economies would remain obscure unless the factors that facilitated the transition of the currently developed economies from stagnation to growth could be identified and modified to account for the differences in the growth structure of less developed economies in an interdependent world.

Unified Growth Theory provides a fundamental framework of analysis for the evolution of individuals, societies, and economies over the *entire* course of human history. The theory – developed by Galor (2005; 2010) based on Galor and Weil (1999; 2000), Galor and Moav (2002) and Galor and Mountford (2008) – captures in a *single* analytical framework the main characteristics of the process of development: *(i)* the epoch of Malthusian stagnation that characterized most of human history, *(ii)* the escape from the Malthusian trap and the associated spike in the

1. The evolution of theories in older scientific disciplines suggests that theories founded on the basis of a subset of the existing observations may be attractive in the short run but are nonrobust and non-durable in the long run. For instance, classical thermodynamics, which lacked micro-foundations, was ultimately superseded by the micro-based Statistical Mechanics. Moreover, attempts to develop unified theories in physics have been based on the conviction that all physical phenomena should eventually be explainable by some underlying unity. In particular, Unified Field Theory proposes to unify by a set of general laws the four distinct forces that are known to control all observed interactions in matter: electromagnetism, gravitation, the weak force, and the strong force.

2. Clearly, the understanding of the contemporary world would be limited and incomplete in the absence of a historical perspective. However, the intensity of recent explorations of the interaction between economic development and economic history could be attributed to increasing frustration with the failure of the ahistorical branch of growth theory to capture some of the most fundamental aspects of the growth process.

growth rates of income *per capita* and population, *(iii)* the emergence of human capital formation in the process of development, *(iv)* the trigger for the onset of the demographic transition, *(v)* the emergence of the contemporary era of sustained economic growth, and *(vi)* the divergence in income *per capita* across countries.[3]

The theory unveils the principal economic forces that have generated the remarkable transition from stagnation to growth and underlines their significance for understanding the contemporary growth process of both developed and less developed economies. Moreover, it sheds light on the role of historical and prehistorical characteristics in the divergence of income *per capita* across regions of the world in the past two centuries.

Unified Growth Theory suggests that the transition from stagnation to growth has been an inevitable by-product of the process of development. It argues that the inherent Malthusian interaction between the rate of technological progress and the size and composition of the population accelerated the pace of technological progress and ultimately raised the importance of education in coping with the rapidly changing technological environment.[4]

The rise in industrial demand for education brought about significant reductions in fertility rates. It enabled economies to divert a larger share of the fruits of factor accumulation and technological progress to the enhancement of human capital formation and income *per capita*, paving the way for the emergence of sustained economic growth.

The theory further explores the dynamic interaction between human evolution and the process of economic development and advances the hypothesis that the

3. The term "Unified Growth Theory" was coined by GALOR O. (2005) to categorize theories of economic growth that capture the entire growth process within a single unified framework of analysis. Some of the six salient characteristics of this process have been explored in the literature focusing on the transition from stagnation to growth (*e.g.*, LUCAS R.E. (2002); HANSEN G.D. and PRESCOTT E.C. (2002); JONES C.I. (2001); DOEPKE M. (2004); FERNÁNDEZ-VILLAVERDE J. (2001); LAGERLÖF N.P. (2003); O'ROURKE K.M. *et* AL. (2008); VOIGTLÄNDER N. and VOTH H.J.(2006); BROADBERRY G. (2007); ASHRAF Q. and GALOR O. (2007); STRULIK M. and WEISDORF J.L. (2008)). However, the only unified theory of economic growth that captures the endogenous evolution of population, technology, human capital, and income *per capita* over the entire course of economic development and generates both a spontaneous transition from Malthusian stagnation to sustained growth and a great divergence is the one developed by GALOR O. (2005; 2010).

4. The increased demand for human capital has not necessarily resulted in an increase in the rate of return to human capital due to institutional changes (*e.g.*, the provision of public education) that lowered the cost of investment in human capital and facilitated a massive increase in the supply of education.

forces of natural selection played a significant role in the evolution of the world economy from stagnation to growth. The Malthusian pressures have acted as the key determinant of population size and conceivably, via natural selection, have shaped the composition of the population as well. Lineages of individuals whose traits were complementary to the economic environment generated higher levels of income, and thus a larger number of surviving offspring, and the gradual increase in the representation of their traits in the population contributed to the process of development and the take-off from stagnation to growth.

2.1 *Origins of Global Disparity in Living Standards*

Unified Growth Theory sheds light on the notable divergence in income *per capita* across the globe during the past two centuries. The theory advances the understanding of three fundamental aspects of comparative economic development. First, it identifies the factors that have governed the transition from stagnation to growth and have thus contributed to the observed worldwide differences in economic development. Second, it highlights the persistent effects that variations in historical and prehistorical conditions have had on the composition of human capital and economic development across countries. Finally, it uncovers the forces that have sparked the emergence of convergence clubs and it explores the characteristics that have determined the association of different economies with each club.

2.2 *Catalysts for the Engine of the Transition from Stagnation to Growth*

The first layer of Unified Growth Theory explores the underlying forces that have determined the timing and pace of the transition from an epoch of Malthusian stagnation to an era of sustained economic growth and have thus contributed to the disparity in economic development across countries. Country-specific characteristics that have affected the intensity of the pivotal interaction between the rate of technological progress and the size and composition of the population have generated variations in the transition from stagnation to growth and contributed to the gap in income *per capita* across countries.

Variation in rates of technological progress has reinforced the differential pace of the emergence of demand for human capital, the onset of the demographic transition, and the shift from stagnation to growth, and has thus contributed to the divergence in income *per capita* in the past two centuries. In particular, worldwide variation in the pace of technological progress has been triggered by cross-country differences in: *(a)* the stock of knowledge and its rate of creation and diffusion among members of society; *(b)* the level of protection of intellectual property rights, its positive effect on the incentive to innovate and its adverse effect on the proliferation of existing knowledge; *(c)* financial constraints and the level of competitiveness of the innovation sector; *(d)* the composition of cultural and religious attributes and their effect on knowledge creation and diffusion; *(e)* the composition of interest groups in society and their incentives to block or promote technological innovations; *(f)* the level of human diversity and the degree to which it complements the implementation and advancement of new technological paradigms; *(g)* the propensity to trade and its effect on technological diffusion; and *(h)* the abundance of natural resources essential for an imminent technological paradigm.

Once the technologically-driven demand for human capital emerged in the second phase of industrialization, the prevalence of characteristics conducive to human capital formation has determined the swiftness of its accumulation, the timing of the demographic transition, the pace of the transition from stagnation to growth, and the observed distribution of income in the world economy. Thus, variations in country-specific characteristics that have contributed to human capital formation have differentially affected the timing and pace of the transition from agriculture to industry and comparative economic development as a whole.

In particular, global variation in human capital formation has been influenced by cross-country differences in *(a)* the prevalence of human capital-promoting institutions or policies (*e.g.*, the availability, accessibility, and quality of public education); *(b)* the ability of individuals to finance the cost of education as well as the foregone earnings associated with schooling; *(c)* the impact of the level of inequality and of the degree of credit market imperfections on the extent of under-investment in education; *(d)* the stock of knowledge in society and its effect on the productivity of investment of human capital; *(e)* the composition of cultural and religious groups in a society and their effects on the incentives of individuals to invest in human capital; *(f)* the impact of geographical attributes on health and thus human capital formation; *(g)* the propensity to trade and the patterns of comparative advantage with respect to the production of skill-intensive goods; and *(h)* preferences for educated offspring that may reflect cultural attributes, the composition of religious groups, and social status associated with education.

2.3 *Persistence of Prehistorical Biogeographical Conditions*

In its second layer, Unified Growth Theory highlights the direct persistent effect that deep-rooted factors, determined as early as tens of thousands years ago, have had on the course of comparative economic development from the dawn of human civilization to the modern era.

The theory captures the thesis that part of the differences in the process of development across the globe can be traced to biogeographical factors that led to regional variation in the timing of the Neolithic Revolution (Diamond, 1997). According to this thesis, favorable biogeographical endowments that contributed to the emergence of agriculture gave some societies the early advantage of operating a superior production technology and generating resource surpluses. They permitted the establishment of a non-food-producing class, whose members were crucial for the development of written language and science and for the formation of cities, technology-based military powers, and nation states. The early dominance of these societies persisted throughout history, being further sustained by geopolitical and historical processes, such as colonization. The significance of the timing of agricultural transitions for *precolonial* economic development has been confirmed empirically, although evidence appears to suggest that over the past five hundred years the initial dominance brought about by an earlier transition to agriculture has dissipated.

Moreover, the theory is consistent with the thesis that the exodus of modern humans from Africa, nearly a hundred thousand years ago, appears central to understanding comparative economic development across the globe (Ashraf and Galor, 2009). In the course of the exodus of *Homo sapiens* out of Africa, variation in migratory distance from the cradle of humankind to settlements across the globe affected the level of genetic diversity and has had a long-lasting, hump-shaped effect on the pattern of comparative economic development that cannot be captured by contemporary geographical, institutional, and cultural factors. While the intermediate level of genetic diversity prevalent among Asian and European populations has been conducive to development, the high degree of diversity among African populations and the low degree among Native American populations have acted as detrimental forces in the development of these regions.

2.4 *Convergence Clubs*

In its third layer, Unified Growth Theory advances the understanding of the forces that have contributed to the existence of multiple growth regimes and the emergence of convergence clubs (*i.e.*, groups of countries among which the disparity in income *per capita* tends to narrow over time). The theory attributes these phenomena to variation in the position of economies across the distinct phases of development. It suggests that the differential timing of take-offs from stagnation to growth has segmented economies into three fundamental growth regimes: slowly growing economies in the vicinity of a Malthusian steady state, fast growing countries in a sustained-growth regime, and a third group of economies in transition from one regime to the other. Moreover, it suggests that the presence of multiple convergence clubs may reflect a temporary state as endogenous forces may ultimately permit members of the Malthusian club to shift their positions and join the members of the sustained-growth club.

3. - Looming Challenges

Unified Growth Theory has planted the seeds for a renaissance in the fields of economic growth and economic history. It has generated novel testable predictions that will enable researchers to revisit their interpretations of existing evidence while guiding them in their important mission of data collection. Recent research on the validity of the Malthusian hypothesis, the sources of the demographic transition, and the role of human capital in the advancement of industrialization is an early indication of the potential impact of Unified Growth Theory on the field of economic history.

Further, Unified Growth Theory suggests that the exploration of the role of cultural, institutional, and geographical factors in the differential pace of the transition from stagnation to growth and the emergence of a great disparity in economic development across the globe could generate significant insights about the growth process and comparative economic development. In particular, the hypothesis that the pace of the transition from stagnation to growth has been influenced by cultural and institutional factors, which may have evolved in response to the economic incentives that the process of development has generated, could benefit from further exploration. Have the institutional and cultural factors that have been associated empirically with the disparity in economic development been the oil that lubrificated the wheels of development once economies emerged from the Malthusian trap, or were they the initial trigger that set those wheels in motion?

Finally, the most promising and challenging future research in the field of economic growth in the next decades will be: *(i)* the examination of the role of historical and prehistorical factors in the prevailing disparity across the globe, and *(ii)* the analysis of the interaction between human evolution and the process of economic development. The exploration of these vast and largely uncharted territories may revolutionize the understanding of the process of economic development and the persistent effect that deep-rooted factors have had on the composition of human capital and economic outcomes across the globe, fostering the design of policies that could promote economic growth and poverty alleviation.

BIBLIOGRAPHY

ASHRAF Q. - GALOR O., «Cultural Assimilation, Cultural Discussion, and the Origin of the Wealth of Nations», *Working Paper*, Brown University, 2007.

-.-,-.-,. «The Out-of-Africa Hypothesis, Human Genetic Diversity, and Comparative Economic Development», *Working Paper*, Brown University, 2009.

BROADBERRY S., «Recent Developments in the Theory of Very Long Run Growth: A Historical Appraisal», *The Warwick Economics Research Paper Series*, no. 818, 2007.

DIAMOND J., *Guns, Germs and Steel: The Fates of Human Societies*, W.W. Norton & Co., New York, NY, 1997.

DOEPKE M., «Accounting for Fertility Decline During the Transition to Growth», *Journal of Economic Growth*, no. 9(3), 2004, pages 347-383.

FERNÁNDEZ-VILLAVERDE J., «Was Malthus Right? Economic Growth and Population Dynamics», *Working Paper*, Department of Economics, University of Pennsylvania, 2001.

GALOR O., «From Stagnation to Growth: United Growth Theory», *Handbook of Economic Growth*, vol. IA, Elsevier North-Holland, Amsterdam, The Netherlands, 2005.

-.-, «The 2008 Lawrence R. Klein Lecture. Comparative Economic Development: Insights from United Growth Theory», *International Economic Review,* no. 51(1), 2010, pages 1-44.

GALOR O. - MOAV O., «Natural Selection and the Origin of Economic Growth», *Quarterly Journal of Economics*, no. 117(4), 2002, pages 1133-1191.

GALOR O. - MOUNTFORD A., «Trading Population for Productivity: Theory and Evidence», *Review of Economic Studies*, no. 75(4), 2008, pages 1143-1179.

GALOR O. - WEIL D.N., «From Malthusian Stagnation to Modern Growth», *American Economic Review,* no. 89(2), 1999, pages 150-154.

-.-,-.-, «Population, Technology, and Growth: From Malthusian Stagnation to the Demographic Transition and Beyond», *American Economic Review*, no. 90(4), 2000, pages 806-828.

HANSEN G. D. - PRESCOTT E.C., «Malthus to Solow», *American Economic Review*, no. 92(4), 2002, pages 1205-1217.

JONES C.I., «Was an Industrial Revolution Inevitable? Economic Growth Over the Very Long Run», *Advances in Macroeconomics*, no. 1(2), 2001, pages 1-43.

KUHN T.S., *The Copernican Revolution*, Harvard University Press, Cambridge, MA, 1957.

LAGERLÖF N.-P., «From Malthus to Modern Growth: Can Epidemics Explain the Three Regimes?», *International Economic Review*, no. 44(2), 2003, pages 755-777.

LUCAS R.E., «The Industrial Revolution: Past and Future», in LUCAS R.E. JR. (ed.), *Lectures on Economic Growth*, Harvard University Press, Cambridge, MA, 2002.

MADDISON A., *The World Economy: A Millennial Perspective*, OECD, Paris, 2001.

O ROURKE K.H. - RAHMAN A.S. - TAYLOR A.M., «Luddites and the Demographic Transition», *NBER Working Paper*, no. 14484, 2008.

STRULIK H. - WEISDORF J.L., «Population, Food, and Knowledge: A Simple United Growth Theory», *Journal of Economic Growth*, no. 13(3), 2008, pages 195-216.

VOIGTLÄNDER N. - VOTH H.-J. «Why England? Demographic Factors, Structural Change and Physical Capital Accumulation During the Industrial Revolution», *Journal of Economic Growth*, no. 11(4), 2006, pages 319-361.

Population Dynamics, Malthusian Crises and Boserupian Innovation in Pre-Industrial Societies: The Case Study of Northern Italy (ca. 1450-1800) in the Light of Lee's "Dynamic Synthesis"

Guido Alfani*
Bocconi University, Milan
Dondena Centre for Research on Social Dynamics and IGIER

This article makes use of Lee's 'dynamic synthesis', which aims to combine the views of Malthus and Boserup, to provide a new interpretation of population dynamics in Northern Italy from about 1450 to 1800. The article analyzes Lee's theory and suggests that, even if it is difficult to test, it is useful both from the point of view of population theory and from that of interpretation of historical cases. Applying it to the Italian case, the article provides a new interpretation of the path that finally led the Italian population to escape long-term limits to demographic growth.
[JEL Classification: N33, N53, N93, J11].

Keywords: Malthus, Boserup, middle ages, early modern period, malthusian crises, plague, famine, agrarian innovation, demographic crises, population theory.

* *<guido.alfani@unibocconi.it>*.

1. - Introduction

Malthus and Boserup are usually considered the main sources of inspiration for different ways of looking at the interaction between humans and resources (or humans and the environment), and at the role technology plays in this. For decades, though, demographers and economic historians have been trying to conciliate them. In economic history, the elaboration of the "Unified Growth Theory" led to the progressive disappearance of any explicit reference to Boserup, whose teaching, however, has been incorporated to a degree into most models. In his turn, Malthus enjoys much wider mention – suffice it to consider how widespread are expressions like "Malthusian stagnation", replacing old favourites such as "Malthusian crisis" or "Malthusian trap". Among demographers, and especially those sharing an interest in demographic theory, Malthusian and Boserupian perspectives tend to remain apart[1], although attempts to combine the two are not lacking. Ronald Lee's "dynamic synthesis", in particular, is quite widely cited – usually as a reminder that, while it is handy to separate Boserup from Malthus, they could also be seen as integrating, and not contrasting.

This article will briefly recapitulate the key points of Malthusian and Boserupian theories and present the views of Lee and others about how they could be reconciled (sections 2 and 3). In sections 4 and 5, the rationale of Lee's model will be applied to the case of Italy, first providing a general picture from the period of the Roman Empire until 1900 (3), and later focussing on the case of Northern Italy in the years 1450-1800, for which an interpretation of the long-term interaction between population, environment and technological innovation will be developed (4). Some concluding remarks will suggest that this specific perspective can be usefully applied also to other parts of Europe. The analysis will not make use of complex formalization, given that some key components of Lee's model (such as the boundaries of the "Boserup space") would not be easy to derive for actual historical examples. Instead, it will favour a more descriptive approach, rich – in the Italian case – in historical detail.

1. See for example the way in which they are presented in the classic book A concise history of World population by LIVI BACCI M. (1997). Also see the recent synthesis by CUFFARO N. (2001) on the different views about the relationship between population, economic growth and technological innovations.

2. - Malthus, Boserup and Lee's Synthesis

«There are two grand themes in macro-demographic theory: the Malthusian one, that population equilibrates with resources at some level mediated by technology and a conventional standard of living; and the Boserupian one, that technological change is itself spurred by increases in population...» (Lee, 1986, page 96). The opening words of Ronald Lee's contribution to an important book debating the current (in 1986) state of population theory, notably in its relationship to Malthus' teaching (Coleman and Schofield, 1986), could not have made the point about the existence of two different sources of inspiration for demographers more clearly. It may be of some use to recapitulate their main points, albeit very succinctly.

For Malthus (1798; 1830), the level of population corresponds to a given technological situation, as well as to social and cultural factors. Despite the fact that imbalances periodically occur between population and resources as a result of their different rhythms of growth, overall the system oscillates around an equilibrium, maintained through repeated episodes of super-mortality. So in order to bring about a lasting growth in population, there must be a substantial improvement in agricultural technology which, however, if not followed by subsequent improvements, over the long term does not rule out the "need" for further interventions of what Malthus called the "positive checks" (famines, epidemics, and similar).

For Boserup (1965; 1981), the population itself, by promoting technological micro-innovations to traditional practices in response to demographic pressure, permits a slow increase in population by starting a chain reaction: it is not necessary to have a periodic re-equilibrium of population and resources. According to this theory therefore, the demographic pressure stimulates technical innovation in a continuous manner. Population is not a dependent variable whose maximum amount is determined by technology and environmental conditions (as in the Malthusian model), but in its turn exerts an influence on technology. Agrarian technology and the rate of innovation then, in "Boserupian" models, are determined endogenously.

Boserup herself never elaborated a formal model, preferring to present her theories in other ways. This task was attempted by others[2] and, in a sense, also Lee's synthesis can be numbered among such attempts. It is not the aim of this article,

2. See MATHIEU J. (2004) for a rare first-hand testimony of Boserup's feelings, late in her career, about the way she had influenced other scholars.

however, to debate whether Boserupian models are really true to Boserup's thought[3], nor to provide any discussion of their respective flaws and merits. Instead, I will focus on Lee's attempt to draw up a model which is able to account for the action of both Malthusian, and Boserupian forces: a model that, I believe, is in itself a relevant contribution to population theory and also a powerful instrument of analysis and interpretation of empirical cases, if one accepts the practical quasi – impossibility of measuring its parameters and variables.

Lee's starting assumption that «the two theories are not contradictory, but rather complementary» was grounded in the fact that «they share the assumption of diminishing returns to labour for a fixed technological level. To this common ground Malthus adds the assumption that population growth rates are endogenous, while Boserup adds the assumption that technological change is endogenous» (Lee, 1986, page 96).

Production, then, expressed as total food output (Q), would be a function of labour (L), the relevant technological level (T) and land or, more generally, natural resources (R):

$$Q = Q(L, T, R)$$

with:

$$Q_L,\ Q_T \text{ and } Q_R \text{ all} > 0$$
$$Q_{LL}^{4},\ Q_{TT} \text{ and } Q_{RR} \text{ all} < 0^{5}$$

As anticipated, there is no reason for presenting here a formal version of Lee's model, given that the reader can simply look for it in his original, excellent article. It is much more interesting, instead, to focus on its final results, which can be easily understood with some graphic support.

According to Lee, the Malthusian view of the relationship between population and technology can be represented as an area on a phase plane[6]. Within this area (the "Malthus space"), positive population growth occurs; outside of it, popula-

3. In Lee's case, this has actually been questioned by McNicoll G. (1988, page 145).
4. As Lee recognized, for small inputs of labour Q_{LL} might be positive, but eventually diminishing returns would set in (after exceeding a threshold defined by T and R).
5. The first derivative is positive and the second is negative because marginal returns to all factors are positive but diminishing (but see the earlier note about marginal returns to labor).
6. Phase planes are visual representations of the temporal evolution of variables.

tion declines[7]. Both the left-hand and the right-hand curves delimiting the area (as can be visualized in Graph 1) correspond to equilibria. In fact, according to the model developed by Lee, for a given level of technology there are usually two equilibrium population sizes (P*): one corresponding to a low-level equilibrium (placed in the region of increasing returns to labour[8]) and the other corresponding to a high-level equilibrium (in the region of decreasing returns to labour). The left-hand curve delimiting the area connects all points of low-level equilibrium; the right-hand one all those of high-level equilibrium. The left-hand curve also corresponds to the minimum population for which a given level of technology is sustainable. To the left of the curve, a shrinking population would be forced to drop to lower technological levels. The curve itself corresponds to unstable equilibria, given that Malthusian forces will drive population away from this line, towards the right-hand boundary[9]. This situation of instability is made clear by the arrows in Graph 1. The right-hand curve delimiting the Malthus space, that we'll call Z(T), corresponds to the population size for which, at a given technological level, marginal product of labour equals subsistence – that is, a "Malthusian" equilibrium in presence of competitive labour markets. This curve, though, would also coincide with the population size maximizing *surplus* produced for a given level of technology[10] (Lee, 1986, page 101): a very relevant circumstance, given that in her later book (1981) Boserup suggested that technological progress was

7. This is either because, for a given level of technology, the population is too large to be fed, or because it is too small to allow the agrarian system corresponding to that level of technology to work efficiently (here the idea is that more complex agrarian systems require larger populations to operate efficiently). As shall be seen, given that the region to the left of the Malthus space is also to the left of the "Boserup space", a population stuck in such region will experience both demographic decline, and technological decline.

8. As explained in note no. 4, for small inputs of labour the marginal returns can be increasing. The size of the labour force at which diminishing returns set in is determined by the available resources (R) and by the level of technology (T). The greater R and T, the larger the threshold labour force (LEE R., 1986, page 103; also see the graphical representation at page 106).

9. In the region immediately to the right of the left-hand curve, returns to labour are increasing, so that an increase in population raises the wage – allowing for a further increase, and so on.

10. More precisely, Z(T) is the right-hand boundary of the Malthus space when the "cultural standards of living" are at the biological subsistence level, *m*, and in presence of effective *surplus*-extracting institutions (village and urban authorities, states…). Only in this case, is the right-hand boundary of the Malthus space coinciding with the *surplus* maximization line: a circumstance which, as shall be seen, is crucial in implying that the Malthus and Boserup spaces are partially overlapping. In this article, we will formulate the hypothesis that this is true for the North Italian pre-industrial economy. It must be noted, though, that it is a definite possibility that the right-hand boundary of the Malthus space does not coincide with Z(T).

partly dependent on the quantity of *surplus* available, used to feed the non-agrarian sectors (people not working directly the land), to which the most innovating elites belonged[11]. Should the population reach a position to the right of the Z(T) curve, Malthusian forces would steer it leftwards. Any position directly on the Z(T) curve, then, is stable (as suggested by the arrows in Graph 1).

GRAPH 1

THE "MALTHUS SPACE" IN THE PHASE PLANE

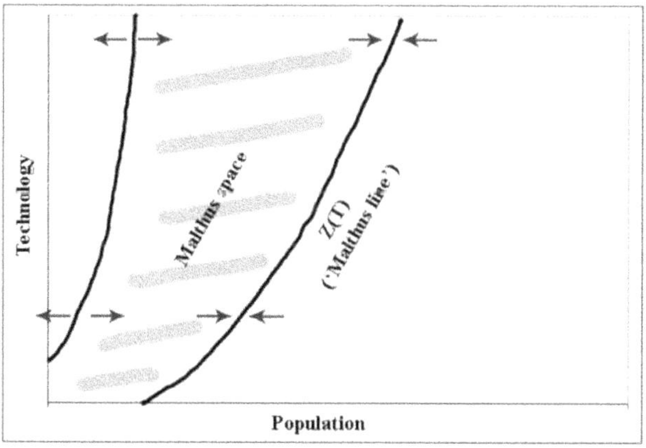

Under fairly realistic hypotheses[12], the Malthus space partially superimposes onto the "Boserup space", the latter being defined as "the *locus* of points for which technology is growing" (Lee, 1986, page 111), or T'>0. Defining the boundaries of such a space, and even defining the shape of it, is a much more complex task than defining the left and right hand curve of the Malthus space. Lee analyzed

Much depends on the "normative standards of living" and on the capacity of institutions to extract *surplus*. In Lee's example, «under a perfectly egalitarian system, with no taxes and a normative standard equal to *m*, the population would tend to equilibrate at the maximum possible level, with an average product of labour equal to subsistence, *m*; in this situation, there is no *surplus* at all. The Malthus line falls entirely to the right of the Boserup space (that is, the space within which technological progress tends to occur), and population constantly tends to a density too great to sustain a technology beyond the most primitive» (LEE R., 1986, pages 108-109).

11. Of course, the existence of *surplus* depends on the existence of institutions able to extract it, for example through taxation. The greater the efficiency of such institutions, the greater the potential *surplus*. Also see note no. 10.

12. The condition of superimposition of the two spaces would be always satisfied when the right-hand boundary of the Malthus space coincides with Z(T), the *surplus* maximization curve.

different possibilities, many of which were consistent with specific approaches to be found in the demographic literature of the time. By combining a number of assumptions, for example about the "forgettability" of technology (implying the possibility that a population could fall to lower technological levels than it had previously reached: as would have happened at the time of the collapse of the Mayan civilization, or in Europe during the "Dark Ages"), or about the fact that total agricultural *surplus* fuelled technological progress, he managed to reduce the possibilities to a fairly limited number of alternative shapes. His conclusion was that the shape of the Boserup space can be either inverted-"U" shaped or elliptical, and it is intersected by the Z(T) line. The boundaries of the Boserup space are the "Boserup line" while the right-hand boundary of the Malthus space, that here we take as coinciding with Z(T), is the "Malthus line". Where they cross, we find equilibrium points of the system for which neither population nor technology is changing (Lee, 1986, pages 111-113).

I have already clarified that if population is placed to the left or to the right of the Malthus line, Malthusian forces will move it horizontally on the phase plane towards the line. If population is placed within the Boserup space (within the boundaries of the Boserup line), it will tend to move upwards, to higher levels of technology. If population is placed outside the Boserup space, which has been defined as the *locus* of points where technology is growing, then inevitably it will move downwards to lower levels of technology. Even if the Boserup space occupies only a limited part of the phase plane (which we can take as the *locus* of all theoretically possible combinations of population and technology), Malthusian forces operating within a much larger space will steer population and technology towards it. The interaction of Malthusian and Boserupian forces on a phase plane in which Malthus and Boserup spaces are represented is shown in Graph 2 (which, as for Graph 1 and Graph 3 in the following, is a slightly simplified version of Lee's original).

In the right-hand part of Graph 2 (elliptical Boserup space), the path from point "a" to point "b" describes a human society enjoying a virtuous interaction of demographic and economic forces, slowly moving towards higher population density and higher technology until it finally reaches a point of equilibrium, on the upper-right boundary of the Boserup line.

To fully understand how Lee's synthesis can be used to interpret historical cases, two points still need to be clarified.

Firstly, inverted-"U" and elliptical Boserup spaces can be thought to coexist in the same phase plane, on which we can also draw *different* Boserup spaces.

GRAPH 2

DYNAMIC BEHAVIOUR ON THE SYSTEM
(INVERTED U OR ELLIPTICAL BOSERUP SPACES)

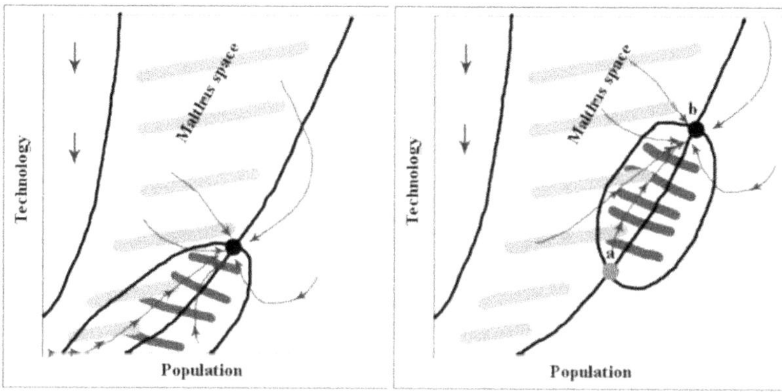

Within each space, population obeys the dynamics described above, while "transitions between them are largely exogenous" (Lee, 1986, page 121). Here, Lee is referring to very long time scales, such as those on which we can trace the movement from hunting and gathering, to agriculture, to industry. However, I believe that we can also visualize the "agriculture" phase as a sequence of Boserup spaces, either separated or connected by narrow spits. On the other hand, Lee himself recognized the possibility that Boserup spaces were not "disconnected… ellipses" but loosely connected ones (see the comment about Graph 3). In particular, as shall be seen, the introduction in Italy of the "new agriculture" and of new crops (especially maize) in the Early Modern period would finally make it possible to overcome a boundary that since Roman times had proved impossible to exceed. Alternatively, we could imagine that in that period the population finally squeezed through a bottleneck whose entry point had repeatedly been missed. The first hypothesis is consistent with the idea of a population moving from one Boserup space to another, separate one, while the second hypothesis (which implies that population *might* have exceeded the long-term Italian limits to demographic growth even before the introduction of maize, but historically failed to do so) is consistent with the idea that the Italian situation would be better described as one of loosely connected Boserup spaces.

Before analyzing in detail the Italian case (sections 4 and 5), it is useful, in order to better understand the relevance of the shape of the Boserup spaces and of their relative positions, to present a Graph (no. 3) analogous to Lee's original.

Graph 3

TECHNOLOGICAL REGIMES AND BOSERUP SPACES
(DISCONNECTED OR LOOSELY CONNECTED SPACES)

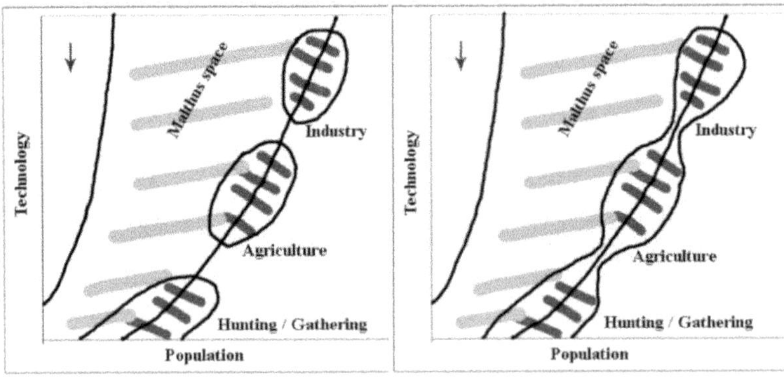

In Graph 3, three different stages in the development of human societies are represented: hunting/gathering; agriculture; industry. This partition has become a classic in demographic theory, although there has been much controversy over how a population can move from one stage to the other. Boserup herself interpreted the introduction of agriculture in a hunter-gatherer society as the consequence of an increase in population density, which made it both necessary and possible to settle in stable villages and begin cultivating the land (Boserup, 1965), and a similar position has been taken by Mark Cohen (1977). Another classic interpretation, by Deevey (1960), suggested (in an essentially Malthusian framework) that human populations moved from lower equilibrium levels to higher ones by means of a series of "technological revolutions". According to Lee, his "dynamic synthesis", as represented in Graph 3, is able to reconcile these contrasting views of the interaction between population and technology: by allowing for Boserupian chain-reactions of innovation *within* specific Boserup spaces, and at the same time explaining why we do not find, historically, a steady upward trend of population and technology. This would be due to the fact that, without a shock (see later), a specific Boserup space can prove to be inescapable (left-hand part of Graph 3: separate Boserup spaces) or very difficult to escape (right hand part: loosely connected Boserup spaces)[13].

---

13. For a more detailed discussion of Graph 3, see Lee's own in the 1986 article, pages 121-123.

Graph 3 is also helpful in clarifying the second point that still needs to be developed, that is, the role played by what Lee called "historical shocks". In general, if a population reaches an equilibrium point, how is it possible that it moves to higher (or lower) levels of technology? If we are in a situation similar to that represented in the left-hand part of Graph 3, how is it possible to move from one Boserup space to another? According to Lee, exogenous forces could displace the system, breaking the equilibrium and forcing it into a path towards restoration of the old equilibrium, or towards another equilibrium (higher or lower)[14]. The typical example of an exogenous factor causing a reduction in population, and potentially also a technological decline, is a very bad epidemic. A historical example of this would be the shrinking of the Mayan population in Mexico, to just 5% of its previous level, after the Conquest (the decline was due mostly, but not solely, to epidemics: Livi Bacci, 2008), while Medieval and Early Modern European epidemics, the Black Death included, would be smaller-scale events determining a huge loss of population, but a limited loss of technology, or none at all. Positive, exogenous shocks to population and technology could be caused by large-scale immigration, lucky discoveries, and so on. As shall be seen in sections 4 and 5, by leaving open space for the action of these "historical shocks", Lee's synthesis allows for the smooth integration into the interpretation of historical cases of events whose occurrence is determined exogenously to the model (events which, at least in the case of some kinds of epidemic and most notably of plagues, we could even consider to be random, or at least placed substantially outside the sphere of control of pre-industrial societies).

3. - Lee's Synthesis and Other Approaches

Almost a decade after it was published, Lee's synthesis was criticized by Noël Bonneuil for having provided us with a "mechanistic" model that failed to consider the fact that human innovation is contingent – and so should not be considered as the automatic consequence of specific combinations of population and technology, nor as the consequence of the random appearance of a genius (Bonneuil,

[14] More precisely, all "regimes" (in Lee's original article: hunting and gathering; agricultural; industrial) have «a catchment area, from within which all paths lead ultimately to the stable equilibrium»; so, «when a shock occurs, we must first determine whether the population has been displaced into a different catchment area», or whether it is still within the catchment area of the old regime, then moving back towards the old equilibrium point (Lee R., 1986, pages 126-127).

1994)[15]. This kind of criticism, which is rooted in the "viability theory" and which leads to the elaboration of even more complex models[16], does not seem to negate the usefulness of Lee's dynamic synthesis as an instrument for interpreting historical developments, in the sense that it is ultimately moving the discussion to a much higher level, challenging the very idea that the notion of causality is adequate to understand human history (Bonneuil, 2001, page 114). In other words, the same criticism could be formulated for all the demo-economic models produced to describe long-run human behaviour (surely in the case of the most widely used), save for Bonneuil's and maybe a few others sharing similar assumptions.

It is not convenient here to discuss further this very complex topic. It is more relevant to underline that Lee's dynamic synthesis has been much cited as "proof" of the fact that Malthusian and Boserupian views have not necessarily to be seen as contrasting, but could integrate (a kind of instrumental use of Lee's work to which I am not extraneous: Alfani, 2007; 2010*a*). On the other hand, as far as I know it has been very rarely used as an instrument for interpreting developments of historical populations, let alone "tested". Also, it should be noted that alternative, explicit attempts at synthesizing Boserupian and Malthusian views do exist[17], but it is not the aim of this article to discuss to any degree of completeness their different characteristics.

More interesting is a brief consideration of how economic historians have incorporated some of Boserup's ideas into their models. Of course, one could think that, in the end, this simply means making the rate of technological progress positive: which, thinking in a Malthusian perspective, would mean allowing for a continuous increase of the maximum sustainable population (or of the "carrying capacity" of the system). An early example of this is the model developed by Karl

15. According to Bonneuil, «the population pressure does not drive technological change in a mechanistic manner, but modifies the set of opportunities left to people, given their capacities for changing their own fate. (...) Population pressure does exist on technological change, but indirectly, and systems are still allowed to do nothing, or even to forget. The shrinking of sets of reachable states, while time passing and population growing, stand, in the view I suggest (...) as the actual incentive to technological progress. The Boserupian theme should thus not be understood as a univocal mechanistic relationship, but as resulting from a consideration of time left to avoid an undesired situation, when things need time and effort to be changed». (Bonneuil N., 1994, page 118).

16. And even less testable: being intrinsically compatible with an even greater range of possible outcomes. But again, in this kind of population theory, requiring testability would be off the point.

17. See for example Atzrouni M. and Komlos J. (1985); Steinman J. and Komlos J. (1988); Tsolouhas T.C. (1992); Capasso S. and Malanima P. (2007).

Gunnar Persson, with help by Peter Skott, which allowed for a slow, but permanent, technological progress (Persson, 1988). As Persson recently regretted, this model did not make technological progress endogenous: a characteristic that would instead be found in New Growth Theory and in Unified Growth Theory (Persson, 2008)[18].

The Unified Growth model elaborated by Oded Galor and David Weil, in particular, «links the size of the population to the rate of technological progress» (Galor and Weil, 2000, page 810), which ultimately can explain the end of Malthusian stagnation and how a "post-Malthusian regime" began. During Malthusian stagnation, at very low levels of population, steady state equilibria can be reached with very low rates of technological change. Over time, «the slow growth of population that takes place in the Malthusian Regime raises the rate of technological progress… generating a qualitative change in the dynamical system». This change corresponds to the movement from small populations to moderate-size populations: «The dynamical system of education and technology, for a moderate population, is characterized by multiple, history-dependent, steady-state equilibria». The final step: «As the rate of technological progress continues to rise in reaction to the increasing population size… the dynamical system experiences another qualitative change. The Malthusian steady-state equilibrium vanishes, and the conditional dynamical system is characterized by a unique globally stable modern steady-state equilibrium… with high levels of education and technological progress» (Galor, 2009, pages 19-21).

By making technological growth endogenous, Unified Growth Theory surely answers some of Boserup's criticism of Malthusian (and even more so, neo-Malthusian) views, even though it does not always explicitly recognize Boserup among its sources of inspiration. So there would be no point in debating to what extent the way it models interaction between population and technology is truly Boserupian. It is more useful to compare it with Lee's synthesis, suggesting the existence of specific strengths and weaknesses in both models.

I believe that the strong points of Lee's model are essentially two. Firstly, it allows us to separate the action of Malthusian forces from Boserupian – a fact that, from the perspective of population theory if not necessarily from that of economic history, is not negligible. Furthermore, it enables us to distinguish situations (visualizable graphically) in which Boserupian forces are unable to operate, but Malthusian forces can and do. This not only makes it easy to account for sit-

18. Also see Persson's treatment of technology in his 2010 synthesis.

uations in which the interaction between population and technology is not virtuous, but also reiterates the usefulness of old notions such as "Malthusian crisis" and "Malthusian traps" (as will be exemplified in the next section). Lastly, if from the broad picture we move to smaller areas, this would help us to understand why, in the same time period, some of them behaved in Boserupian ways, while others seemed to be much more constrained by Malthusian forces.

The second point is that Lee's synthesis accounts for the possibility that Boserup spaces are unconnected and that populations can move from one to the other only by means of exogenous shocks. A more moderate position would be to suggest that they are connected, but through narrow spits (remember the discussion of Graph 3 in section 2). I believe that this can help us to understand the fact that historical populations encountered specific limits to growth, or population levels which they repeatedly failed to overcome, rebounding from them as a result of Malthusian crises, or of negative exogenous shocks. As shall be seen, Italy was seemingly faced with such a situation from the times of the Roman empire until the seventeenth century, later finding its way through a very narrow spit (or jumping to a different Boserup space).

This being said, Lee's synthesis, when compared to Unified Growth theory, has one very serious drawback: testability. In the perspective of economic history, at least in its more formalized or cliometric version, this is a key point (which, by the way, Lee himself had openly recognized, later using other models to work on empirical cases[19]), and with this article I do not intend to suggest in any way that we should abandon Unified Growth theory in favour of this older model, nor is it my aim to state its superiority. My intent is simply to suggest that it allows us to look in a slightly different way at historical cases, providing us with further useful insights. I shall make my point more clearly by analyzing the Italian case.

4. - Italy's Long-Lasting Limit to Demographic Growth

In one of his concluding remarks, Lee stated: "it would be difficult to test the theory by examining historical episodes. A wide variety of patterns of behaviour is consistent with it. In many ways this is unfortunate, since it weakens the theory's predictive power" (Lee, 1986, page 127).

Surely, such a statement was meant to induce caution in any scholar willing to make use of the theory in his own research. The nature of what will be at-

[19] See for example LEE R. and ANDERSON D. (2002).

tempted in this section and in the following one, then, must be clearly spelled out: it is not my aim to "demonstrate" that the Italian case corroborates the theory. Much more modestly, I will make use of the theory as a tool for interpreting how Northern Italy, between 1450 and 1750-1800, was finally able to overcome a kind of ceiling to demographic expansion, from which it had repeatedly rebounded since the times of the Roman empire. The theory, I believe, has much to offer in terms of helping us to interpret the path followed by population and agrarian innovation (technology) in what was still, until at least the early seventeenth century, a leading area in the European economy[20].

To clearly understand Italian population dynamics in the Late Medieval and Early Modern period, it is necessary to start with some considerations about a longer time frame. According to a recent reconstruction of the population of Italy between the late Roman Empire and the Contemporary Age (Lo Cascio and Malanima, 2005), there is a population level that the peninsula repeatedly came close to, and then rebounded from. This level, corresponding to about 14 or 15 million people[21], allows us to roughly identify the maximum carrying capacity of the Italian demographic system, at least before 1700 after when, as shall be seen, it was breached for the first time. The level, reached at the time of the Roman Empire and then lost during the second century AD due to the Antonine Plague of 160-180 AD (that killed at least 20-30% of the population, with the high estimate being 50%) and to subsequent epidemiological crisis (Lo Cascio and Malanima, 2005; Little, 2007), would be regained by around 1300. It was lost again due to the outbreak of plague in 1347-48, reacquired by the last decades of the sixteenth century (Alfani, 2010*a*), and lost again during the seventeenth be-

20. The reconstruction proposed here can be usefully compared with that developed by CAPASSO S. and MALANIMA P. (2007), using a different, more formalized approach for studying long-term economic and demographic developments for the whole of the Italian peninsula. More recently, CHIARINI B. (2010) tested some "Malthusian" implications for Italy in years 1320-1870, concluding that in this specific case they do not seem to be verified.

21. It should be noticed that these new estimates, especially as regards Antiquity, are a marked revision of older (and much lower) ones, mostly based on Beloch's reconstructions (1886) and also more or less accepted by other syntheses about Italian population in the long run, and particularly DEL PANTA L. *et* AL. (1996). Even more recently, the old estimates have been defended by SCHEIDEL W. (2004). It is well possible, then, that future research will bring more data in favour of one or the other extremes, but for the sake of this article the most recent hypotheses formulated by Lo Cascio and Malanima will be accepted (save for some revision as regards the Early Modern period, in order to take into account even more recent research and particularly ALFANI G., 2007; 2010*a* for the sixteenth century and ALFANI G., 2010*b*; 2010*c*; FUSCO I., 2007; 2009 for the seventeenth; see later, discussion of Graph 6).

cause of the plague pandemics of 1629-30, in the North, and 1656-57, in the centre and South (Alfani, 2010*b*; 2010*c*).

GRAPH 4

ITALIAN POPULATION 200 BC - 1900 AD AND THE ITALIAN MAXIMUM CARRYING CAPACITY BEFORE 1700[22]

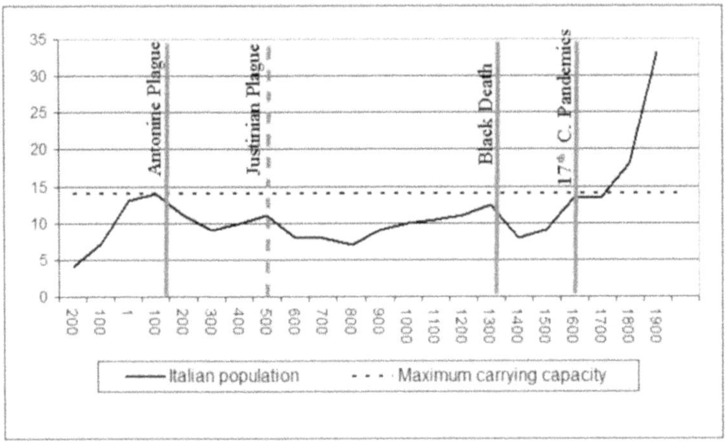

The existence of a recognizable maximum carrying capacity of the Italian demographic system implies (in a Malthusian perspective) that, if and when it is exceeded, positive checks will bring population back to lower levels. Hypothetically, and referring solely to the estimates represented graphically in Graph 4, we could place this threshold somewhere between 14 and 15 million people.

The Graph shows, by means of vertical lines, the three moments when positive checks apparently came into action: 160-180; 1348-1349; 1629-1657 (1629-1630 focussing on the North). Maybe we should add to this list also 541-544 (the fragmented vertical line in Graph 4), when the Justinian plague pandemic raged (Little, 2007), but in this period the overall population was well below the threshold, in spite of the considerable increase in the previous decades. For this reason, the case of the Justinian plague will not be developed further.

The vertical lines separate specific cycles of demographic decline and growth (the last one is not clearly visible in Graph 4 given that it happened mostly between the 1600 and 1700 estimates, but it can be seen in Graph 7). In all three instances (or four, including the Justinian Plague), these "checks" were epidemic

[22] I would like to thank Paolo Malanima for having provided me with the data used in the Graph.

in nature: smallpox in the case of the Antonine "plague", bubonic plague[23] in the other two (or three) cases. While epidemics were surely among Malthus's short list of possible demographic checks, it is not clear in which way population growing beyond specific limits could trigger pandemics of plague (if this were the case, they could be considered as endogenously determined by population growth). As a matter of fact, for the case of the Black Death, which was preceded by very severe famines around Europe, it has been suggested that we should consider both epidemics and famines as part of a phase of acute environmental instability, in which demographic, epidemiologic and climatic factors interacted in complex ways (Campbell, 2010*a*; 2010*b*). Probably, something similar could be said about Northern Italy for the period 1590-1631 (see later, about the occurrence of famine and plague at the peak of the Little Ice Age, and Alfani, 2010*d*). Here it is not possible to develop further this point. Suffices it to note that, in our case study, plague pandemics will be considered as exogenous shocks, coherently with the hypotheses of Lee's model and with the traditional identification of the agent of plague with the *Yersinia Pestis* bacillus[24].

If we consider the first two long-term cycles of demographic recovery (those following the Antonine Plague and the Black Death), it is quite easy to interpret them in the context of Lee's model. Before the pandemics, population had reached the upper boundary of the Boserup space and maybe, led by the inertia regulating demographic systems, had exceeded them, entering the area of the phase plane in which Malthusian forces cause population to drop (famines; insufficient nutrition determining greater susceptibility to infectious diseases[25]). Alternatively, we can hypothesize that the population had reached a Malthusian equilibrium of high population and relatively low average standards of living (an equilibrium of the kind represented in Graph 2, at the intersection of Malthus

23. This article will not discuss the complex issue of the agent of plague, with the traditional identification with the *Yersinia Pestis* now being questioned. About such debate, suffices it to cite Cohn S.K. (2002); Alfani G. and Cohn S.K. (2007); Del Panta L. (2007); Theilman J. and Cate F. (2007); Alfani G. (2010*a*).

24. Research into twentieth century epidemics caused by *Yersinia Pestis*, mainly in Asia, tends to rule out the possibility that lack of nutrition could make people more susceptible to catching the disease (in this regards, Cohn S.K., 2002). However, I believe that we should openly consider the possibility that "historical plague" was something different from *Yersinia Pestis:* a different disease, or a different strain or biovar of the same disease (Alfani G. and Cohn S.K., 2007; Alfani G., 2010*a*). If the agent of historical plague was not *Yersinia Pestis,* then it might be possible that low levels of nutrition made people more susceptible to the disease.

25. But not to *Yersinia Pestis;* see note no. 24.

and Boserup lines), from which it rebounded due to exogenous shocks. Whatever the case, the existence of a recognizable maximum carrying capacity of the Italian demographic systems suggests that either: *a)* population growth during different cycles happened within a closed Boserup space; *b)* even if the relevant Boserup space was not closed, the spit allowing escape from this to another loosely connected, more advanced Boserup space was very narrow and was repeatedly missed. The first case implies that it would have been quite impossible, for the Italian population, to exceed specific limits to growth. After the high-population equilibrium was reached, demographic growth was possible only after an exogenous shock had moved the overall population to a lower level – but with no possibility of escaping the closed Boserup space. The second case implied that, in Italy, it would have been theoretically possible to reach population levels higher than the 14-15 million threshold, had specific paths of demographic growth and agrarian innovation been taken, leading to a different Boserup space where further growth was possible. However, historically the Italian population simply did not manage to do this. The complex interaction of many factors prevented it from entering these very narrow paths (constituting a "spit" which loosely connected different Boserup spaces), and population got "stuck at relatively low-level equilibria", to use Lee's words to describe this kind of situation (Lee, 1986, page 122).

Data about the population of Italy from Antiquity to the Early Modern period, then, suggests that, whatever the stimulus to agrarian innovation, technological growth was incapable of determining continuous population growth beyond well-defined limits. Key to this article is to provide an interpretation of the end of the story: explaining, in the light of Lee's synthesis, how it was possible that, after rebounding for a third time during the late sixteenth - early seventeenth century, the Italian population finally managed to grow beyond its millenary limits, by moving from one Boserup space to another. As anticipated, I will focus on Northern Italy: a much more homogeneous area than the whole peninsula, and an area for which it will be possible to detail how human beings reacted to a situation of increasing scarcity of resources.

5. - The Case Study of Northern Italy, ca. 1450-1800

As suggested by the most recent reconstructions (Alfani, 2007; 2010*a*), during the sixteenth century the population of Northern Italy was characterized by a long phase of stagnation during the Wars of Italy (1494-1559), followed by a very quick growth completed before 1589[26]. Afterwards, it went through what was probably the worst famine to strike the peninsula since the times of the Black Death (1590-1593). The famine did not have long-lasting consequences for the total population. The overall mortality levels, even though they were exceptionally high for a famine[27], were much lower than those characterizing the plague pandemics. Indeed, the impact of the famine is barely visible on the estimates used here (in Graph 7, it appears more as a temporary stop to growth than as a drop in population, given that the aggregate data cover short-term phases of decline), but it should be pointed out that it is much more apparent in reconstructions based on time series of births and deaths (see for example Graph 5) and probably this should be taken into account by future revisions of the estimates. The same can be said for the phase of stagnation during the Wars of Italy.

GRAPH 5

RECONSTRUCTION OF BIRTHS AND DEATHS IN NORTHERN ITALY, 1550-1628 (INDEXES, BASE 100 = AVERAGE OF YEARS 1601-1628)[28]

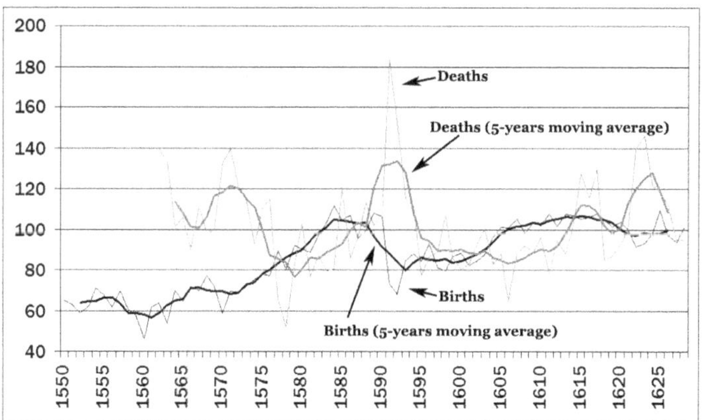

26. In 1560-89, it is possible to calculate a rate of growth of the level of births – that can be treated as a rough proxy for population levels – of a yearly 15.7-17.7 per thousand ALFANI G. (2010*a*).

27. As suggested by LIVI BACCI M. (1998), literally dying of hunger is a fairly rare event. About the exceptional mortality rates of the great famine of the 1590s, see ALFANI G. (2009*a*; 2009*b*; 2010*a*).

28. For a full comment on the graph and information about the database and the methods of reconstruction used, see ALFANI G. (2010*a*, pages 244-252) (an early version of the reconstruction, only including births, has been published and commented in ALFANI G., 2007).

However, even the most "unfavourable" reconstructions suggest that by the beginning of the seventeenth century all damage caused by the famine to total population levels had been recovered.

North Italian populations (the plural here is justified both by the fragmentation of the area into different political entities, from the Duchy of Savoy to the West to the Republic of Venice to the East, and by the existence of quite different agrarian and economic-social-demographic regimes) were generally aware of a rising imbalance between the number of people and the potential for food production. In Emilia, for example, we know that the slow transformation of rural areas from the cultivation system of the "*chiusura*" to the more intensive "*piantata*"[29] was linked to the need to produce greater quantities of food, even at the cost of sacrificing variety and focusing on two fundamental resources: grapes and wheat (Cattini, 1984). This transformation, which took decades to be completed and required changes in mentality and social customs (for example, about what to eat, and how), is the kind of agricultural innovation stimulated by demographic pressure, that Boserup (1981) postulated for times of shrinking supplies of land and food resources. The transformation did not involve Emilia only, but covered a larger area including much of Veneto and part of Lombardy (Sereni, 1961, pages 177-178; Rombai and Boncompagni, 2002, pages 200-201; Cazzola, 2002, page 231). Not by chance was this area also among the most densely populated of the peninsula.

In other parts of Northern Italy, however, innovations in farming techniques did not always lead to the production of more calories per hectare. In the countryside of the lower Milanese and Lodigiano, where during the sixteenth century the meadow spread in order to allow for larger bovine herds (to produce the leather, meat and dairy products required by large urban markets such as that of Milan), but mostly without becoming part of those systems of crop rotation which in due course would be considered as inherent to much of the very advanced "wet farming" of Lombardy[30], we find increasing concerns about the actual capacity of this very market-oriented agrarian system to feed a quickly growing population (Alfani, 2010*a*, pages 238-240). According to an estimate, the population of the State of Milan (which at the time comprised most of Lombardy) increased, overall, from

29. "*Chiusure*" and "*piantate*" are surrounded by hedges, fences or ditches to keep out animals grazing in surrounding fields. The changeover to the "*piantata*" is characterised by the progressive reduction of the grazing area in favour of the cultivated area with the consequent abandonment of semi-nomadic animal husbandry (CATTINI M., 1984, pages 28-37).

30. About the spread of these "stable meadows", see CHITTOLINI G. (1988); DI TULLIO M. (2010).

about 770,000 in 1542 to about 1,240,000 around 1600 (+61%), with a particular dynamic trend in the rural areas (+66%). This estimate, which is probably too high, is nevertheless consistent with other reconstructions, based on more reliable data, in suggesting that a very significant increase in population was taking place[31].

The famine of the 1590s was the final benchmark of the capacity of the kind of agrarian innovation characterizing the sixteenth century to feed a population that tended to exceed its millenarian maximum level. Occurring in one of the coldest periods of the Little Ice Age[32] (see Graph 6 for the most recent reconstruction of the trend of global temperatures), characterized by high meteorological instability, the famine was caused by several years of bad weather (more precisely, weather particularly unfavourable to wheat and other cereals) causing an impressive sequence of back-to-back harvest failures. The crisis was so acute that, in spite of the steps taken by markets and by institutions attempting to bring in provisions from outside the peninsula, a situation of mass starvation in the Po Plain could not be avoided (Alfani, 2009*b*; 2010*a*; 2010*d*).

GRAPH 6

RECONSTRUCTED GLOBAL TEMPERATURE ANOMALIES, 1350-1800 (MEASURED IN CELSIUS DEGREES OF VARIATION FROM THE MEAN 16AD TO 1935AD)[33]

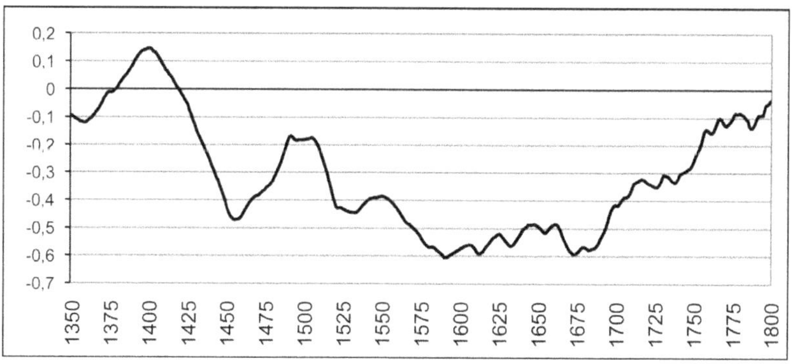

31. The estimates are based on the data provided by BELOCH K.J. (1994, pages 503-504). Also see my reconstruction of the demographic trend of Lombardy based on Parish data, in ALFANI G. (2010*a*, page 247).

32. Temperatures dropped during the fifteenth century; recovered at the beginning of the sixteenth; then around 1550 began a final phase of decline that brought them to a minimum in 1591 (incidentally, at the peak of the famine striking Northern Italy). About this, see LE ROY LADURIE E. (2004); LOEHLE C. and MCCULLOCH J.H. (2008); ALFANI G. (2010*d*).

33. Elaboration based on data by LOEHLE C. and MC CULLOCH J.H. (2008); see the article for the methodology that led to the definition of "anomalies" as divergences of 29-year mobile averages from the mean 16AD to 1935AD. Also see, for a detailed comment on the graph and on its implications for the Italian population, ALFANI G. (2010*d*).

If we consider how different agrarian systems fared during the famine, we have to admit that the areas in which we can find recognizable Boserupian-style processes of agrarian innovation did not do any better than those where innovation was supposedly detrimental to food production. In other words, even if they had been moving within the Boserup space (that, as shall be remembered, is the space within which technological innovation can happen), most Northern-Italian populations were driven outside the boundary of the Boserup space by the inertia characteristic of many demographic systems (see later), and had entered the Malthusian space dominated by the positive checks restraining population growth. In this sense, the great famine of the 1590s can be considered a "Malthusian crisis": even though it was triggered by climatic-meteorological factors, it was so acute because demographic growth had already made the population-resources equilibrium very precarious. Furthermore, Malthus himself pointed out that, when a population has grown too much, the actual occurrence of a famine is tied to random accidents such as an unfavourable season.

The case study of Northern Italy has already given us a first lesson: that agrarian innovation is not always favourable to improving the survival of the population living on the land. A key point is to identify who took the decisions to innovate. In Emilia, these were small-holding farmers and sharecroppers, who, obviously, had a direct interest in not starving and therefore, were careful about subsistence. In Lombardy, they were the new haute bourgeoisie owners and large renters, anxious to exploit their land investments to the utmost, according to a logic of profit. In this period and in this region, maximizing profit meant replacing fields with stable meadows, then reducing production of foodstuffs.

Another relevant lesson comes from the fact that, while most North Italian populations, and notably all of those settled in the Po Plain, suffered badly from the famine, there were also some who were spared. This is chiefly the case of Alpine and pre-Alpine populations, in Western Piedmont, North Lombardy or the Western Apennines of Liguria[34]. Studying the Alps in general, Jon Mathieu (2000) suggested that there, in the long run, the population was subject to a slow but continuous growth, without the ups and downs characterizing other areas of Europe. According to him, this result shows that positive chain-reactions of demographic stimuli and agrarian innovation were at work, in exactly the same way as was postulated by Boserup.

---

34. About this see ALFANI G. (2010*a*), and particularly the maps on pages 100-101.

How did the Alpine populations manage to avoid the painful occurrence of Malthusian positive checks? Of crucial importance was the precocious establishment in the mountains of a "low pressure" demographic regime, characterized by moderate birth and mortality rates, no greater than 30-35 per thousand (Viazzo, 1990). While some aspects of this story are still unclear (especially concerning the original causes of this particularly favourable condition[35]), we can also interpret the Alpine situation as one characterized by particularly strong preventive checks. This condition of the Alps has been recognized and praised by Malthus himself.

To sum up: in the second half of the sixteenth century we find a variety of situations across Northern Italy:

1) areas in which population is growing quickly and agrarian innovation of a non-Boserupian kind is taking place, which does not help preventing a Malthusian crisis, and maybe the contrary (by "non-Boserupian agrarian innovation" I mean a kind of innovation which neither considers, nor is fostered by, the needs of an increasing number of human beings);
2) areas in which population is growing quickly and Boserupian agrarian innovation is taking place, which helps feeding more people in the short run but ultimately proves inadequate in preventing a Malthusian crisis;
3) areas in which population is growing slowly and Boserupian agrarian innovation is taking place, effectively avoiding Malthusian crises.

The first situation characterized the Milanese and the Lodigiano in Lombardy, and probably part of the Western areas of the Republic of Venice (especially on the left bank of the river Po). The second situation was to be found in Emilia, in Romagna, in much of Veneto, in part of Lombardy, and more generally in that area of the Po plain where, in the first place, population had grown a lot between the second half of the fifteenth century and the late 1580s and, secondly, decisions to innovate were taken mostly, or entirely, by small owners or by sharecroppers whose survival was directly dependent on their own crops. It is possible that further research on this topic will suggest that cases of this kind were the most widespread. Lastly, the third situation, which characterized the Alps, many pre-Alpine areas, the Western Liguria Apennines and probably other hill or mountain regions. These areas had very specific environmental conditions that differed enor-

35. Many elements have been underlined, such as the regulatory role of nuptiality, the forms of organization of the family, the way the work force was used (with large-scale seasonal migration), etc. For a short synthesis, Fornasin A. and Zannini A. (2002, pages 11-15).

mously from the other two situations which were related to the Po Plain, where the vast majority of the population of Northern Italy lived. Given that the Alpine physical environment strongly influenced the agrarian-technological options available, we can consider that Boserupian and Malthusian spaces were shaped differently in the mountains and in the plain. For this reason I shall now focus on the non-mountain areas.

As shown by Graph 7, in which the population trend in Central-Northern Italy during 1450-1800 is represented, the demographic damages caused by the crisis of the 1590s were very quickly mended and population continued to grow beyond the risky levels it had already reached before the famine. By the 1620s we find, again, frequent dearth, triggered by bad weather but "caused" just as much by the precarious *ratio* of population and food resources. This situation was resolved, so to speak, by the great pandemics, and especially by that of 1629-30 (which involved all of Northern Italy, save for Liguria, plus Tuscany) which was the one affecting most the area covered by the Graph.

GRAPH 7

CENTRAL-NORTH ITALIAN POPULATION, 1450-1800[36]
(LAZIO AND ABRUZZO EXCLUDED)

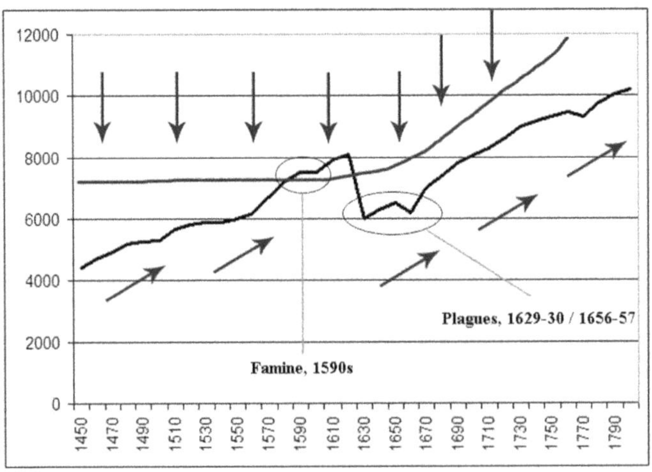

36. As for Graph 4, I wish to thank Paolo Malanima for having provided me with his estimates of population in central-north Italy during the period examined here. Such estimates are represented in Graph 7, with small corrections around the crisis years in order to take into account recent research which, especially for the two plague pandemics, suggests an overall mortality higher than previously thought ALFANI G. (2010*c*); FUSCO I. (2009).

In the North, the 1629-1630 plague killed 30-35% of the overall population (Alfani, 2010*c*): a catastrophe whose consequences, in terms of long-lasting demographic damage, were on a scale entirely different from that of the famine of the 1590s. In fact, the plague opened a time span during which agrarian innovations could be completed which, by the time the earlier population levels had been recovered (end of the seventeenth/beginning of the eighteenth century[37]), would allow growth beyond the old maximum carrying capacity. According to fairly recent estimates (Sonnino 1996, 79), the population of Northern Italy amounted to 6.5 million people in 1600 and was about the same (6.7 million) in 1700, but by 1750 it had already grown to 7.7 million people[38]. In the graph, the changing condition allowing for growth beyond the old limit is represented by the grey line separating the space dominated by Malthusian forces (whose action is shown by the downwards-orientated arrows). Below this line, we find the Boserup space in which interaction of population growth and agrarian innovation can be virtuous. Of course, this representation differs from that used in section 1 because time, and not population, is represented on the *x* axis. The fact that the boundary between areas within which the population can grow or is forced to shrink (the grey line in Graph 7) curves upwards after the 1590s famine tends to suggest that a new path is being tested: one which ultimately will lead to a different Boserup space (connected or unconnected to the previous one, as shall be seen), allowing for demographic growth beyond the sixteenth or early seventeenth century maximum. However this did not happen without the occurrence of another crisis: the plague pandemic. As already suggested, even though it is tempting to formulate the hypothesis that plague is endogenously determined in the system, it is more prudent[39] to treat it as an exogenous shock.

We can think, then, that this exogenous shock brought the population back

---

37. See for example the estimates proposed by SONNINO E. (1996).

38. In the centre of the peninsula, Sonnino estimated population to be equal to 2.2 million in 1600; 2.1 in 1700; 2.4 in 1750. It should be noticed that Sonnino's estimates for the central-north Italian population are different from those by Malanima used in Graph 7 (this is also because Malanima did not include Lazio and Abruzzo as part of the centre-north). Both sets of estimates, though, as well as others (see the summary table of different estimates in ALFANI G., 2010*a*, page 297), suggest that after 1700 the Italian population reached levels higher than any to be found during the Middle Ages and the first two centuries of the Early Modern period.

39. As a matter of fact, the Italian seventeenth century pandemics were exceptional events, both compared to Italian plagues of earlier periods (save for the Black Death) and compared to contemporary epidemics elsewhere in Europe. About this, and for some hypotheses about possible explanations of such an occurrence, see ALFANI G. (2010*b*; 2010*c*).

to a sub-area of the Boserup space which was sufficiently distant from the boundary to spare Northern Italian populations the risk of being projected into the Malthus space – which could quite possibly have happened otherwise, as a result of unfavourable climatic conditions, considering that the coolest phase of the Little Ice Age included the whole of the seventeenth century (Alfani, 2010*d*). If this explains why slow, large-scale agrarian innovation could be completed without further Malthusian crises, it still does not explain how it was possible to breach the old population limit. In fact, if the potential for exceeding the millenary maximum carrying capacity of the Italian demographic system was within the technological possibilities of the populations living in the peninsula, we could wonder why they did not accomplish such a result much earlier. As shall be seen, it is probable that they *could not* have obtained this, before an exogenous shock (the discovery of the New World) took place.

A number of factors cooperated in exceeding the limit. As shown by Domenico Sella (1997) and others, the seventeenth century was a period of great dynamism in the countryside of Northern Italy, balancing, at least to a degree, the concurrent crisis of the urban economies. Heavy investment in rural areas was needed to complete a thorough restructuring of the system of agrarian production. The water, distributed by the same network of capillary canals that had permitted the spread of irrigated meadows in the sixteenth century, was now used for the needs of the rapidly expanding paddy fields. These produced rice, a product widely requested by European markets and, consequently, a very profitable investment for the rich landowners of some of the greatest Northern Italian cities (particularly Milan). Economic interests, then, were safeguarded, but without damaging the capacity for food production of the territory (and thus eliminating the difference found, in the sixteenth century, between areas characterized by Boserupian or non-Boserupian agrarian innovation). The importance of rice does not lie mainly in its yield per hectare, but in the fact that it contributed to the elimination of fallow and limited the excess of irrigated meadows that had developed during the fifteenth and sixteenth centuries, a result that was also obtained through new systems of crop rotation (Alfani, 2010*e*)[40].

The solution to a productive dilemma (calories or profit?) characterizing one of the most advanced Italian rural areas during the sixteenth century and the introduction of innovating crop rotation are not sufficient to explain how it was

40. During the seventeenth century, the "stable meadows" widespread in earlier periods progressively disappeared. Meadows then became a component of complex systems of continuous rotation of crops.

possible to break free from the long-term constraints on population growth. Nor is it enough to include in the picture the expansion of the cultivation of mulberry trees, whose leaves were key in raising silkworms to feed a growing rural proto-industry[41] (while silk surely provided peasants with a relevant and very valuable resource, to overcome the ancient limits to demographic growth in Italy a greater production of food for humans[42], not for silkworms, was needed). Climate probably played a role given that, as suggested by Graph 6, during seventeenth century the Little Ice Age entered into its warming phase. Climate, though, had been more favourable in the past without allowing to breach long-term limits to demographic growth[43]. The main factor, in Northern Italy as elsewhere in the peninsula, was almost certainly maize. This new product, coming from the New World like another, the potato, which arguably played a similar role in Central and Northern Europe[44], began to spread at the time of the great famines of the late sixteenth and early seventeenth century. Earlier it had been considered mainly as a garden plant (Doria, 2002, pages 570-573). It has been suggested that the famines and the 1629-30 plague pandemic provided the cultural shock necessary to overcome any residual resistance to cultivation of this "foreign" plant[45]. Maize then came to be associated with all the main crops of seventeenth and eighteenth century Northern Italy (wheat, rice, irrigated meadows) and in time came to be used in the new forms of crop rotation that eliminated fallow. Maize not only provided extra calories and food diversity (even though its nutritional defects are well known), but also represented a means of protection from bad weather, given that it reacted quite favourably to the kind of weather harmful to crops of wheat (Coppola, 1979; Finzi, 2002; 2009; Alfani, 2010*d*).

---

41. About the expansion of the cultivation of the mulberry tree (which, in certain areas, became part of the system of the "*piantata*") in Early Modern Italy, see MALANIMA P. (2002, pages 132-135); BATTISTINI F. (2003); CORRITORE R.P. (2010).
42. About the issue of "distribution *versus* production" as factors explaining the famines of the late sixteenth and early seventeenth century in Northern Italy, see ALFANI G. (2010*d*).
43. See ALFANI G. (2010*d*) for a more detailed analysis of the relationship between climate and demographic trends in Italy during the period 1450-1800.
44. See NUNN N. and QUIAN N. (2008), who, however, are wrong in suggesting that the potato was playing in Italy a role similar to the North of the continent. In Italy, we know that the potato spread late (nineteenth century) and was mostly confined to marginal (hilly, mountainous) areas (DORIA M., 2002, pages 570-573).
45. About early cultivation of maize, see LEVI G. (1991) and FINZI R. (2009).

As rightly suggested by Paolo Malanima[46], in Early Modern Italy maize was the most important innovation regarding calories, given that its productivity was double that of other grains. Differently from rice, which had been present in the Italian peninsula since the Middle Ages, when it was introduced by the Arabs into the South, and spread slowly in the following centuries (not by chance, with a marked increase in pace after the years of dearth and famine of the late sixteenth century), maize was a new plant that became available to Europe only during the sixteenth century. Hence the question: should we consider maize, together with other factors such as the spread of rice and improvements in agronomic theories (crop rotation), simply as part of the explanation why, after repeated failures, Northern Italian populations were finally able to get onto the narrow path to a higher-level Boserup space, or should we consider it, maybe also in association with other factors, as characterizing a separate Boserup space, unconnected with the earlier one?

This is not an idle question, given that it influences how we define the action of exogenous shocks in our case study. The discovery of the New World and the import of maize to Europe is something that is surely exogenous to our model. When this new plant arrived in Italy, it opened up new possibilities and consequently changed the shapes of possible Boserup spaces. However the mere availability of maize does not imply that it was cultivated, and this simply because people were initially quite reluctant to eat this new food, fearing that its spread would damage more "noble" crops and particularly wheat. Should we believe traditional interpretations, according to which the famine of the 1590s and the plague of 1629-1630 both furnished, in Northern Italy, a key incentive to overcome all resistance to a plant that some even suggested was *too* productive to be good? In this case, we could imagine that another exogenous shock (the plague) displaced what was in the first place a precarious equilibrium, and helped to bring Northern Italian populations within a new Boserup space that had only recently appeared on the horizon. It must be noted that this dynamic might be not entirely coherent with Lee's original implications, but in our perspective it is an entirely acceptable use of his synthesis as an aid to interpret actual historical dynamics.

46. MALANIMA P. (2002, pages 126-129); LO CASCIO E. and MALANIMA P. (2005, page 29).

6. - Conclusions

This article has made use of Lee's dynamic synthesis as a theoretical support to the interpretation of the case study of Northern Italy from the Middle Ages to around 1800. It has suggested that Lee's synthesis, by allowing us to make a distinction between "Boserupian" and "Malthusian" forces, and by pointing out that the area in which a virtuous interaction of demographic forces and technological innovation can happen is limited (in other words, explicitly accounting for situations in which technological innovation is not possible, or cannot prevent Malthusian forces from coming into action), has much to offer as an aid to interpretation of actual historical dynamics. While Lee himself recognized in the lack of "testability" the most serious drawback of his model, here his work has been used simply to place into perspective a specific case study, without any formal empirical test. This article, then, does not intend to propose Lee's synthesis as an alternative to other models currently the object of greater attention and particularly those related to Unified Growth Theory. It does, however, attempt to make the point that a clear distinction between different demographic forces, which population theory separates much more neatly than most contemporary economic history, is useful when studying the past.

In the case of Northern Italy, this led to identifying a Boserup space from which, from the Roman Era to the Early Modern period, population could not escape. In this period high-population equilibrium levels close to the maximum carrying capacity were reached, and repeatedly rebounded from due to exogenous shocks (with hints that specific pandemics might have to be considered as endogenous, if and when support is provided in favour of the idea that they were caused by diseases triggered by poor nutrition levels). It also allowed for interpreting the final overcoming of these millenary limits as a movement towards a different Boserup space. A space "created" by the discovery of the New World and the import of new crops (an exogenous event), together with relevant advances in agronomic theory which ultimately led to the integration of those crops into complex systems of rotation, and with new techniques for the use of water. Furthermore, it suggested that non-Boserupian agrarian innovation may have hindered rather than favoured the survival of the people living on a territory (as in sixteenth century Lombardy), when market incentives overcame what we could label "demographic incentives"[47]. Such a situation can last only until positive

[47] Of course, it is also possible that market incentives orientate agrarian innovation in the same direction as demographic incentives (or "Boserupian forces"). In Northern Italy, this was the case after the critical years 1590-1630 – but not before the great famine of the 1590s, or at least, not in key regions such as Lombardy.

checks make economic actors recognize the problem of sustainability, inducing them to change their strategies. Lastly, this article has demonstrated that even when Boserupian innovation does take place, as in Emilia, it is not always enough to prevent the abandonment of the area of virtuous interaction (the boundaries of the Boserup space), and consequently Malthusian crises can happen in spite of such innovation, as at the time of the 1590s famine.

The first section of the article has already provided information both about criticism of Lee's synthesis, and about alternative ways of modelling the (originally Boserupian) idea that population growth by itself provides a stimulus to agrarian innovation. However some concluding words about the possibility of applying this conceptual framework to other areas of Europe (and potentially, of the world) are necessary. One exceptional case has already been underlined: that of the vast Alpine region comprising part of South-East France, Northern Italy, Southern Germany, all of Switzerland and most of Austria. Here, the most recent synthesis interested in long-term developments (Mathieu, 2000) has suggested that Boserupian forces were able to act, almost undisturbed, from the late Middle Ages up until the age of industrialization and the demographic transition. Explaining how this could happen, means looking for the origins of the characterizing "low-pressure" demographic regime of the Alps, a topic which is still the object of much debate. It is even more relevant to compare Northern Italy with the area of Europe whose population dynamics in the past have been more comprehensively reconstructed: England. The classic *The Population History of England* by Tony Wrigley and Roger Schofield (1981), which provided the data used in most subsequent recontructions, was basically Malthusian in interpreting the data. Malthusian, or even arch-Malthusian (Clark, 2007), views of English population history have been prevalent until now[48]. Lee himself interpreted the case mainly in the light of variations of "Malthusian" models (Lee, 1981; 1985), even though he explicitly recognized the possibility that «population growth drove technological progress» (Lee and Anderson, 2002, page 198)[49]. The presence of "Boserupian causality" in the English case has been suggested with the greatest force by Theofanis Tsoulouhas, who even stated that it was "dominant". He concluded that "exoge-

48. It is not convenient to discuss here the quite sizeable literature on the English case: by far the most studied, and also the one subject to most debate.

49. It is significant, I think, that in this late work the 1986 article is not cited, apparently due to the already mentioned impossibility of testing it with econometric analyses. The views expressed there, though, are considered in Lee's less empirical, more theoretical works: for example, LEE R. (1987; 1990).

nous mortality changes determined the population changes which, in turn, drove the technological changes" (Tsoulouhas 1992, page 169). Tsoulouhas related this statement to the exogenous decline in mortality determining a demographic growth of eighteenth century England, which in its turn "caused" a trend change in the growth rate of technology. It is significant, though, that we could use the same statement to describe how climatic and environmental instability determined the exogenous mortality shocks which ultimately caused North Italian populations to exceed their millenary limit (the famine of the 1590s and the dearth years that preceded and followed it orientated the choices towards the production of more calories per hectare[50]). In other words, according to specific situations, both declining and rising mortality can provide a "Boserupian" stimulus to technological change. This conclusion suggests that, when focusing on specific case studies and on well defined time periods, accurate historical analysis is needed to apply population theory correctly (and it should be noted that up to now, the generalizability of English results to the rest of Europe has proven, at best, very dubious). In this perspective, this article has suggested that for historical analysis, and without negating the usefulness of more generalizing approaches in understanding long-term macroscopic transformations, it is still helpful, when explaining actual historical developments, to distinguish between "Malthusian" and "Boserupian" dynamics, as properly done by most population theory.

50. As shall be remembered, it is possible to suggest that also the plague pandemic of 1629-1630 provided a stimulus to agrarian innovation, by inducing people to overcome reluctance to change patterns of food consumption and planting crops of maize. However, the plague also cancelled, for many decades, the demographic pressure on resources that, in a Boserupian perspective, would have stimulated agrarian innovation. In this article, inertia in patterns of innovation has been implied: with conversion of fields to new crops, and particularly to paddy, requiring a lot of effort over many years once the decision has been taken to change crops. In such perspective, it has been suggested that the plague pandemic offered to North Italian populations the time span needed to complete an agrarian conversion, stimulated by high population levels since the late sixteenth century, without the need for further intervention of Malthusian positive checks.

BIBLIOGRAPHY

ALFANI G., «Population and Environment in Northern Italy during the Sixteenth Century», *Population*, no. 4, 2007, pages 1-37.

-.-, «Crisi demografiche, politiche di popolazione e mortalità differenziale (ca. 1400-1630)», *Popolazione e Storia*, no. 1/2009, 2009*a*, pages 57-75.

-.-, «The Famine of the 1590s in Northern Italy: An Analysis of the Greatest "System Shock" of the 16th Century», paper given at the World Economic History Congress, Utrecht, August 2009, forthcoming in *Histoire et Mesure*, 2009*b*.

-.-, *Il grand tour dei cavalieri dell'apocalisse. L'Italia del "lungo Cinquecento" (1494-1629)*, Marsilio, Venezia, 2010*a*.

-.-, «Pestilenze e "crisi di sistema" in Italia tra XVI e XVII secolo», in CAVACIOCCHI S. (ed.), *Le interazioni fra economia e ambiente biologico*, Florence University Press, Firenze, 2010*b*, pages 219-244.

-.-, «Plague in Seventeenth Century Europe and the Decline of Italy: An Epidemiological Hypothesis», *Working Paper*, 2010*c*.

-.-, «Climate, Population and Famine in Northern Italy: General Tendencies and Malthusian crisis, ca. 1450-1800», *Annales de Démographie Historique*, no. 2/2010, 2010*d*, pages 23-54.

-.-, «Malthus or Boserup? Agricultural Innovation in Early Modern Italy and the "Rice Revolution"», in VAN DER BURG M. - MAAT H. (eds.), *Fifty Years of IRRI and Global Food Strategies through International Rice Research, 1960-2010*, forthcoming, 2010*e*.

ALFANI G. - COHN S.K., «Nonantola 1630. Anatomia di una pestilenza e meccanismi del contagio», *Popolazione e Storia*, no. 2/2007, 2007, pages 99-138.

ATZROUNI M. - KOMLOS J., «Population Growth through History and the Escape from the Malthusian Trap: A Homeostatic Simulation Model», *Genus*, no. 41, 1985, pages 21-39.

BATTISTINI F., *L'industria della seta in Italia nell'età moderna*, Il Mulino, Bologna, 2003.

BELOCH K.J., *Die Bevölkerung der griechisch-römischen Welt*, Leipzig, 1886.

-.-, *Storia della popolazione italiana*, Le Lettere, Firenze, first ed. *Bevölkerungsgeschichte Italiens*, Gruyte, Berlin-Leipzig 1937-1961, 1994.

BONNEUIL N., «Malthus, Boserup and Population Viability», *Mathematical Population Studies*, no. 5, 1994, pages 107-119.

-.-, «History, Differential Inclusions, and Narrative», *History and Theory*, vol. 40, no. 4, 2001, pages 101-115.

BOSERUP E., *The conditions of Agricultural Growth*, Allen and Unwin, London, 1965.

-.-, *Population and Technology*, Blackwell, Oxford, 1981.

CAPASSO S. - MALANIMA P., «Economy and Population in Italy. 1300-1913», *Popolazione e Storia*, no. 2/2007, 2007, pages 15-40.

CATTINI M., *I contadini di S. Felice. Metamorfosi di un mondo rurale nell'Emilia dell'Età moderna,* Torino, Einaudi, 1984.

CAZZOLA F., «Colture, lavori, tecniche, rendimenti», in PINTO G. - PONI C. - TUCCI U. (eds.), *L'Italia agricola dalle origini ad oggi*, vol. II, *Il Medioevo e l'età moderna*, Accademia dei Georgofili, Polistampa, Firenze, 2002, pages 223-253.

CHIARINI B., «Was Malthus Right? The Relationship between Population and Real Wages in Italian History, 1320 to 1870», *Explorations in Economic History*, no. 47, 2010, pages 460-475.

CHITTOLINI G., «La pianura irrigua lombarda fra Quattrocento e Cinquecento», *Annali Cervi*, X, 1988, pages 207-222.

CLARK G., *A Farewell to Alms*, Princeton University Press, Princeton, 2007.

COHEN M.N., *The Food Crisis in Prehistory. Overpopulation and the Origin of Agriculture*, Yale University press, New Haven, 1977.

COHN S.K., *The Black Death Transformed*, Arnold, London, 2002.

COLEMAN D. - SCHOFIELD R.S. (eds.), *The State of Population Theory: Forward from Malthus*, Blackwell, Oxford, 1986.

COPPOLA G., *Il mais nell'economia agricola lombarda (dal secolo XVII all'Unità)*, Il Mulino, Bologna, 1979.

CORRITORE R.P., *Storia economica, ambiente e modo di produzione. L'affermazione della gelsibachicoltura in Lombardia nell'ultima parte del Cinquecento*, paper given at conference *Storia economica e ambiente italiano. Ca. 1400-1850*, Bocconi University, Milan, January 2010.

CUFFARO N., *Population, Economic Growth and Agriculture in Less Developed Countries,* Routledge, London, 2001.

DEEVEY E., «The Human Population», *Scientific American*, vol. 203, no. 3, 1960, pages 195-204.

DEL PANTA L., «Per orientarsi nel recente dibattito sull'eziologia della "peste"», *Popolazione e Storia*, no. 2/2007, 2007, pages 139-149.

DEL PANTA L. - LIVI BACCI M. - PINTO G. - SONNINO E., *La popolazione italiana dal Medioevo ad oggi*, Bari, Laterza, 1996.

DI TULLIO M., *La ricchezza delle comunità,* PhD dissertation, Bocconi University, 2010.

DORIA M., «Le colture del Nuovo Mondo», in PINTO G. - PONI C. - TUCCI U. (eds.), *L'Italia agricola dalle origini ad oggi*, vol. II, *Il Medioevo e l'età moderna*, Accademia dei Georgofili, Firenze, Polistampa, 2002, pages 569-577.

FINZI R., *"Sazia assai ma dà poco fiato". Il mais nell'economia e nella vita rurale italiane, secoli XVI-XX*, Bologna, CLUEB, 2009.

FORNASIN A. - ZANNINI A. (eds.), *Uomini e comunità delle montagne. Paradigmi e specificità del popolamento dello spazio montano (secoli XVI-XX)*, Udine, Edizioni Forum, 2002.

FUSCO I., *Peste, demografia e fiscalità nel regno di Napoli del XVII secolo*, Franco Angeli, Milano, 2007.

-.-, «La peste del 1656-58 nel Regno di Napoli: diffusione e mortalità», forthcoming in *Popolazione e Storia*, no. 1/2009, 2009, pages 115-138.

GALOR O., «Comparative Economic Development: Insights from Unified Growth Theory», 2008, Lawrence R. Klein Lecture, *http://ideas.repec.org/p/bro/econwp/2009-10.html*, 2009.

GALOR O. - WEIL D.N., «Population, Tecnology and Growth: From Malthusian Stagnation to the Demographic Transition and Beyond», *American Economic Review*, no. 4/2000, 2000, pages 806-827.

LEE R.D. «Short-Term Variation: Vital Rates, Prices and Weather», in WRIGLEY E.A. - SCHOFIELD R.S. (eds.), *The Population History of England 1541-1871: A Reconstruction*, Harvard University Press, Cambridge MA, 1981, pages 356-401.

-.-, «Population Homeostasis and English Demographic History», *Journal of Interdisciplinary History*, vol. 15, no. 4, 1985, pages 635-660.

-.-, «Malthus and Boserup: A Dynamic Synthesis», in COLEMAN D. - SCHOFIELD R.S. (eds.), *The State of Population Theory: Forward from Malthus*, Oxford, Blackwell, 1986.

-.-, «Population Dynamics of Humans and Other Animals», *Demography*, vol. 24, no. 4, 1987, pages 443-465.

-.-, «The Demographic Response to Economic Crisis in Historical and Contemporary Populations», *Population Bulletin of the United Nations*, no. 29, 1990, pages 1-15.

LEE R.D. - ANDERSON M. «Malthus in State Space: Macro Economic-Demographic Relations in English History, 1540 to 1870», *Journal of Population Economics*, no. 15, 2002, pages 195-220.

LE ROY LADURIE E., *Histoire humaine et comparée du climat*, vol. I: *Canicules et glaciers XIIIe-XVIIIe siècles*, Paris, Fayard, 2004.

LEVI G., «L'energia disponibile», *Storia dell'economia italiana*, vol. 2, Torino, Einaudi, 1991, pages 141-168.

LITTLE L.K. (ed.), *Plague and the End of Antiquity. The Pandemic of 541-750*, Cambridge University Press, Cambridge, 2007.

LIVI BACCI M., *A Concise History of World Population*, 2nd ed., Blackwell, Oxford, UK, 1997, pages 195-220.

-.-, *La popolazione nella storia d'Europa*, Laterza, Bari, 1998.

-.-, *Conquest: The Destruction of the American Indios*, Polity Press, Cambridge, 2008.

LOEHLE C. - MCCULLOCH J.H., «Correction to: A 2000-year Global Temperature Reconstruction Based on Non-Tree Ring Proxies», *Energy and Environment*, vol. 19, 2008, pages 93-100.

LO CASCIO E. - MALANIMA P., «Cycles and Stability. Italian Population before the Demographic Transition», *Rivista di Storia Economica*, no. 3, 2005, pages 197-232.

MALANIMA P., *L'economia italiana. Dalla crescita medievale alla crescita contemporanea*, Bologna, Il Mulino, 2002.

MALTHUS T.E., *An Essay on the Principle of Population, as it Affects the Future Improvement of Society*, J. Johnson, London, 1798, ed. it. *Saggio sul principio di popolazione*, Einaudi, Torino, 1977.

-.-, *A Summary View on the Principle of Population*, John Murray, London, 1830, ed. it. *Saggio sul principio di popolazione*, Einaudi, Torino, 1977.

MATHIEU J., *Storia delle Alpi 1500-1900*, Bellinzona, Casagrande, 2000.

-.-, «Il cerchio interdisciplinare: un ricordo ticinese», *Archivio Storico Ticinese*, XLI, vol. 135, 2004, pages 139-148.

MC NICOLL G., «Review to The State of Population Theory: Forward from Malthus», *Population Studies*, vol. 42, no. 1, 1988, pages 144-146.

NUNN N. - QUIAN N., «Columbus's Contribution to World Population and Urbanization: A Natural Experiment Examining the Introduction of Potatoes», *Working Paper*, 2008.

PERSSON K.J., *Pre Industrial Economic Growth*, Blackwell, Oxford, 1988.

-.-, «The Malthus Delusion», *European Review of Economic History*, no. 12, 2008, pages 165-173.

-.-, *An Economic History of Europe. Knowledge, Institutions and Growth, 600 to the Present*, Cambridge University Press, Cambridge, 2010.

ROMBAI L. - BONCOMPAGNI A., «Popolazione, popolamento, sistemi colturali, spazi coltivati», in PINTO G. - PONI C. - TUCCI U. (eds.), *L'Italia agricola dalle origini ad oggi*, vol. II, *Il Medioevo e l'età moderna*, Accademia dei Georgofili, Polistampa, Firenze, 2002, pages 171-219.

SCHEIDEL W., «Human Mobility in Roman Italy, I: The Free Population», *Journal of Roman Studies*, XCIV, 2004, pages 1-26.

SELLA D., *Italy in the Seventeenth Century*, London, Longman, 1997.

SERENI E., *Storia del paesaggio agrario italiano*, Laterza, Bari, 1961.

SONNINO E., «L'età moderna (secoli XVI-XVIII) », in DEL PANTA L. - LIVI BACCI M. - PINTO G. - SONNINO E., *La popolazione italiana dal Medioevo ad oggi*, Laterza, Roma-Bari, 1996, pages 73-130.

STEINMAN J. - KOMLOS J., «Population Growth and Economic Development in the Very Long Run: A Simulation Model of Three Revolutions», *Mathematical Social Sciences*, no. 16, 1988, pages 46-63.

THEILMAN J. - CATE F., «A Plague of Plagues», *Journal of Interdisciplinary History*, no. 3/2007, 2007, pages 371-393.

TSOULOUHAS T.C., «A New Look at Demography and Technological Changes: England, 1550 to 1839», *Explorations in Economic History*, no. 29, 1992, pages 169-203.

WRIGLEY E.A. - SCHOFIELD R.S., *The Population History of England 1541-1871: A Reconstruction*, Edward Arnold Publishers, London, 1981.

Energy and Economic Growth in Europe. The Last Two Centuries

Silvana Bartoletto*
University of Naples "Parthenope",
Department of Economic Studies S. Vinci

The aim of this article is to analyze the role of energy in long-term economic growth. Particular attention will be paid to the relation between energy and GDP. Energy productivity, that is the ratio *of output to energy (Y/E), will be reconstructed and, through a decomposition analysis, I will try to show the relative importance both of rising consumption and of changes in the productivity of energy in growth of* per capita *output.*
[JEL Classification: N130, N140, N730, N740, O130].

Keywords: economic growth, energy consumption, energy productivity, decomposition analysis.

* *<silvana.bartoletto@uniparthenope.it>*.

1. - Introduction

Energy was of central importance in the transition from the old to the modern economy. However, the role of energy in economic growth is still poorly researched in comparison with the traditional factors, capital and labour. Business and financial economists pay remarkable attention to the impact of oil and other energy prices on economic activity, but the mainstream theory of economic growth gives little or no attention to the role of energy or other natural resources in promoting or enabling economic growth.

The key factors that could reduce or strengthen the linkage between energy use and economic activity over time are:

- technological change;
- shifts in the composition both of energy input and of economic output;
- substitution of energy with other forms of inputs.

According to the neoclassical growth theory, the only cause of continuing economic growth is technological progress that makes it possible to produce greater quantities or a better quality of output from the same quantity of input. Energy transition and improvements in energy quality[1] became possible only when the technological obstacle was overcome. We could say that changes in the composition of the energy balance reflect the changes in energy technology through the ages. It was only during the 18th century, with the invention of the steam engine by Thomas Newcomen and James Watt, that the Age of Machines actually began. This made the exploitation of new energy sources possible and hence the growth of *per capita* energy consumption and GDP. In the previous article in this same journal, Malanima presented the main trends of European energy consumption from 1800 to the present day and showed the strong link between energy transition and economic growth. With his results as a starting point, I will deal with a little-known central theme; efficiency in long-term energy consumption over a long period. Energy intensity, that is the *ratio* between energy and GDP (E/Y), is an important concept in research on the well-analysed energy-economy relationship. Almost unknown is the reciprocal of energy intensity, (Y/E), that we could call *productivity of energy*, which represents the output created in relation to a certain amount of consumed energy. A decomposition analysis of rates of growth of *per capita* GDP will be carried out in order to specify the relative im-

1. Energy quality is the relative economic usefulness per heat equivalent unit of different energy carriers. The shift to higher quality fuels, reduces the amount of energy required to produce GDP.

portance of the input of energy and the efficiency of its exploitation in Europe during the 19th and 20th centuries.

2. - The Present Energy Balance

The last two centuries have been a period of unprecedented economic growth throughout Europe and the world. Both the size of the economy and the level of energy consumption have expanded at a faster rate than world's population. As a consequence, modern economies are able to produce goods and services on a scale unconceivable in pre-industrial economies, and do so by utilising a vastly increased *per capita* supply of energy. In 2007, on the eve of the economic and financial crisis, world energy consumption was about 12,071 Mtoe and *per capita* energy consumption was about 1.82 toe; that is 76,19 Gigajoules. More than 80 percent was represented by fossil energy carriers: coal, oil and natural gas (Table 1). Nuclear energy represented 6 per cent and hydroelectricity 2 per cent. The remaining 10 per cent consisted of biomass *i.e.* organic vegetable sources and waste. Food for men and working animals, today a marginal source of power, are not included. Firewood is still an important item of consumption but only in relatively backward countries.

TABLE 1

WORLD TOTAL AND *PER CAPITA* ENERGY CONSUMPTION IN 1973, 2007 (TOE)

	1973			2007		
	Mtoe	Toe per c.	%	Mtoe	Toe per c.	%
Coal/peat	1,500.90	0.38	24.36	3,186.32	0.48	26.40
Crude oil	2,866.25	0.73	46.52	4,131.97	0.62	34.23
Gas	978.90	0.25	15.89	2,519.87	0.38	20.87
Nuclear	53.05	0.01	0.86	709.14	0.11	5.87
Hydro	110.23	0.03	1.79	264.74	0.04	2.19
Renewables and waste	646.05	0.16	10.49	1,176.39	0.18	9.75
Other	6.00	0.00	0.10	82.93	0.01	0.69
Total	6,161.38	1.56	100.00	12,071.36	1.82	100.00

1 Toe=10,000,000 Kcal= 41,868 Gigajoules; 1 Mtoe=10^6 Toe
Source: our processing of data from the International Energy Agency (IEA) 2009.

During the last two centuries, the energy balance has undergone several changes and its present composition reveals the strata of a long history of technical changes. Before the modern growth, the energy sources were food for men and working animals, wood, along with water and wind employed to drive mills and sails. These sources are classified as traditional energy sources. Modern growth, from about 1800 until today, has marked a sharp rise in the amount of energy consumption, when fossil energy sources, first coal, then oil and later natural gas, multiplied in the economy. *Per capita* energy consumption in Europe increased from 15,000 kcal per day in 1800 to 101,882 in 2000[2]. The passage from organic vegetable sources to organic mineral sources represented only one aspect of the energy transition. Even more important was the technological change which allowed new kinds of use of these fuels. Until the end of the 1940's, the world energy balance was dominated by coal which still represented more than 50 per cent of total consumption.

In the meantime, oil consumption grew and since oil was abundant and cheap, its consumption rose at a very fast rate, especially from the beginning of the 1950's.

GRAPH 1

CRUDE OIL PRICES 1861-2008
(US DOLLARS PER BARREL)

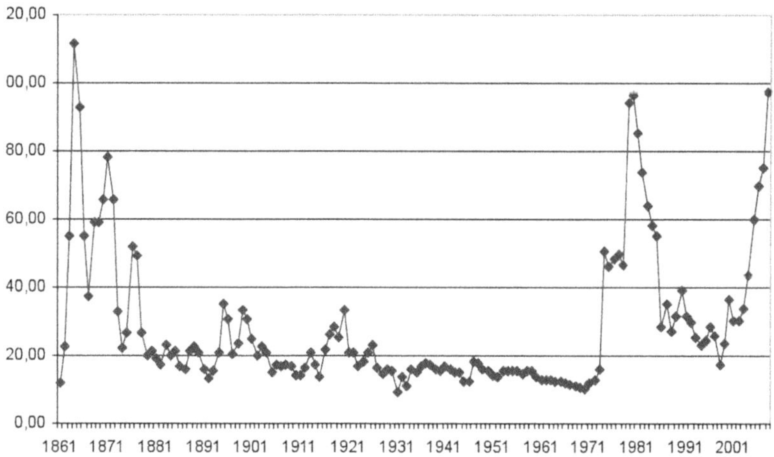

Source: BP, *Statistical review of world energy 2009.*

After the energy crises of the 1970's, the composition of the world energy balance changed once more (Table 1) and oil prices increased by 130-140 per cent (Graph 1)[3]. In 1973, just before the oil crises, the main energy source was oil,

2. See Malanima, Table 3, previous article in the same journal.

3. The average official prices fixed by Opec between December 1978 and December 1979 rose from 12.8 to over 26 dollars per barrel. The following year, they peaked at 45 dollars per barrel, about 20 times the price of ten years earlier (CLÔ A., 1994, pages 61-125).

with a share of 46.5 per cent of the total. Then, the oil consumption diminished significantly, while natural gas consumption rose from 15 per cent in 1973 to 21 per cent in 2007. Since the oil crises, some countries have invested heavily in nuclear power, whose share rose from 0.86 percent in 1973 to 6 percent in 2007. In spite of the 1970s oil crisis, which exposed the dramatic vulnerability of the economic system of industrialized countries, our energy problems, far from improving, have become even greater. High levels of *per capita* energy consumption by a world population of several billions and current environmental concerns, especially regarding the increase of CO_2 emissions, make it necessary to realize a new energy transition so as to avoid a new Malthusian trap. As also argued by Maddison (2008), the proved reserves of fossil fuels are likely to be inadequate to sustain the growth of the world economy to the end of the present century.

3. - The Constraints of the Traditional Energy System

In the transition from old to modern economy, energy is of central importance. In recent studies energy has been recognized as a main determinant of the divergence of Europe from the rest of the world in the 19th century and as the main cause of its success (Pomeranz, 2000; Allen, 2009; Malanima, 2010). The introduction of new energy carriers and engines able to transform energy into mechanical work were the necessary, although not the only condition of modern growth in Europe and subsequently in the rest of the World. Notable and rapid changes accelerated the transition from one energy system to another especially from the 17th to the 19th century. Without this transition, modern growth could not have occurred. Although some other significant changes took place in the use of energy before the modern era, the transition to an energy system based on fossil fuels is often, because of its rapidity and intensity, considered the most important transition. A first move towards the change derived from the population growth. Over a period of 200 years, from 1650 to 1850, world population doubled from about 600 to 1200 million. The rate of increase was about 10 times higher than in the previous 1600 years. In Europe population also grew with virtually no interruptions from about 1450 onwards. From 1600 to 1800, while European agricultural production grew by 54%, the population grew by 64%. This led to a reduction of the *per capita* agricultural income, especially from 1750

---

4. Malanima P. (2006*b*, pages 101-121).

to 1820[4]. The cutting down of forests to obtain new cultivable land had already greatly reduced the availability of wood. The acceleration of growth brought on a true shortage of wood. Food, glass, and soap industries consumed huge quantities of wood, but the greatest demand came from shipyards and ironworks.

Variations in climate conditions were another important factor towards the change. From the end of the high Middle Ages, in the 13th century, temperatures gradually dropped. The so-called Little Ice Age lasted until the first half of the 19th century. The negative effects of colder temperatures on vegetable energy sources were remarkable after 1550, when the lowest levels in the past 1,000 years were reached: 1 degree less than the average of the last millennium[5].

The increase of energy prices represented another stimulus towards change. From the second half of the 16th century wheat prices began to increase rapidly and, after a period of stability or decline, did so again from about 1730-50 onwards. Moreover, there is no consensus on the role of energy prices in energy transition.

Allen argued that if we look at the real prices of fuel, the increase ceases to exist during the early modern age. He deems the theory of the whole of Europe facing an energy crisis by the 18th century to be false, since an energy crisis simply did not happen. There was no general crisis but only local adjustments[6]. However, Malanima replied that Allen's conclusions were only correct if we look at pre-modern energy sources in a partial way; that is if we consider firewood and fuels as the only sources of energy, excluding others. If, on the other hand, we consider energy in a wider perspective, including food for humans and animals, Allen's conclusions can no longer be considered valid.

Two significant changes influence the transformation taking place in the energy system, the first is aimed at saving land and the second, thanks to inanimate machines, labour. Both played a central role in the start of modern growth. The consumption of greater quantities of coal was an important way to save land, together with the introduction into European agriculture of new, more productive, crops and new forms of crop rotation.

From the end of the 16th century onwards, coal and peat began to be used to overcome the lack of wood. Overall, the use of coal in Europe during the 17th and the greater part of the 18th century remained modest and was not important for the economy as a whole. The situation in England or in the northern areas of the Netherlands was different, as in these areas from the 17th century onwards much of the economy's success depended on the exploitation of new energy resources.

5. Malanima P. (2009, pages 49-94).

6. Allen R.C. (2003, page 477).

The shift to new fuels represented one aspect of the energy transition then in progress. However, it was not the most important. The transition to a modern economy and society required the introduction of inanimate machines, first achieved in the form of steam engines. The introduction of machines able to convert heat into mechanical power was the main change in the energy system, comparable in importance to the discovery of fire.

Energy transition is often associated with the Industrial Revolution. In this perspective Allen argued in a very recent work that the transition to coal and the adoption of the steam engine and other breakthrough technologies of the Industrial Revolution, such as the coke blast furnace, the water frame and the spinning jenny, happened earlier in Britain than in other countries because coal in Britain was cheap and labour was expensive[7]. In particular, he argued that since wages in Britain were high and coal cheap in comparison to other countries in Europe and Asia, it was profitable to adopt new technologies that replaced workers by machines. Zeira reasons in a similar way, showing that the adoption of such technologies is not beneficial everywhere, but depends crucially on the prices of production factors[8]. However, as we have seen, Paolo Malanima emphasizes the role of the energy crisis (referring especially to wood), in the energy transition[9].

The enormous growth in the number and size of towns was both the result of, and a factor in, the changes that have occurred in the energy system over the last two centuries because a town can only survive if it can draw on the energy it needs. In the 19th century in particular, when coal gradually replaced firewood, towns began to change and grow rapidly. The growth of a city such as London from 50,000 inhabitants in the 16th century, to about 600,000 in the 18th century and 1 million in the 19th century would have been impossible without coal, considering the limits imposed by the availability of wood[10].

4. - The Growth of Energy Consumption

From 1800 to the present day energy consumption in Europe has risen considerably more than population. As shown by Malanima in the previous article, if we only consider Western Europe, the increase in *per capita* terms was 6-fold

7. ALLEN R.C. (2009).
8. ZEIRA J. (1998, pages 1091-1117).
9. MALANIMA P. (2006*b*, page 101). See also WRIGLEY E. (1962; 1988).
10. For the case of London, see ALLEN R.C. (2009, especially pages 84-90); HAYAMI A., DE VRIES J., VAN DER WOUDE A. (1990, page 12). For Naples and other Italian cities see BARTOLETTO S. (2009; 2004).

and, overall, 26 fold. Until 1840, energy consumption per head did not increase in Europe, because coal consumption rose at the same rate as the population. In the subsequent period, fossil fuels consumption grew at a faster rate than population. On the world scale, the increase of energy consumption was even higher than Europe, about 10-fold in *per capita* terms, 63 times on the whole.

Although the transition from traditional energy sources to the fossil energy carriers was a crucial watershed, we know very little about it and there is the false impression that industrial economies made a swift transition from vegetable energy sources to fossil energies in the late 19th century or in the early 20th century at the latest. Nothing is farther from the truth. Until well into the 20th century, most Western economies remained vastly dependent upon traditional forms of energy (human and animal labour, firewood, wind and waterpower). Animals carried out most agricultural tasks and provided transportation. In urban and rural dwellings, people mainly relied on firewood, peat, and organic oils for cooking, heating and lighting. Early industrialization was based on firewood and wind and waterpower, and in some areas these remained the main sources of energy for the industry until the late 19th century. Even during the coal period of the industrial revolution, human and animal power continued to play a significant role. In 1860, traditional energy sources on a world scale represented about 75-80 per cent of total consumption and until the beginning of the XX century, about 40 per cent of the total (Graph 2). However, we can suppose that the percentage of traditional energy sources was much higher, especially during the second half of the 19th century and the first decades of the 20th century, when huge quantities of wood consumption were not accounted for. If they were included, the percentage of modern energy sources would be much lower, especially during the period 1860-1900.

It is important, however to consider the difference in consumption of the various regions. While energy transition took place rapidly in Northern Europe, especially in England and Wales, this was not the case in Southern Europe, where on the eve of the 20th century traditional energy carriers represented 70-80 per cent of total energy consumed[11]. In Italy and Spain, in particular, the contribution of traditional energy to total energy input became less than 50 percent only immediately before World War II. Moreover, in the 1960's a fourth of the total energy input was still of vegetable origin[12].

11. In Italy firewood consumption varies considerably between the Southern regions and the Alpine area. Some estimations concerning Naples and Rome confirm an average of about 1.5-2 kg *per capita* per day during the XIX century (Bartoletto S., 2009; 2004).

12. Bartoletto S. - Rubio M. (2008).

GRAPH 2

PERCENTAGE OF MODERN ENERGY SOURCES ON TOTAL ENERGY CONSUMPTION WORLDWIDE (1860-1953)

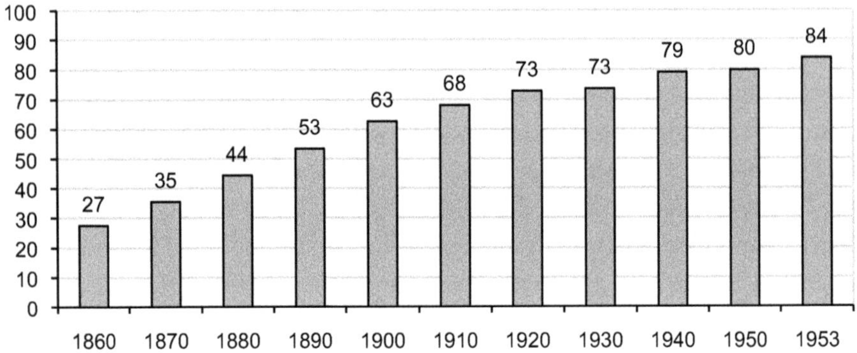

Source: UNITED NATIONS (1955, page 307). These estimates are lower than those in the previous article by Malanima, since here only firewood is included (without food for humans and fodder for working animals).

TABLE 2

COMPOSITION OF ENERGY CONSUMPTION IN ENGLAND AND WALES 1600-2000 (%)

	1600	**1700**	**1800**	**1900**	**1950**	**2000**
Firewood	28.7	13.4	4.4	0	0	0
Food for human beings	27.5	19.9	7.4	2.5	3	1.5
Feed for animals	25.6	16.4	8.8	1.7	0	0
Wind, Water	1.5	1.4	2.5	0.33	0	0
Fossil fuels	16.7	48.6	77	95.5	97	90.6
Primary electricity	0	0	0	0	0	7.9

Source: WARDE P. (2008, page 69).

TABLE 3

COMPOSITION OF ENERGY CONSUMPTION IN ITALY 1870-2000 (%)

	1870	**1913**	**1950**	**1973**	**2000**
Firewood	50.04	21.17	16.50	3.08	2.39
Food for human beings	22.89	19.77	15.37	4.56	3.89
Feed for animals	18.74	15.99	11.62	0.50	0.00
Wind, Water	1.04	0.28	0.11	0.00	0.00
Fossil fuels	7.29	41.67	46.94	88.70	88.19
Primary electricity	–	1.11	9.46	3.16	5.53

Source: MALANIMA P. (2006*b*); BARTOLETTO S. - RUBIO M. (2008).

It may also be noted that a census report for 1911 stated that about 58 per cent of the total horsepower installed in Italian industries (1,603,836 hp) was represented by water power, while only 29 per cent was represented by steam.

The energy balance in England and Wales was very different. Water power never accounted for more than 1 per cent of aggregate energy consumption. By the beginning of the 18th century, wood provided only 13 per cent of the total consumption and about 4 per cent a century later (Table 2). By the beginning of the 20th century energy consumption was almost entirely comprised of coal.

The dominance of coal among countries varied considerably. In Italy, the maximum was around 40 per cent in 1935-40 (Table 3) and in Spain coal consumption peaked in the years 1927-30 with levels of 46-40 per cent. In Sweden, the peak was only 45 per cent in 1909. In England and Wales, in 1700, coal consumption already represented more than 48% and in 1800 more than 70 per cent. The maximum was around 95% starting from the beginning of the 1880s.

GRAPH 3

PER CAPITA ENERGY CONSUMPTION IN SOME EUROPEAN COUNTRIES (1850-2005)

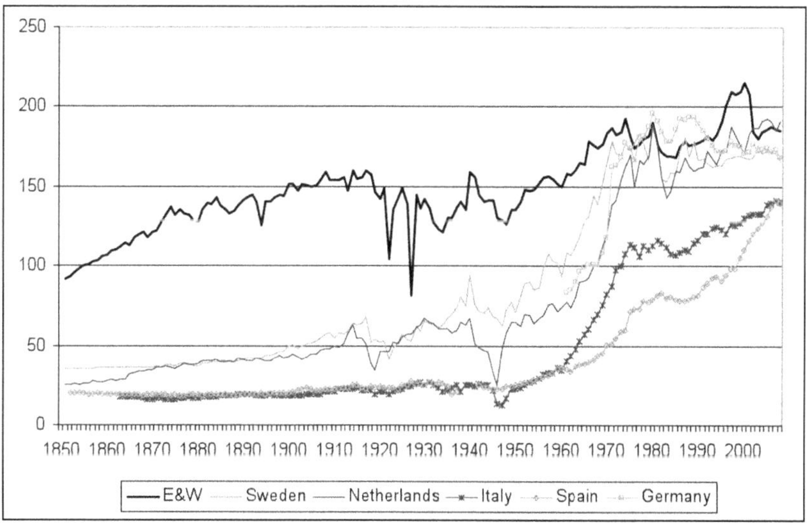

Source: For Italy, BARTOLETTO S. (2005), MALANIMA P. (2006); for Sweden, KANDER A. (2002); for England and Wales, WARDE P. (2008); for Netherlands and Spain, GALES B. *et* AL. (2007). For the period 1960-2007 our data processing on IEA 2009.

While structures of the energy systems are different, we can observe similarities in the long-term pattern of energy consumption (Graph 3). There were modest rates of increase until the World War II, a period of faster growth rates in 1950-73 and declining growth rates between 1973 and 2000.

In Europe, Britain retained its supremacy. Other countries such as Belgium, Germany, France and above all Sweden, Italy and Spain lagged far behind during the period between 1850-1950. Towards 1865, energy consumption of 100 gigajoules per person per year appears to have been reached in the United Kingdom, but in Germany this level was attained only shortly before World War I and in France and Italy only after the Second World War, at the beginning of the 1960's.

A convergence between countries in *per capita* energy consumption has taken place during the last half century, after the strong economic growth during the period 1950-1970.

5. - Energy Productivity in Europe

The advantage of machinery and technological change are immediately visible in the trend of energy productivity (*Y/E*), which is the reciprocal of energy intensity formula (*E/Y*). While energy intensity refers to the amount of energy used to produce a certain amount of output, energy productivity inform us about how much value has been created in relation to a certain amount of energy. This is because the measure of energy flow, that is the energy converted in the production of goods, is not correlated with the economic output value. Very small amounts of energy conversion can create considerable value and *vice versa*. At the same time, there is a difference between the thermodynamic efficiency of the physical conversion of energy from one form to another and the economic efficiency in turning energy into value. Energy carriers, whether primary or secondary, are converted into energy services; heat, motion and light. In line with the second law of thermodynamics, all these conversions of energy from one form to another entail losses. As shown by Malanima (2009), thermodynamic efficiency (E_u / E_i) can be expressed through a *ratio* where in the numerator we find the useful energy or energy services (E_u) and in the denominator the input of energy in the form of a primary or secondary source (E_i). If 90 per cent of the energy of wood is lost when it is burnt in an open stove and only 10 per cent remains as heat in the room we say that the thermal efficiency is 10.

The measure of economic, and not only thermodynamic, efficiency is sometimes called *energy productivity* (*Y/E*), where *Y* is output in monetary terms and *E* is the raw input of energy (expressed in joule, toe etc.) into the economic flow.

Increases in thermodynamic efficiency imply increases in energy productivity. For example, the transition from biological engines to mechanical engines, which is the main recent change in the energy system, implied both a rise in energy yield or efficiency and productivity. However, while thermodynamic efficiency deals with the mere technical structure of an engine or a series of engines, energy productivity is more comprehensive and contemporaneously includes technical, organisational and institutional changes. More precisely, productivity of energy is not only influenced by technical capacity of conversion, but also by other variables, such as the specialisation of economy in particular sectors and sub-sectors. If parts of the economy that are more energy efficient than others grow faster and provide a greater share of national income, the energy productivity of the economy will increase although technical knowledge may not have changed. The climate, the level of gross output and changes in the institutions that rule the economy, the society and the performance of economic variables also influence energy productivity.

TABLE 4

ENERGY PRODUCTIVITY, ENERGY CONSUMPTION AND POPULATION IN THE WHOLE OF EUROPE (1830 2000)

	Energy productivity (GDP/GJ)	Energy consumption (PJ)	Population (million)
1830	48.69	5,382	234
1900	38.55	24,181	422
1950	52.71	39,675	548
1970	60.22	89,806	656
1989	78.36	111,240	720
2000	82.90	113,350	728

Petajoules (PJ) corresponds to 1 million GJ.
Source: for energy productivity, our data processing. For energy consumption and population in the whole of Europe, MALANIMA P. (2010); for GDP, MADDISON A. (2003; 2008).

From the analysis of energy productivity in Europe (Table 4-5, Graph 4), it may be may noted that the introduction of modern energy carriers and machines only implied a rise in energy productivity only starting from the end of the XIX century onwards. If we consider the whole of Europe (Table 4), the reduction of energy productivity from 48.69 (GDP/GJ) in 1830 to 38.55 (GDP/GJ) in 1900 is evident. We could say that during this period of time, a biological converter was still more efficient than a machine, so the GDP increase depended totally on the growth of energy consumption.

TABLE 5

ENERGY PRODUCTIVITY, ENERGY CONSUMPTION AND POPULATION IN 12 WESTERN EUROPEAN COUNTRIES (1820-2001)

	Energy productivity (GDP/GJ)	Energy consumption (PJ)	Population (million)
1820	52.71	2,707	115
1850	56.48	4,222	144
1870	52.57	6,450	162
1890	48.24	10,259	187
1913	47.72	17,617	228
1921	53.27	13,832	222
1931	58.27	16,467	237
1941	69.80	17,941	248
1951	67.67	20,107	258
1961	84.75	25,794	276
1971	83.29	40,107	298
1981	99.60	43,133	306
1991	117.76	45,503	314
2001	127.04	51,242	325

Source: for energy productivity and energy consumption, our data processing. For data on population and GDP, MADDISON A. (2003; 2008). This table includes 12 Western European countries: Austria, Belgium, Denmark, Finland, France, Germany, Italy, Netherlands, Norway, Sweden, Switzerland and The United Kingdom.

GRAPH 4

ENERGY PRODUCTIVITY IN WESTERN EUROPE 1820-2001 (GDP/GJ)

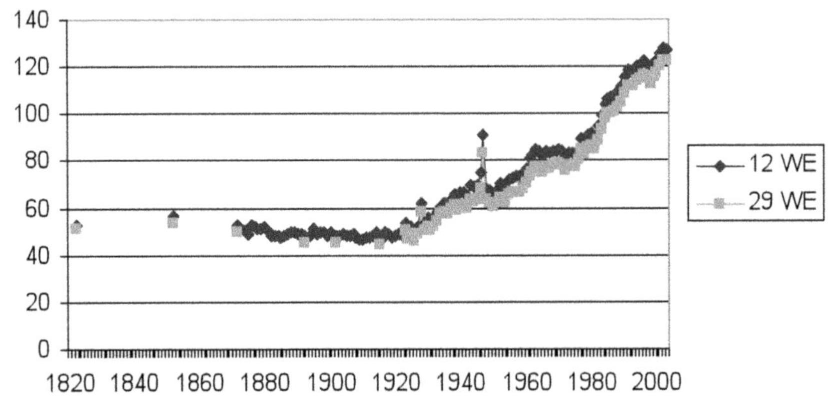

Source: our data processing.

6. - Decomposition Analysis

In order to evaluate the actual increase in the available useful energy in these last two centuries, the energy consumed must be multiplied by the efficiency in energy consumption. A decomposition of *per capita* GDP can be useful in order to specify the relative importance of the input of energy and the efficiency of its exploitation (Malanima, 2009). *Per capita* GDP (*Y/P*) is, in fact, the result of energy consumption *per capita* (E/P) by the productivity of energy (*Y/E*):

$$\frac{Y}{P}=\frac{E}{P}\cdot\frac{Y}{E}$$

If we assume:

y as the rate of growth of *Y/P*;

e as the rate of growth of *E/P*; and

π as the rate of growth of *Y/E*;

we can specify the relative importance of *e* and π in the growth of *y*, during the period concerned; that is the years from 1820-30 until 2000. Thus:

$$y=c+\pi$$

If we consider the whole of Europe (Table 6) we can see that the increase of *per capita* GDP during the first period (1830-1900), depended totally on the growth of energy consumption, while as a consequence of low efficiency of the first steam engines energy productivity slowly diminished (-0.14).

TABLE 6

RATES OF GROWTH OF *PER CAPITA* GDP (*Y*), *PER CAPITA* ENERGY CONSUMPTION (*E*) AND PRODUCTIVITY OF ENERGY (*Π*) 1830-2000 IN EUROPE

	y	e	π
1830-1900	0.42	0.56	-0.14
1900-1950	0.47	0.20	0.27
1950-1970	1.67	1.38	0.29
1970-1989	0.88	0.28	0.60
1989-2000	0.25	0.03	0.22

Source: our data processing.

Between 1900 and 1950, the rate of growth of energy productivity was remarkable in Europe. The input of energy contributed less than the productivity of energy in the growth of *per capita* product. Acceleration of modern growth was determined by the so-called Second Industrial Revolution whose main developments were the internal combustion engine, the electricity and the transition from coal to oil. Between the two World Wars, particularly during the twenties and thirties, there was a marked acceleration of technological progress in Europe. New machines were introduced on a larger scale than ever before. The growth of output of manufactured goods took place in many countries where the increase in the number of workers was zero or at least minimal. Many of the innovations made since the First World War had their origins in the previous period, but were improved and became more widespread during the period between the wars. Moreover, technical advances in fields such as chemistry, production of motor vehicles and aeronautics was greatly stimulated by the war. Of the many technological developments of the period, two were of exceptional importance: electricity and motor vehicles for transport. These two advancements led to a huge increase in economic efficiency dramatically reducing costs and increasing production flexibility. The electric motors revolutionized low-cost power for industry and agriculture and stimulated the mechanization of production. Cars, trucks and tractors transformed the cost and the means of transport for both people and goods.

If we do not consider the whole of Europe, but only 12 Western European countries, a deeper analysis is possible (Table 7).

TABLE 7

RATES OF GROWTH OF PER CAPITA GDP (*Y*), PER CAPITA ENERGY CONSUMPTION (*E*) AND PRODUCTIVITY OF ENERGY (*Π*) 1820-2000 IN WESTERN EUROPE

	y	e	π
1820-1850	0.42	0.32	0.10
1850-1870	0.50	0.65	-0.16
1870-1890	0.51	0.70	-0.19
1890-1913	0.63	0.65	-0.02
1913-1921	-0.58	-1.18	0.60
1921-1931	0.86	0.47	0.39
1931-1941	0.96	0.18	0.78
1941-1951	0.19	0.32	-0.13
1951-1961	1.76	0.78	0.98
1961-1971	1.51	1.59	-0.08
1971-1981	0.98	0.20	0.78
1981-1991	0.84	0.11	0.73
1991-2001	0.70	0.37	0.33

Source: our data processing.

From 1830 until the First World War, a remarkable decline took place in energy productivity, especially during the period 1850-1890. The input of energy contributed more than the productivity of energy to the growth of GDP. From 1913, both the contribution of rising consumption and its more efficient use determined a growth in GDP, with some differences. The rate of growth of energy productivity was much higher than the rate of growth of *per capita* energy consumption during the periods 1913-1921, 1931-1941 and 1971-1991 reaching a maximum during the decade 1951-1961. During the 1960s energy productivity slowly diminished because energy, especially oil, was both abundant and cheap and energy use was less efficient. After the severe oil crisis of 1970, the higher price of energy encourages more efficient exploitation and a decline of energy consumption in the industrial sector. Compared to other continents, Europe, today, has the highest productivity of energy and the lowest energy intensity. The scarcity of fossil fuels and the high prices of energy, together with environmental concerns, helps Europe to proceed in the direction of energy saving.

7. - Conclusions

The transformation of the energy system was the necessary condition to overcome the Malthusian limits for growth. Without the transition to fossil fuels economic growth could not occur. However, the consumption of higher quality energy sources has only been possible since the technological obstacle was overcome.Thanks to the employment of the steam engine, the first technology for the direct conversion of fossil fuels into work, the transition to an energy system based on the exploitation of fossil fuels began. Later, with the introduction of electricity, another important transition in energy consumption occurred. It was the first energy carrier that could be converted to light, heat and work, *in situ*[13]. At the same time, the possibility of exploiting new energy sources once again stresses the importance of technical change as the engine of economic growth. Productivity growth, resulting from technical change, can be considered as a fundamental source of economic growth. This means that GDP growth was determined not only by the rise in energy consumption but also by an increasing technical efficiency, *i.e.*, the *ratio* of useful energy to consumed energy. Moreover after the oil crises of the 1970s, concerns between ecologists and many natural

13. Ruttan V.W. (2001, page 235).

scientists about the constraints imposed by a scarcity in natural resources have taken a more pessimistic view on possibilities of sustainable growth especially. In very recent years, a Malthusian perspective is once again spreading. Coal, oil and natural gas are non-renewable energy sources and produces a number of environmental problems, firstly CO_2 emission and the rise of global warming. Recent estimations demonstrate that proven reserves of fossil fuels are likely to be inadequate to sustain the potential growth of the world economy to the end of the present century. The transition to fossil fuels, that was the fundament of modern growth during the last century, now risks triggering a new Malthusian trap, if we do not reduce our dependence on fossil fuels and encourage the consumption and development of alternative energy sources.

BIBLIOGRAPHY

ALLEN R.C., «Was There a Timber Crisis in Early Modern Europe?», in CAVACIOCCHI S. (ed.), *Economia e energia secc. XIII-XVIII*, Istituto Internazionale di Storia economica "F. Datini", Firenze, Le Monnier, 2003.

-.-, *The British Industrial Revolution in Global Perspective*, Cambridge, Cambridge University Press, 2009.

BARTOLETTO S., «Dalla legna al carbon fossile. I consumi di combustibile a Napoli nel corso dell'Ottocento», *Mélanges de l'Ecole française de Rome*, no. 116, 2004.

-.-, «I combustibili fossili in Italia dal 1870 ad oggi», *Storia Economica*, no. 2, 2005.

-.-, «Energy Consumption in Naples between the 19th and the 20th Centuries», *Working Papers*, Department of Economic Studies, University of Naples Parthenope, December 2009.

BARTOLETTO S. - RUBIO M., «The Energy Transition in Southern Europe: Italy and Spain (1850-2000)», *Global Environment*, no. 2, 2008.

CLÔ A., «Crisi energetica: consumi, risparmi e penetrazione elettrica», in ZANETTI G. (ed.), *Storia dell'industria elettrica in Italia,* vol. 5, *Gli sviluppi dell'Enel 1963-1990,* Roma-Bari, Editori Laterza, 1994.

GALES B. - KANDER A. - MALANIMA P. - RUBIO M., «North versus South. Energy Transition and Energy Intensity in Europe over 200 Years», *European Review of Economic History*, no. 11, 2007.

HAYAMI A. - DE VRIES J. - VAN DER WOUDE A. (eds.), *Urbanization in History. A Process of Dynamic Interactions,* Oxford, Clarendon Press, 1990.

KANDER A., *Economic Growth, Energy Consumption and CO_2 Emissions in Sweden 1800-2000,* Almqvist & Wicksell international, Stockholm, 2002.

MADDISON A., *The World Economy, Historical Statistics*, OECD, 2003.

-.-, *Contours of the World Economy, 1-2030 AD, Essays in Macro-Economic History,* Oxford University Press, 2008.

MALANIMA P., «Energy Crisis and Growth 1650-1850: The European Deviation in a Comparative Perspective», *Journal of Global History*, no. 1, 2006*a*.

-.-, *Energy Consumption in Italy in the 19th and 20th Centuries. A Statistical Outline,* CNR, Rome, 2006*b*.

-.-, *Pre-Modern European Economy. One Thousand Years (10th-19th centuries)*, Leiden-Boston, Brill, 2009.

-.-, «Pre-Modern Economies», in KANDER A. - MALANIMA P. - WARDE P., *Power to People,* in print, 2010.

POMERANZ K., *The Great Divergence. China, Europe and the Making of the Modern World Economy,* Princeton University Press, 2000.

RUTTAN V.W., *Technology, Growth and Development. An Induced Innovation Perspective*, Oxford University Press, 2001.

SCHURR S., *Energy in the American Economy, 1850-1975. An Economic Study of its History and Prospects,* The Johns Hopkins Press, Baltimore, 1960.

STERN D., «Economic Growth and Energy», *Encyclopedia of Energy*, vol. 2, no. 00147, Elsevier, 2004.

UNITED NATIONS, *L'utilisation de l'énergie atomique à des fins pacifiques,* Atti della Conferenza internazionale di Ginevra, voll. I, III, 1955.

WARDE P., *Energy Consumption in England and Wales*, CNR, Istituto di Studi sulle società del Mediterraneo, Rome, 2007.

WRIGLEY E., «The Supply of Raw Materials and the Industrial Revolution», *Economic History Review*, II s., XV, 1962.

-.-, *Continuity, Chance and Change. The Character of the Industrial Revolution in England,* Cambridge, Cambridge University Press, 1988.

ZEIRA J., «Workers, Machines and Economic Growth», *The Quaterly Journal of Economics*, vol. 113, no. 4, Nov. 1998, pages 1091-1117.

The Path Towards the Modern Economy The Role of Energy

Paolo Malanima*
ISSM-CNR, Naples

The transformation of the energy system during the period between the 16th and 19th centuries was the necessary, although not sufficient, condition of modern growth, first in Europe and then in the rest of the World. The transition to alternative forms of energy was prompted by the decline in per capita *energy availability in early modern Europe during the phase of population rise from the late Middle Ages onwards. The transformation taking place in the energy system was composed of two significant changes, the first aimed at saving land, and the second labour.*
[JEL Classification: N130, N140, N370, N740, O130].

Keywords: energy, energy transition, modern growth.

* *<www.paolomalanima.it>*; *<paolo.malanima@issm.cnr.it>*.

1. - Introduction

The strong direct link between coal, steam power and growth in the last decades of the 18th century and the first half of the 19th century might seem quite obvious to modern observers. Yet looking at coeval economists and even modern scholars, it is not so. We know that the English classical economists did not single out the importance of this linkage. «None appreciated the revolutionary possibilities for the scale and speed of expansion in industrial output (and at a later date in agricultural output) made available to an economy that switched from sole reliance upon organic raw materials to an increasing dependence upon mineral raw materials» (Wrigley, 1988*b*, page 34).

John Nef (1954 and 1932) was the first modern historian who looked at energy as the main support of the industrial revolution. In his opinion, the industrial revolution was a long-term development, which started at the end of the 16th century, when a first industrial revolution occurred in Britain and strengthened during the following two centuries. His view on the energy-economy interplay did not reach the centrality it deserved.

The explanation of world economic history by Carlo M. Cipolla (1961 and 1962), based on energy changes, was appreciated, but not followed by the historians working on the beginning of modern growth. In his opinion, two economic revolutions took place in the history of mankind and both were correlated to deep changes in the energy endowment: the Agricultural Revolution in the Neolithic and the Industrial Revolution in the 18th and 19th centuries. Both marked discontinuity in demographic evolution and productive capacity.

More recently Antony E. Wrigley proposed a reconstruction of British economic history founded on the passage from an "organic" to a "mineral-based" economy supported by coal and steam power (1988*a* and 2004). Although the approach by Wrigley has been appreciated by the scholars, it has not been so widely followed by the historians dealing with pre-modern European economy. Among the several constraints of past agrarian economies, the "organic" character is seldom mentioned.

Only in recent years has the emphasis on energy within the transition from the old to the modern economy received new attention (Pomeranz, 2000; Allen, 2009). Its central importance has been recognized as a main determinant of the divergence of Europe from the rest of the world in the 19th century and as the main cause of its success (Tello, Jover, forthcoming).

It is not my aim to discuss the complex interrelationships among the many variables involved in the process of transition to modern economy. Much more modestly the purpose of the following pages is to stress an immediate determinant of growth. More remote extra-economic determinants are outside the picture I will present. In the following pages the transition to modern growth will be explained as a discontinuity founded on the increase in productive capacity, due to the introduction of new energy carriers and engines able to transform energy into mechanical work. This change, on the other hand, will be correlated to the pressure of population on the agrarian system and the ensuing increase in prices both of the traditional energy sources and of labour. In the second section I will present the endowment with energy sources of pre-modern agrarian societies and the theoretical approach; in the third the stimuli to change in the energy system together with the constraints; in the fourth the beginning of the transition towards modern growth.

2. - The Energy System of the Agrarian Civilisations

2.1 *Pre-Modern Energy Systems*

From the viewpoint of energy, the long history of mankind could be divided into two main epochs:

- the 5-10 million years from the birth of the human species until the early modern age, that is about 5 centuries ago, and
- the recent history of the last 500 years, which has witnessed a fast acceleration in the pace of energy consumption.

In the first long epoch, energy sources were represented by *food* for humans, *firewood* and *fodder* for animals; with a small addition of *water* and *wind* power. The second epoch witnesses the rapid almost complete replacement of the old sources by fossil carriers, which became and still constitute the main energy source. Since organic vegetable sources of energy were transformed into work by biological converters (animals) and fossil sources are transformed by mechanical converters (machines), we are able to distinguish past economies according to the system of energy they employed and the prevailing kind of converters as:

1. *organic vegetable economies* or *biological economies*;
2. *organic fossil economies* or *mechanical economies.*

Although the energy system prevailing today is apparently wholly different from the simple digestion of food, the original energy source, or from the burning of firewood by our primitive ancestors, it is, however, based on the same principle, that is the oxidation of Carbon compounds by breaking their chemical ties. Looking at their energy system, not only are past economies organic economies, as suggested by A. Wrigley (1988*a*; 2004) in important contributions to the topic of energy, but our economies too are so. Actually, since carbon compounds are defined in chemistry as organic compounds and organic chemistry is the chemistry of organic compounds, we could define all the energy systems which have existed until today as organic and the economies based on those organic sources as *organic economies*. Coal, oil and natural gas, the basic sources oxidized today in order to bring about organized, that is mechanical, work, heating or light are carbon compounds such as bread or firewood. The difference between pre-modern and modern energy systems depends on the fact that, until the recent energy transition, organic vegetable sources were exploited, whilst from then on organic fossil energy sources became the basis of our economy.

The analysis of the passage from the first economic system to the second is the aim of the present paper.

2.2 *Phytomass and Energy*

In past agricultural societies more than 95 percent of the energy input was represented by phytomass, that is, vegetable products. The problem any economy had to face was the combination of soil exploitation in order to cover the primary needs of mechanical power and heating. Food demand is the most inelastic. Food, however, is not enough. Working animals were the main capital of many past economies, essential both to work the land and transport goods…; and animals need pastures. According to the different systems of cultivation, a percentage of land varying in size had therefore to be subtracted from the arables and employed to feed the animals. However, fields and pastures were still not sufficient. Although with significant differences, depending on the location and climate, forests played an important role in the economies of past societies since they produced firewood, the main carrier of most past societies. The specific combination of these three essential needs distinguishes the several pre-modern agricultural systems. In any case, the availability of energy resources in pre-modern energy systems required soil and soil is not infinite (Malanima, 2006).

Low power and low energy consumption characterizes the energy systems based on phytomass. The power of a man in everyday work is the same as that of a 40 watts lamp, or 0.05-0.07 HP. The power of a horse is 15-20 times higher. The maximum power attainable on the land, in past agrarian economies, was that of a wind-mill, that is 10 HP at the best, while, on the sea, that of a sailing ship with a tonnage of 1,000, was 100-150 HP. Today a maximum power of several millions of HP is attainable by a nuclear power plant. We have here a measure of the effectiveness of work on the environment in order to transform it according to the needs and wishes of human beings.

In 1750, the daily *per capita* energy consumption in Europe (without Russia) was about 15,000 kcal for a population of 121 million. It reached almost 40,000 kcal in 1900, when the population was 295 million. In 2000 it was 100,000, with a population of 523 million. A simple calculation shows that, if the energy system had been based for the last 250 years on the same sources exploited in 1750 – assuming the same efficiency – the need for fertile land would have grown to more than 3 times the entire surface of Europe – Alps and Pyrenees included – in 1900 and to 20 times that surface in 2000.

2.3 *The Constraints of the System*

The system of energy based on land product is represented through the following Graph 1. In the left part, we see the combination of *L* and *K* to produce the output levels $Q_1 < Q_2 < Q_3$. *K* includes not only capital, but also natural resources, which represent the main part of *K* in pre-modern economy. A feature of these economies is, in fact, that, in order to produce the main energy carriers (food, fodder, and firewood), land is necessary and land availability can scarcely be modified. We assume then that *K* is represented in the graph by the vertical line. Some increase or decrease of *K* is in fact possible. New lands can be cultivated and their productivity increased thanks to investments of capital and labour; exogenous climatic changes can actually modify land availability. High temperatures permit the cultivation of hilly soils and lands in more northern regions. On the other hand, diminishing temperatures imply a subtraction of cultivable land. Land supply can oscillate from K^* to K_1 in this second case and from K^* to K_2 in the first.

Graph 1

COMBINATION OF PRODUCTION FACTORS (ON THE RIGHT)
AND AGGREGATE DEMAND AND SUPPLY (ON THE LEFT)

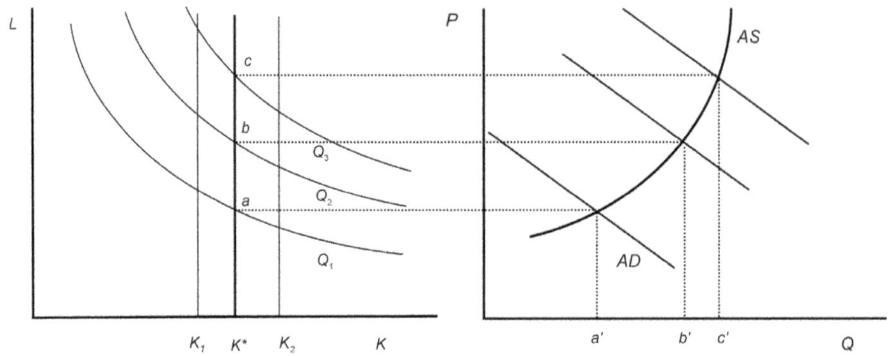

Possibilities of producing more vegetable energy do not lack, but they require an intensification of labour (more people work and more hours are devoted to labour by any worker). We see that, as soon as the system needs a higher level of output in order to feed and heat more biological converters, more labour is employed and the intersection of *L* with the given supply of land is higher and higher (at first in *a*, then in *b* and *c*). However, decreasing returns to labour impend on the agricultural energy system of past agrarian civilisations.

This is the reason why the price of energy rises, as soon as more labour is employed in order to raise the level of agricultural product. On the right side of the graph in fact, prices of agricultural goods (in real terms, that is divided by the consumer price index) can be seen corresponding to the quantities Q_1, Q_2, Q_3. Aggregate supply (*AS*) of energy, on the right of the previous graph, rises less and less (from *a'* to *b'* to *c'* on the horizontal axis), as soon as more labour is employed on *K* and the price of energy (*P*) rises.

On this background, the mean features of the change occurring between the late Middle Ages and the start of modern growth are represented by the following trends of the main variables:

1. *L* population and workers rise;
2. *K* resources, mainly natural resources, are stable (with the exceptions due to climatic changes);
3. p_e the real price of energy (agricultural commodities) rises;
4. MP_L marginal labour productivity diminishes and then $\frac{w}{pe}$, the real wage, diminishes;

5. w nominal wage rises (once the level of subsistence has been reached by the real wage), and then production costs of the entrepreneurs rise;
6. p_i the real price of industrial goods diminishes;
7. $\pi=p_i-w$ profits (π), the difference between prices of manufactured goods and labour costs, shrink and represent an incentive towards innovation.

Assuming 1. and 2., the others are merely developments of these assumptions (with the exception of the decline of real industrial prices, as we will see). The start of modern growth consists in the removal of the constraints represented by the vertical line *K*, that is the limited availability of natural resources. This significant change took place in two waves. The first occurred in England, and, to a lesser extent, in The Netherlands, after the second half of the 16th century and consisted in the development of coal and peat consumption, that is of fuels that did not need soil for their production. It was a way of saving land. The second developed in England after the 18th century and consisted in the introduction of artificial resources, that is non biological energy converters. These resources were represented by steam engines, in other words by thermal machines. Fossil fuels and machines marked a sharp rise both in the sources used and in the efficiency of their exploitation; that is a true *energy transition.* Modern growth, from about 1820 until today, was the consequence of this big change.

3. - The Stimuli Toward a Change

3.1 *Population Growth (L)*

World population doubled in the 1600 years after the birth of Christ: from 250 to 500 million. The rate of increase in this long period was, on average, 0.04 per cent per year: imperceptible, that is. The phase of population growth started at the end of the 15th century, accelerated in the 16th, slowed down in the 17th century and became ever faster from the end of this century. Over a period of 200 years, from 1650 to 1850, world population doubled: from about 600 to 1,200 million. The rate of increase was 0.4 per cent, or 10 times higher than in the previous 1600 years. These figures are, however, far from conclusive: their margins of uncertainty are wide, especially for earlier periods. No doubt, on the other hand, exists on the trend.

On the whole, the European population grew almost without interruptions from about 1450 onwards. The first wave of the *demographic transition* (Chesnais, 1986), starting from about 1670-1700, meant the acceleration of an already upward trend (Table 1).

Table 1

THE EUROPEAN POPULATION FROM 1400 TO 1900
(WITHIN PRESENT BORDERS) (MILLIONS)

1400	67.9
1450	71.2
1500	84.9
1550	86.6
1600	107.1
1650	105.3
1700	121.9
1750	143.2
1800	188.6
1870	310.3
1900	422.3

Source: Malanima P. (2009, page 9).

This acceleration was not a European event. The sudden demographic wave began, from the second half of the 17th century onward, to submerge the existing agrarian structures. Such a fast population growth had never occurred on a world scale. The same demographic trend was shared by other Eurasian regions such as India and China (Biraben, 1969). Although scholars do not agree on the reasons for this demographic wave, the opinion expressed by Braudel on the basis of the contemporary rise in several parts of the world would suggest a linkage with climatic changes, that is temperature increase in several regions at the same time (Braudel, 1979, I, chap. I; Galloway, 1986). Another reason (at least for Europe) is certainly the disappearance of the plague.

3.2 *Climate (K)*

When we look at energy in past agrarian civilizations, we often forget the importance of climatic changes in those traditional worlds where all forms of energy came directly from sunlight. Recent reconstructions by paleoclimatologists of temperatures over the last two millennia have shed light on the influence of variations in the sun's irradiation on energy sources. The effects of sudden climatic changes on harvests, agricultural prices and mortality have been repeatedly stressed in agrarian history. As to long-term climatic variations and their influence, historians have been much more cautious, especially because of our superficial knowledge of the subject until a few years ago and the few available series relating to climate over the very long term. However, energy availability in past agrarian civilizations not only depended on human technological ability to tap known sources, but also, and to a greater extent, on variations in the sun's irradiation reaching the Earth. To neglect this side of the problem when looking at energy in past agrarian civilizations means to neglect an important part of the whole story. A mere drop of 1 degree C° for several years can entail important effects on the energy balance of an agrarian civilization (Bozhong, 1998). The main consequences can be summarized as follows:

- kcal from solar radiation diminish by about 10 per cent per cm^2;
- hours of solar light decrease in the temperate zone from a yearly average of more than 2,000 to less than 1,900, with a consequent ca. three-week decrease in the growing periods of crops, pastures and forests (Marks, 1998, page 217). In cold northern European regions cereal cultivation becomes ever more difficult;
- microbial activity in the soil declines, and with it the decomposition of organic material and the activation of latent fertility;
- the altitude of cultivated land diminishes by 150-200 metres and the negative effects on cultivation can be serious especially in mountainous regions;
- it is harder to feed livestock in late winter and early spring: stored grass and hay may be insufficient until pastures grow again in April or May (Pfister, 1988, pages 38 ff).

Higher temperatures, on the other hand, mean the formation of free capital and the prospect for humans to exploit a wider range of natural energy resources. A correlation exists between long-term population movements and climatic variations. In general, warmer temperatures imply more energy from fields and woods and thus the possibility of supporting a wider population.

3.3 *The Little Ice Age: The Last Phase (K)*

It seems that in the 2000 years before 1900 annual temperatures varied within a narrow range and that long-term changes depended principally on variability of solar irradiation and volcanic eruptions (Crowley, 2000). The decline in temperatures, ordinarily defined as the Little Ice Age, occurred from the end of the 13th century, after the so-called Medieval Climatic Optimum (Graph 2). The effect on the economy is represented in the previous Graph 1 by the swing of the constraints of the natural resources from K^* towards K_1.

It seems highly probable that the negative effects of colder temperatures on vegetable energy sources were remarkable in the 17th century, when the lowest levels in the past 1,000 years were reached: 1 degree less than the average of the last millennium. «During the cooling period from around 1590 to 1670, grain yield, measures of fertility, and life expectancy were low, and the population growth rate declined» (Galloway, 1986, page 12). The formerly mentioned rise in population occurred from the end of the so-called Maunder minimum, in the second half of the 17th century (Eddy,1977*a*; 1977*b*; Eddy, Gilman, Trotter, 1976). Demographic transition started in the last phase of the Little Ice Age, which ended during the 19th century. However, recent research has shown that temperatures rose, to some extent, from the very last years of the 17th century; although the modern rise in temperatures only took place in the second half of the 19th century. After all, even within an unfavourable climatic phase, the first wave of population growth was accompanied by milder temperatures. Only from the 1760s was a standstill reached, followed by a decrease in the first two decades of the 19th century. This decline, while population was still growing, contributed to determine a reaction to offset the worsening in the standard of living.

GRAPH 2

AVERAGE TEMPERATURES IN THE NORTHERN HEMISPHERE 1300-1900

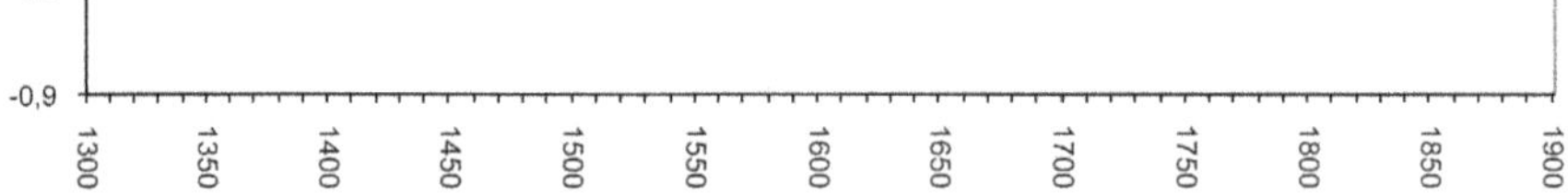

Source: LOHELE C. (2007); LOHELE C. - MC CULLOCH H. (2008).

3.4 *Energy Prices (p_e)*

Up to this point the relationship between humans and land and the relative scarcity of land following the rise in population during an unfavourable climatic age have been highlighted. The trend of energy prices contributes to specify the conjuncture of energy availability. Since we can avail of longer series of prices and wages for England and Italy, we will refer mainly to these countries.

GRAPH 3

WHEAT PRICES IN ITALY AND ENGLAND 1550-1860
(FLORENTINE SOLDI PER KG-ITALY AND PENCE PER KG-ENGLAND)

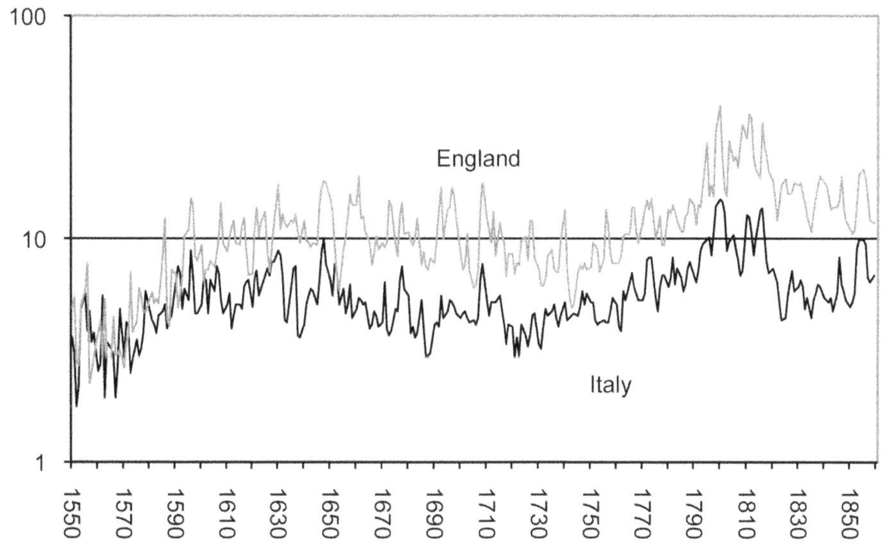

Source: for England CLARK C. (2004); for Italy MALANIMA P. in *www.paolomalanima.it.*

Evidence on the rise in prices is firstly provided by wheat (Graph 3). The correlation between the series is high (0.75), as can be seen on the graph: higher than might be expected. In the second half of the 16th century wheat prices began to increase rapidly and, after a period of stability or decline, did so again from about 1730-50. The rate of increase in the second half of the 18th century and the first two decades of the following century was more or less the same as during the Price Revolution two centuries earlier. From about 1820 wheat prices fell or stabilized. The growth in agricultural productivity allowed a larger population to be supported without any rise in prices. Previously the opposite had occurred.

Despite considerable differences amongst the various regions, price trends in the south, north and east of the continent show similar long-term trends: the 16th century rise, the 17th century decline or stability and the new 18th century increase (Graph 4).

GRAPH 4

CONSUMER PRICE INDEX IN EUROPE 1500-1850 (1500-50=100)

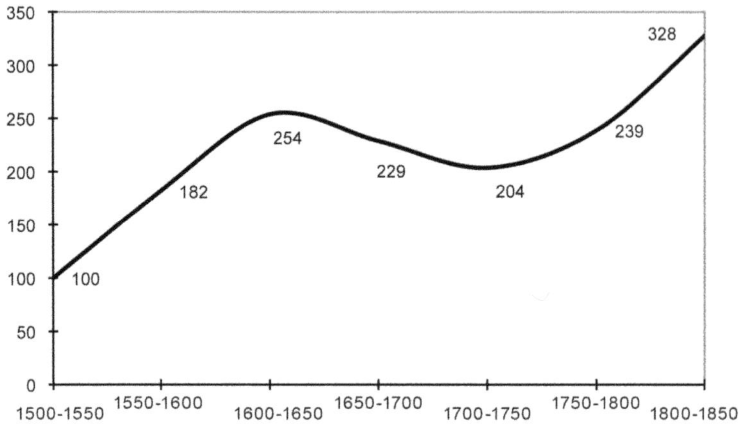

Source: MALANIMA P. (2009, chap. VI).

If we take fuel prices (that is firewood in most European regions, coal in England and peat in Holland from the 17th century onwards), we note the same trend of the primary energy input, food. All Carbon compounds exploited by the Europeans as sources of energy were growing in price from the 16th century onwards. Firewood prices rose about 2-3 times from 1500 until 1700. The increase was modest in the first half of the 18th century and became much stronger in the second (Table 2).

TABLE 2

INDICES OF FUEL PRICES IN SOME EUROPEAN CITIES 1500-1800 (1700=1).

	1500	1550	1600	1650	1700	1750	1800
Antwerp	0.39	0.80	0.79	0.90	1.00	0.91	0.93
Amsterdam	0.37	0.54	0.92	0.92	1.00	1.31	2.38
London	0.35	0.51	0.62	0.95	1.00	1.23	1.55
Paris	-	-	0.98	0.96	1.00	1.09	-
Strasbourg	0.36	0.70	0.87	0.88	1.00	1.60	3.31
Florence	-	0.56	0.83	1.13	1.00	0.99	1.82
Naples	-	1.42	1.68	-	1.00	1.14	1.63
Valencia	0.78	1.32	1.55	1.50	1.00	1.32	-
Madrid	-	1.43	1.89	1.57	1.00	1.34	1.88
Leipzig	-	0.83	1.16	0.72	1.00	0.88	-
Vienna	0.43	0.69	0.88	0.89	1.00	1.20	1.27
Danzig	0.56	0.97	1.00	1.06	1.00	1.68	2.73
Warsaw	-	0.59	1.25	1.05	1.00	1.71	-
Lwow	0.90	1.08	1.14	1.07	1.00	1.49	-

Source: ALLEN R.C. (2003, page 479) (fuel prices on which the Table is based are expressed in grams of silver per BTU).

Allen noted that if we look at the real prices of fuel, that is at fuel prices divided by the consumer price indices of any country, the rise disappears completely and «what impresses is the narrowness of the range of the real price of energy across Europe» (2003, page 474) during the early modern age. His conclusion is that «the theory that all of Europe faced an energy crisis by the 18th century is an attractive theory since it makes the Industrial Revolution the solution to a contradiction in the pre-industrial economy». This theory is, however, false in his view, since an "energy crisis" simply «did not happen. There was no general crisis, only local adjustments» (Allen, 2003, page 477).

Allen's conclusion is only correct if we look at pre-modern energy sources in a partial way; that is if we consider firewood and fuels as the only sources of energy, excluding others. However considering energy in a wider perspective, including, that is, food for humans and animals, we can not but disagree with Allen's view. In this case, since both food and fodder were rising in the 18th as were fuels, and food is the main component of the basket used to compute consumer price indices, in real terms fuel prices were stagnant. Actually, however they rose as did the other sources of energy.

3.5 *Energy Consumption per Head (Q/L)*

Rise of population, hard climatic conditions, decline of agricultural output per head and increasing prices of energy sources resulted both in a diminishing availability of energy *per capita* and in reactions aimed at compensating this decline.

The fall in energy availability from the soil per head by about 25 per cent over the period 1500-1800, and 15 per cent over the period 1750-1820, is apparent in every European region (Graph 5). Until a few years ago, one could still entertain doubts on agricultural product in England. Today it may be seen that a remarkable growth in labour and land productivity had also occurred in England in the 17th century, however the second half of the 18th century was not a prosperous period, at least from the point of view of agricultural output in *per capita* terms. During this half century «food consumption per person fell, reaching its nadir during the Napoleonic wars. In terms of food consumption, the idea of absolute immiseration during the early industrial revolution was no myth» (Allen, 1992, page 217). It appears that *per capita* agricultural product probably dropped less in England than elsewhere in Europe, including Italy, Belgium and the Netherlands.

GRAPH 5

PER CAPITA ENERGY CONSUMPTION IN EUROPE 1500-1850
(GJ PER YEAR)

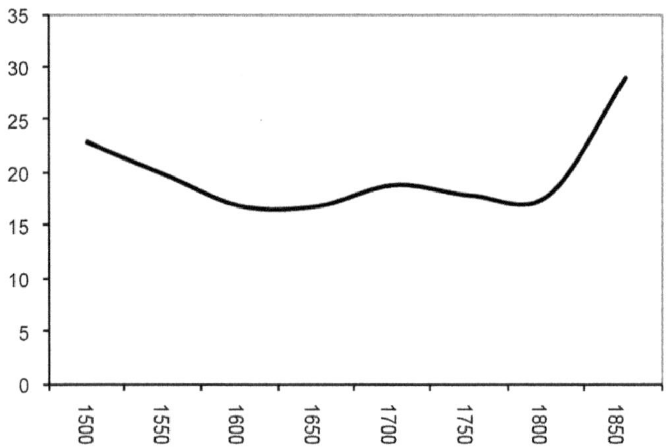

Note: Before the 19th century, we lack direct estimates of energy production and consumption (with the exception of England and Wales) (in WARDE P., 2006). This graph is based on the series of agricultural product in ALLEN R.C. (2000). We assume that, since energy consumption in pre-modern economies coincides with real agricultural product, the trend of agricultural output represents quite well the trend of energy consumption. On the basis of the relationship energy-agricultural output in the first half of the 19th century, I went back in time and reconstructed the curve presented in the Graph.

3.6 *Real Wages and Living Conditions* (MP_L *and* w/p_e)

Series of real wages witness a declining trend from the 15th century onwards. Rising population and declining per-worker resources within a relatively stationary technical framework implied a fall in labour productivity and subsequently in wage rates. Data referring to wages in different European cities reveals a 16th century slump which continued into the first half of the 17th century. Losses even reached 50 per cent. Stability followed for about a century, but subsequently, during the second half of the 18th century, a uniform decline, although of different intensity, brought real wages to a level between 20-60 per cent lower than that of the beginning of the 16th century.

Expressed in terms of wheat, in Western Europe the wage in building industry «fell from about 12 to 15 litres of grain in 1500-20, to 6 to 10 litres in 1780-1800» (Van Zanden, 1999, page 188). This trend is not very different from that of agricultural real wages.

The average European trend can summarise more clearly the phases of decline and growth in urban real wages (Graph 6). In the first half of the 17th century,

European real wage-rates were 23 percent lower than during the period between 1500-50. They recovered between 1650 and 1750. Subsequently they fell again between 1700-50 and 1800, reaching their lowest level since the late Middle Ages in 1780-1818. After 1818 prices began to diminish and wages to rise. From the perspective of the wage trend, the decades around 1800 can be considered a period of crisis.

GRAPH 6

TREND OF THE EUROPEAN REAL WAGE-RATES 1500-1850 (1500-50=100)

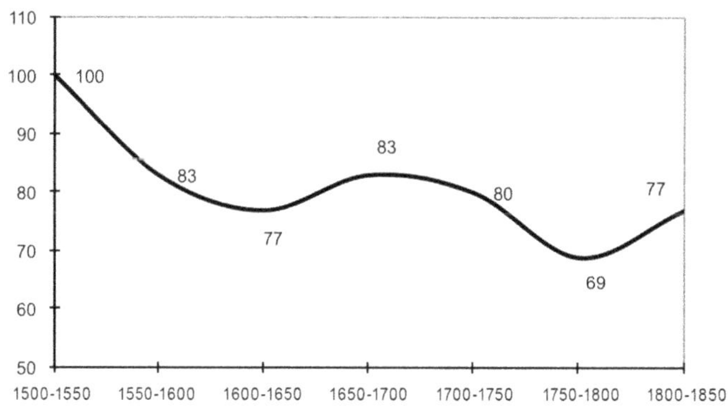

Source: MALANIMA P. (2009, chap. VI).

3.7 *Nominal Wages and Labour Costs (w)*

Whenever real wage is near the subsistence level, rising prices of agricultural goods can not but be followed by some rise in nominal wage. Increases in nominal wages occurred all over Europe during the second half of the 18th century. Since any input of energy was rising in price, there was no alternative for the entrepreneurs, either in the cities or the countryside, than to grant their workers a rise in their nominal wages; in reality the rise was not sufficient to keep their standard of living stable. The consequence was the rise in cost paid by the entrepreneurs in order to carry out their activity. Prices of the commodities produced, on the one hand, and wages in money paid out, on the other, are the basic elements of their economic calculation.

Graph 7

NOMINAL WAGE RATES IN EUROPE AND IN SOME EUROPEAN CITIES 1700-1850 (GR. OF SILVER)

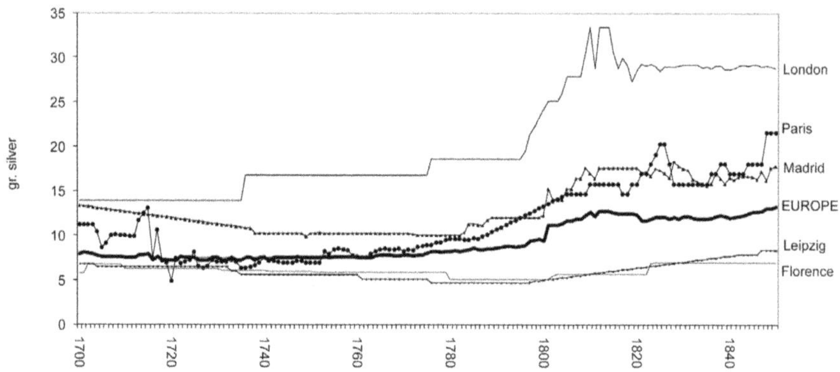

Source: based on data in Allen R.C., *www.iisg.nl/hpw*

Nominal wages, that is wages expressed in the silver content of the currency of any country, show that, in silver, British wages were already sensibly higher during the second half of the 18th century than before and than those of other regions (Graph 7). When the value of something expressed in precious metal rises, it means that the commodity or service purchased is more expensive, or that precious metals are cheaper, in that country; and probably, in the case of England during the so-called commercial revolution, both things were true. On the other hand, we know that the purchasing power of English wages was higher than that of other European workers. It can also be seen that everywhere in the continent nominal wages were increasing, during the second half of the 18th century.

3.8 *The Price of Manufactured Goods (p_i) and Profits (π)*

In every branch of activity, the difference between prices and costs and then the margins of profit were diverse. It seems reasonable to suppose that agricultural entrepreneurs were favoured by an upward trend of agricultural prices, followed, but only with some delay, by nominal wages. However, in the case of industrial entrepreneurs it was different. Prices of secondary commodities were in fact growing much less than agricultural prices. In the case of industry, margins of profit could be endangered by the rising trend of nominal wages, primarily determined by the rising prices of food.

If industrial real prices in England and agricultural real prices (deflated by means of the consumer price index) are observed, it can be discerned that although the 18th century trends were fairly similar, at the end of the century industrial prices relatively fell, as a consequence of the ongoing increase of productivity in textile production (Graph 8). In other European countries, the divergent trend was similar to that of England (Malanima, 2009, chap. VI).

GRAPH 8

REAL PRICES OF AGRICULTURAL AND INDUSTRIAL GOODS IN ENGLAND
1600-1830 (1600-10=1)

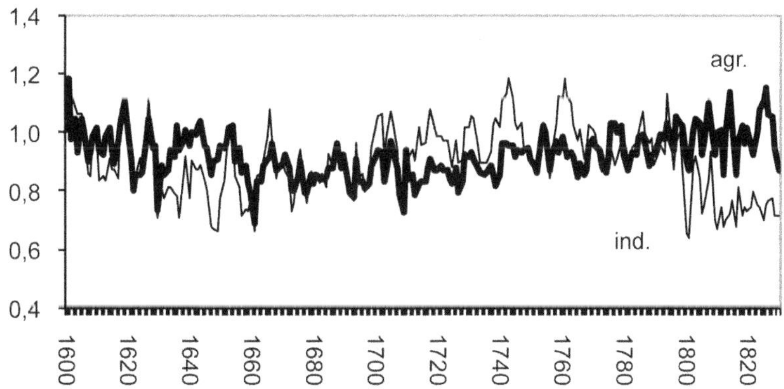

Source: based on data in ALLEN R.C., *www.iisg.nl/hpw.*

As David Ricardo showed, this different behaviour of agricultural and industrial prices can be explained as the consequence of the influx of innovations in industry and trade. «The natural price of all commodities...», Ricardo wrote, «has a tendency to fall, in the progress of wealth and population», thanks to «improvements in machinery», «better division and distribution of labour», and «increasing skill both in science and art of the producers». On the other hand, the diminishing returns in agriculture tend to enhance «the natural price of the raw material of which they are made» (Ricardo, 1821, chap. V).

4. - The Start of the Energy Transition

4.1 *Saving Land*

Under the pressure of population and in the face of declining *per capita* availability of natural resources and rising prices, any traditional agricultural society reacts by trying to intensify the use of land, and especially the arables, in order to meet the most inelastic need: food. Intensification means a higher ratio between harvest (in quantity or value) and cultivated soil (Boserup, 1965). It is a way of increasing the productive value of the soil, since less soil is needed to meet the same volume of the harvested calories. It represents a land-augmenting innovation.

The developments allowing land intensification in Europe began in the 16th century. These were as follows:

a. colonization of new lands;

b. introduction into European agriculture of new, more productive, crops;

c. new forms of rotation.

The other more important development, which will require particular attention, is the resort to coal.

a. *Colonization.* Colonization of new lands accompanied the rise in population and often meant deforestation. On the one hand new arables supported the growing demand for food, but, on the other, they implied a reduction in the availability of the main fuel: firewood. On the basis of contemporary literature on forest degradation and the frequent attempts to control and limit wood destruction, Pomeranz (2000) wrote of a European ecological crisis during the 18th and 19th centuries. Throughout the 19th century, not only did this process of conquering new space for agriculture continue, but it also spread outside Europe, opening up new lands on other continents, especially the Americas. These vast areas of natural resources were for the most part entirely unexploited.

b. *Maize and potato.* Although already known in some European regions in the 16th century, it was not until the end of the 17th century that maize spread across a part of Europe extending from the North of Spain and Provence, through the whole of the North of Italy (especially the Po Plain) to Slovenia and Hungary and subsequently to the Balkans. Another vegetable which originated in America was the potato. One hectare cultivated with potatoes could supply a caloric value two to three-fold that of a hectare cultivated with grain; sometimes even higher (Grigg, 1982, page 84). It spread particularly in northern Europe where in many cases it became the first agricultural product.

c. *Convertible husbandry.* The spread of convertible husbandry in England represented an important change, not only increasing land productivity, but labour productivity as well. According to Wrigley, this progress in labour productivity which occurred in England was still within the "organic" economy and was connected, in the 17th century, to the exploitation of more mechanical energy from animals than before (Wrigley, 2006). This progress in agricultural productivity was an aspect of the first stage of the energy transition in England.

These three reactions to the decline in *per capita* energy were able to partially compensate the decline in *per capita* terms. Only after 1820 did productivity of land rise faster than population. Agricultural prices, as we have seen, clearly witness this change.

4.2 *Coal*

Another way of saving land was through the greater use of coal. England was the first country in Europe to resort to coal on a wide scale. Looking at the dynamics of firewood and coal prices, we notice a scissor movement between the price of charcoal and that of coal after about 1530, when a true transition to coal started. Between 1500 and 1700, the rate of increase of charcoal prices was twice that of the consumer price index and the differential among these series became wider and wider in the 18th century (Wilkinson, 1973, page 114). Only at the beginning of the 19th century, when charcoal consumption had almost disappeared, did the prices of these fuels begin to draw closer to each other (Graph 9).

GRAPH 9

PRICES OF CHARCOAL AND COAL IN THE SOUTH-EAST OF ENGLAND
1440-1830
(000 POUNDS PER TOE)

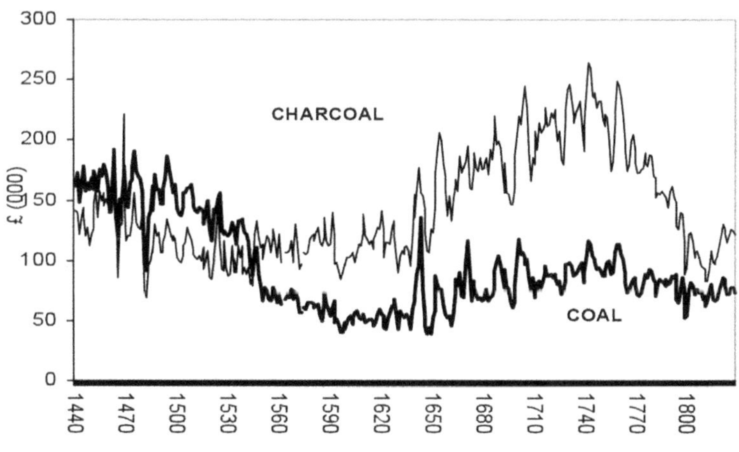

Source: FOUQUET R. (2008). *Note:* a Toe (ton of oil equivalent) = 10 million kcal.

Coal resources are distributed among 2,000 areas throughout the world. Within Europe, coalfields are virtually inexistent in the Mediterranean countries.

They are almost completely localized in the centre, north and east, and especially England, where the main deposits were and are located. In many places these coal deposits were easy to exploit. There is little wonder that they have been exploited since remote times.

The existence of fossil fuels had been known in Europe since the times of ancient Rome. During the late Middle Ages, in those northern European regions where coal was easily available, its consumption spread, as its price was far lower than that of firewood. In China coal was also widely used in metallurgy during the late Middle Ages (Hartwell, 1966; 1967). From the second half of the 16th century, the use of coal increased above all in England. The rising population and particularly that of London represented a strong stimulus towards the consumption of a much cheaper fuel than firewood. In the whole of England the production of coal increased 7-8 times between 1530 and 1630, thanks to the greater depth of the shafts and better drainage of the mines and by the 1620s it had become more important than wood as a provider of thermal energy. For a long period, England was by far the main producer of coal. Only at the end of the 19th century, the rest of Europe was able to compete with England. The proportion of coal consumed in England was 12 per cent of the total energy consumption in 1560, 20 per cent in 1600, and 50 per cent in 1700. Its consumption from 1560 until 1900 reveals an almost stable rate of growth, as a graph in log scale shows (Graph 10).

Graph 10

COAL CONSUMPTION IN ENGLAND & WALES 1560-1900
(IN PETAJOULES; LOG SCALE)

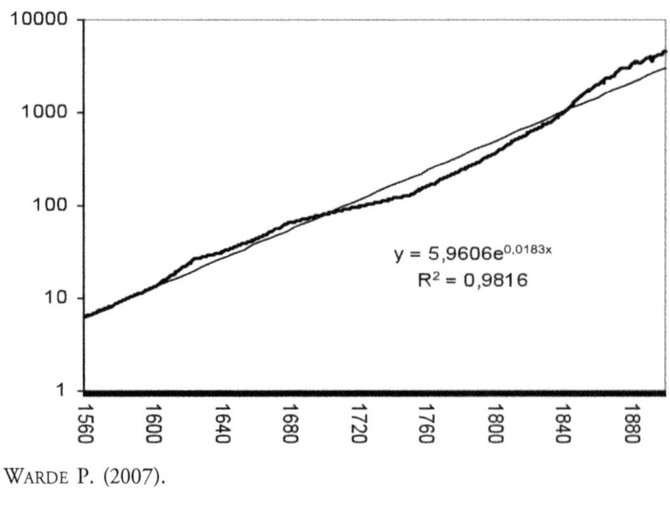

Source: Warde P. (2007).

In The Netherlands another fossil fuel, peat, began to be used on a wide scale from the 17th century onwards (De Vries, Van Der Woude, 1995). It was an important support of the Dutch Golden Age. England and The Netherlands were the countries in Europe endowed with fewer woods in relation to their extent. At the end of the 19th century these were 4.1 per cent of the total surface in England and 7.5 per cent in The Netherlands, while the European average was 25-30 per cent (excluding or including Russia) (Lunardoni, 1904, page 81; Chierici, 1911, pages 258-259). The *per capita* area of woodland was 0.03 hectares in England and 0.05 in The Netherlands, while the European average was 0.75 including Russia, and 0.39 excluding Russia. By means of the use of peat, «the Dutch lived as if their country was twice its actual size» (De Zeeuw, 1978, page 24). It was really a land-augmenting innovation.

Wrigley calculated that 1 ton of coal could replace the calories of 1 acre of forest (Wrigley, 1988*a*, pages 54-55). If we follow this calculation, coal extraction in Britain was replacing in 1700 12,000 square kilometres, which we could call "ghost square kilometres", that is 5 percent of the extent of Great Britain, and in 1800, with 15 million tons of coal annually extracted, 60,000 square kilometres, that is one-fourth the extent of the island. Thanks to these innovations, natural resources (included in K in our previous Graph 1) were no longer fixed. On the other hand, convertible husbandry, with the elimination of fallow land allowed the widening of the arables and contributed to the increase both of food and fodder production. These changes were taking away the constraint of the fixed resources, that is the main obstacle of any agrarian civilisation on the path towards growth. As represented in Graph 11, a lower investment ($L_2E_1K_10<L_1EK0$) made possible to reach the same level of product (Q), thanks to the rise in capital (K) from K^* to K_1 and the decline in labour (from L_1 to L_2).

4.3 *Saving Labour*

It has recently been sustained that the British Industrial Revolution was the consequence of the level of British wages, which were higher than those of continental workers (Allen, 2009). Since wages represent marginal labour productivity and since productivity was higher in 18th and 19th century England than in other European countries, the obvious consequence is that growth had already taken place in the country. We can also hypothesize that the British growth, although slow, derived from ongoing energy transformation, both in food production and industry. The Industrial Revolution only accelerated this change in progress.

GRAPH 11

COMBINATION OF LABOUR AND CAPITAL (LAND INCLUDED) TO PRODUCE Q

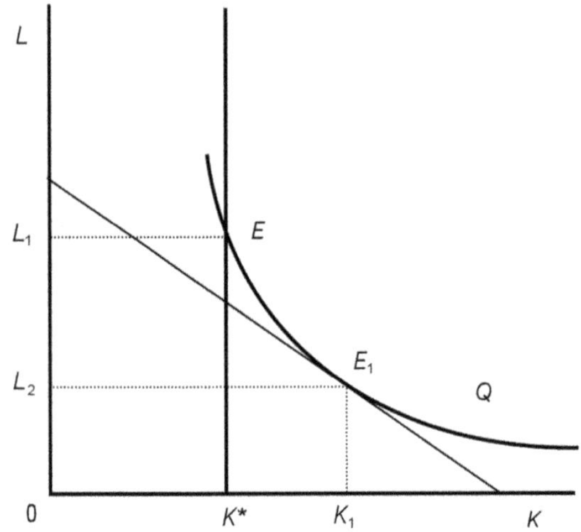

The shift to new fuels represented one aspect of the energy transition then in act. However, it was not the most important. The main technological change was the new utilisation of fuels, that is, the techniques designed to employ the heat of these organic sources to different ends. For about one million years, fuels were utilized for heating, lighting and melting metals, while work, in economic terms, that is organized movement in order to produce commodities and services, was only provided by men and animals; apart from wind and water (whose mechanical work, in any case, was not a conversion of fuel power). The only engines capable to provide work were biological machines. The introduction of machines able to convert heat into mechanical power was the main change in the energy system, comparable in importance to the discovery of fire. It was only during the 18th century, with the invention of the steam engine by Thomas Newcomen and James Watt that the *Age of the Machines* really began. The fundamental technological obstacle that had for millennia limited the capacity of the economic systems to perform work was only then overcome. In 1824, the French physicist Sadi Carnot clearly pointed out the great novelty represented by what he called the "machines à feu", the thermal machines. In his opinion they would replace both the force of animals and that of water and wind. This is precisely what has happened over the last two centuries (Carnot, 1978). The age of machinery began with the steam engine and such energy transition resulted in great changes in the volume of energy consumption, the process of substitution of energy carriers, the geography of energy production, the price of energy, and the energy-economy relationship.

Technical change is always the answer of a producer to a specific problem, and it aimed at saving labour, raw materials or energy sources. Chance plays an important role in finding this solution. Sometimes economic changes generalize the utility or need of the new discovery and the discovery spreads. More often the novelty or mutation is relegated to a specific niche and cancelled by the following development; such as a new tool set in a toolbox and then forgotten being of modest utility or even completely useless. Population growth, decline of soil *per capita,* unfavourable climatic conditions, price increase, diminishing real wages but rising nominal wages all pushed entrepreneurs and workers towards the replacement of traditional biological converters of energy with machines. We could also say that a "latent demand" existed for the replacement of labour with capital. To this purpose, the economic necessity had to meet exogenous developments taking place in technical knowledge.

The invention of thermal machines was a slow development which depended on the increasing know-how in metallurgy and the construction of mechanical instruments. The strong interdependence between energy, on the one hand, and science, on the other, took place during the so-called Second Industrial Revolution in the last decades of the 19th century, but did not exist during the First Industrial Revolution. Protagonists of this first phase of development in energy and technique were able craftsmen (Ruttan, 2001, pages 70-74). «In the Industrial Revolution the knowledge that lay behind the economic success appears to have been largely craft skills and Britain was spectacularly successful in exploiting them. In the 20th century, formal qualifications and formal education increasingly became the source of success» (Harley, 2009, page 334).

4.4 *Main Changes*

The main changes from the 19th century onwards can be represented by the following graph (Graph 12).

With the introduction of mechanical converters of energy, in the 18th and 19th centuries, the novelty was the availability of a technical solution: the replacement, that is, of biological converters fed by means of food, with mechanical converters fed with coal. Technical evolution and capital accumulation implied the possibility of reaching the same value of product Q_1 with lower costs (the line of the isocosts was nearer the intersection of the vertical and horizontal axis) and a different combination of production factors: relatively much more capital (K) and less labour (L). This shift allowed the same volume of product to be obtained but with reduced investment (the rectangle of the first combination of production factors was bigger than that of the second combination). Since labour was endowed with more capital than before (incorporating a more advanced technique) labour became more productive. All this meant an increase in wages and then labour costs and a tendency to replace labour with capital. Technical progress in the production of capital goods implies a decreasing price of capital as regards labour (Salter, 1966). The replacement of labourers by machines became a strong tendency of the economy and was the basis of the continuous replacement of biological converters (workers) with mechanical converters (machines) fed by means of new energy sources. The energy transition has been and still is a process of substitution of capital, both fixed and circulating, for labour. On the lower part of the graph it can be seen that the new combination of production factors was able to provide the same supply as before (Q_1) at a lower price.

GRAPH 12

COMBINATION OF PRODUCTION FACTORS
AND AGGREGATE DEMAND AND SUPPLY

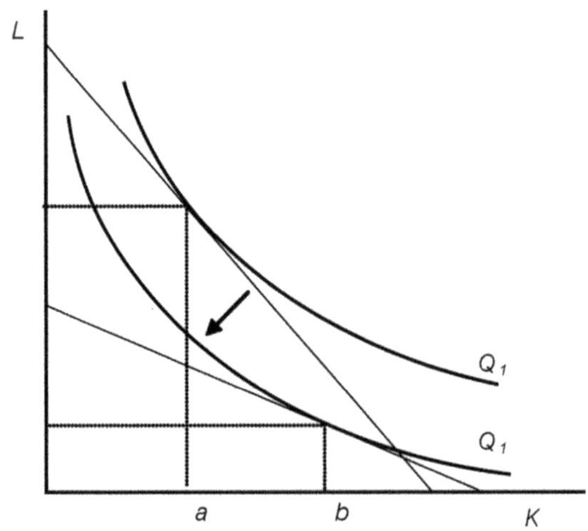

4.5 *The Rise in the Consumption of Energy*

Energy consumption per head diminished in Europe during the 18th century, whilst, from 1800 until 2005, it rose considerably more than population: 9-fold from 1800 until 2000: from 23 Gigajoules to 156. Since at the same time population increase was 3.8 fold, total energy consumption registered a 36-37-fold rise (Table 3).

TABLE 3

ENERGY CONSUMPTION IN EUROPE FROM 1800 UNTIL 2000 (IN KCAL *PER CAPITA* PER DAY, IN TOE PER YEAR, EUROPEAN POPULATION AND TOTAL ENERGY CONSUMPTION IN MTOE)

	kcal. per c. per day	Toe per c. per year	Traditional sources %	Rate of growth (%)	European population	Total Mtoe
1800	15,000	0.6	87		189	104
1830	15,150	0.6	80	0.09	234	129
1900	37,590	1.4	25	1.31	422	578
1950	47,430	1.7	15	0.47	548	948
1970	89,560	3.3	5	3.23	656	2,145
1989	101,057	3.7	5	0.63	720	2,680
2000	101,882	3.7	5	0.07	728	2,707

Source: MARTIN J.-M. (1990); MALANIMA P. (1996).

Until about 1840, energy consumption per head did not increase in Europe, since the input of fossil fuels rose at the same rate as the population. However, from 1840 until the First World War, growth was remarkable. After a period of stability between the two World Wars, a significant increase took place from the 1950s onwards, with a slower increase occurring from the 1970s onwards. (Graph 13).

On the World scale, the rise of *per capita* consumption was even higher than in Europe. It increased 10 times. Since population growth was 6.3-fold, the aggregate rise was 63 times (Table 4). It can be seen that modern or commercial sources overcame traditional sources, or the phytomass, in the last decades of the 19th century or the epoch of the second industrial revolution.

GRAPH 13

PER CAPITA ENERGY CONSUMPTION IN EUROPE 1800-2005 (GJ)

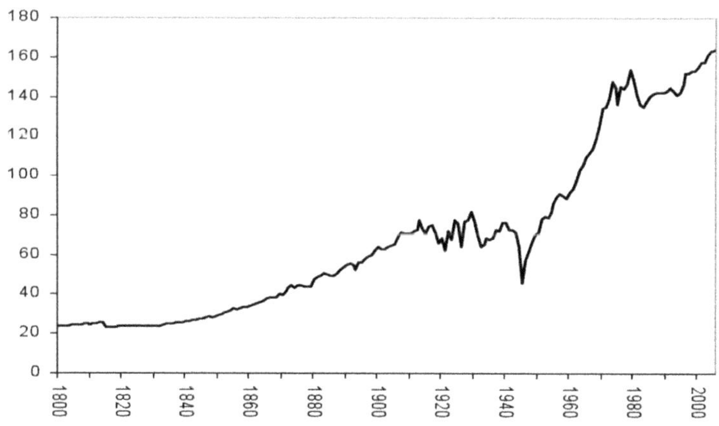

TABLE 4

WORLD ENERGY CONSUMPTION FROM 1800 UNTIL 2000 IN KCAL PER CAPITA PER DAY, IN TOE PER YEAR, WORLD POPULATION AND TOTAL IN MTOE

	kcal. per c. per day	Toe per c. per year	Traditional sources %	Rate of growth (%)	World population	Total Mtoe
1850	9.500	0.3	80		1,241	430
1880	12.300	0.4	50	1.35	1,330	597
1900	17.500	0.6	45	2.26	1,634	1,044
1950	25.600	0.9	30	1.42	2,530	2,364
1970	41.380	1.5	20	2.57	3,637	5,493
1985	41.100	1.5	20	0.12	4,815	7,223
2000	50.400	1.8	15	0.81	6,000	11,038

Source: MARTIN J.-M. (1990); MALANIMA P. (1996); IEA data for 1990.

5. - Conclusion

The escape from the economy of poverty: so could be summarized the change taking place in early modern Europe. Increase of population in front of given resources implies a decline of labour productivity and wages. Low wages do not drive the economy towards the replacement of labour with mechanical engines. We followed, in the previous pages, some main reasons that pushed towards the increase of mechanical converters per worker, which represented the main support of the modernisation of the European economy from the beginning of the 19th century onwards.

The marked increase of mechanisation and the wide use of coal, at first in England and then in Western Europe, contributed to expand the productive capacity. The effect of this expansion was the rise in output *per capita* rather than population. We have seen, however, that the main changes setting the background for this great transformation were: increase in population, increase in energy prices, decrease in marginal productivity and real wages, but rise in nominal wages and diminishing profits. The background was set for a new combination of production factors, with a reduction of natural resources and the rise of produced resources, that is capital. In England the environment was more favourable to this development than elsewhere. However, this great transformation was a European phenomenon and spread fast on the continent. Everywhere the rate of growth began to rise wherever new energy carriers began to be exploited by means of machines.

BIBLIOGRAPHY

ALLEN R.C., «Economic Structure and Agricultural Productivity in Europe, 1300-1800», *European Review of Economic History*, no. 4, 2000, pages 1-26.

-.-, «The Great Divergence in European Wages and Prices from the Middle Ages to the First World War», *Explorations in Economic History*, no. 38, 2001, pages 411-447.

-.-, «Was There a Timber Crisis in Early Modern Europe?», in CAVACIOCCHI S. (ed.), *Economia e energia secc. XIII-XVIII*, Istituto Internazionale di Storia economica "F. Datini", Firenze, Le Monnier, 2003, pages 469-482.

-.-, «Agriculture during the Industrial Revolution», in FLOUD R. - MC CLOSKEY D. (eds.), *The Economic History of Britain since 1700*, I, Cambridge, Cambridge University Press, 1994, pages 96-122.

-.-, *The British Industrial Revolution in Global Perspective*, Cambridge, Cambridge University Press, 2009.

BIRABEN J.-N., «Essai sur l'évolution du nombre des hommes», *Population*, no. 34, 1969, pages 13-25.

BOSERUP E. [1965], *The Conditions of Agricultural Growth*, London, Earthscan, 1993.

BOZHONG L., «Changes in Climate, Land, and Human Efforts. The Production of Wet-field rice in Jiangnan During the Ming and Qing Dynasties», in ELVIN M. - TS'UI-JUNG L. (eds.), *Sediments of time. Environment and society in Chinese history*, Cambridge, Cambridge University Press, 1998, pages 447-487.

BRAUDEL F., *Civilisation matérielle, économie et capitalisme;* I, *Le structures du quotidien;* II, *Les jeux de l'échange;* III, *Les temps du monde*, Paris, Colin, 1979.

CARNOT S. [1824], *Réflexions sur la puissance motrice du feu*, Paris, Vrin, 1978.

CHESNAIS J.-C., *La transition démographique*, Paris, Presses Universitaires de France, 1986.

CHIERICI R., *I boschi nell'economia generale d'Italia. Loro stima*, Caserta, Tipografia della Libreria Moderna, 1911.

CIPOLLA C.M., «Sources d'énergie et histoire de l'humanité», *Annales (E.S.C.)*, XVI, 1961, pages 521-534.

-.-, *The Economic History of World Population*, Harmondsworth, Penguin, 1962.

CLARK G., «The Price History of English Agriculture, 1209-1914», *Research in Economic History*, no. 22, 2004, pages 41-124.

CROWLEY TH., «Causes of Climate Change over the Past 1000 Years», *Science*, no. 289, 2000, pages 270-277.

DE VRIES J., VAN DER WOUDE A. [1995], *The First Modern Economy. Success, Failure, and Perseverance of the Dutch Economy, 1500-1815*, Cambridge, Cambridge University Press, 1997.

DE ZEEUW J.W., «Peat and the Dutch Golden Age. The Historical Meaning of Energy-Attainability», *A.A.G. Bijdragen*, no. 21, 1978, pages 3-32.

EDDY J.A., «Climate and the Changing Sun», *Climatic Change*, I, 1977*a*, pages 173-190.

-.-, «The Case of the Missing Sunspots», *Scientific American*, vol. 236, no. 5, 1977*b*, pages 80-95.

EDDY J.A. - GILMAN P.A. - TROTTER D.A., «Solar Rotation during the Maunder Minimum», *Solar Physics,* XLVI, 1976, pages 3-14.

FOUQUER R., *Heat, Power and Light*, Cheltenham-Northampton WA, Edward Elgar, 2008.

GALLOWAY P., «Long-Term Fluctuations in Climate and Population in the Preindustrial Era», *Population and Development Review*, no. 12, 1986, pages 1-24.

GRIGG D., *The Dynamics of Agricultural Change*, London and Melbourne, Hutchinson, 1982.

HARLEY C.K., «Economic History and Economics over a Generation», *Rivista di Storia Economica*, n.s., XXV, 2009, pages 331-367.

HARTWELL R.M., «Markets, Technology, and the Structure of Enterprise in the Development of the Eleventh-Century Chinese Iron and Steel Industry», *Journal of Economic History*, XXVI, 1966, pages 29-58.

-.-, «A Cycle of Economic Change in Imperial China: Coal and Iron in North-East China, 750-1350», *Journal of the Economic and Social History of the Orient*, X, 1967, pages 478-492.

LOHELE C., «A 2000-Year Global Temperature Reconstruction Based on Non-Treering Proxies», *Energy and Environment*, no. 18(7-8), 2007, pages 1049-1058.

LOHELE C. - MC CULLOCH J.H., «Correction to: A 2000-Years Global Temperature Reconstruction Based on non-Tree Ring Proxies», *Energy and Environment,* no. 19, 2008, pages 93-100.

LUNARDONI A., «Vini, uve e legnami nei trattati di commercio», *Italia Moderna*, Maggio 1904.

MALANIMA P., *Energia e crescita nell'Europa preindustriale*, Roma, La Nuova Italia Scientifica, 1996.

-.-, «Energy Crisis and Growth 1650-1850. The European Deviation in a Comparative Perspective», *Journal of Global History*, I, 2006, pages 101-121.

-.-, *Pre-Modern European Economy. One Thousand Years (10th-19th centuries),* Leiden-Boston, Brill, 2009.

MARKS R., *Tigers, Rice, Silk and Silt. Environment and History in Late Imperial South China,* Cambridge, Cambridge University Press, 1998.

MARTIN J.-M., *L'économie mondiale de l'énergie,* Paris, La Decouverte, 1990.

NEF J., *The Rise of the British Coal Industry*, London, Routledge & Sons, 1932.

-.-, *La naissance de la civilisation industrielle et le monde contemporain*, Paris, Colin, 1954.

PFISTER CH., *Klimageschichte der Schweiz von 1525-1860. Das Klima der Schweiz und seine Bedeutung in der Geschichte von Bevölkerung und Landwirtschaft,* Bern, Haupt, 1988.

POMERANZ K., *The Great Divergence. Europe, China, and the Making of the Modern World Economy*, Princeton, Princeton University Press, 2000.

RICARDO D., *On the Principles of Political Economy and Taxation,* London, Murray, 1821.

RUTTAN V., *Technology, Growth, and Development. An Induced Innovation Perspective*, New York-Oxford, Oxford University Press, 2001.

SALTER W.E.G., *Productivity and Technical Change*, Cambridge, Cambridge University Press, 1966.

TELLO E. - JOVER R. G., «Economic History and the Environment: New Questions, Approaches and Methodologies for the Environmental and Economic History of Preindustrial and Industrial Societies», in *Encyclopaedia of Life Support Systems*, forthcoming.

VAN ZANDEN J.L., «Wages and the Standard of Living in Europe, 1500-1800»>, *European Review of Economic History*, no. 3, 1999, pages 175-197.

WARDE P., *Energy Consumption in England and Wales 1560-2000,* Napoli, ISSM CNR, 2007.

WILKINSON R.G., *Poverty and Progress. An Ecological Model of Economic Development,* London, Methuen, 1973.

WRIGLEY E.A., *Continuity, Chance and Change. The Character of the Industrial Revolution in England*, Cambridge, Cambridge University Press, 1988*a*.

-.-, «The Limits to Growth. Malthus and the Classical Economists», in TEITELBAUM M.S. - WINTER J.M. (eds.), *Population and Resources in Western Intellectual Traditions*, Cambridge, Cambridge University Press, 1988*b*, pages 30-48.

-.-, *Poverty, Progress, and Population*, Cambridge, Cambridge University Press, 2004.

Accounting for Child Mortality in the Pre-Industrial European Economy

Bruno Chiarini
University of Naples "Parthenope"

Massimo Giannini*
University of Rome "Tor Vergata"

Different factors are often assigned an important role in the emergence of modern growth, such as the relationship between demographic factors and changes in institutions that promote innovation, the production of new ideas, the development of education or improvements in technology. In this paper we examine a basic factor, the probability of child survival. We find a negative relationship between child mortality and birth rate. Our results conflict with works which argue that with stochastic mortality a large precautionary demand for children arises, which would lead to mortality decline having a negative effect on net fertility.
[JEL Classification: J11; J13].

Keywords: child mortality, fertility, old age security motive, demographic transition.

* <*chiarini@uniparthenope.it*>; <*massimo.giannini@uniroma2.it*>. The authors thank Paolo Malanima and an anonymous referee for their useful comments.

1. - Introduction

In this paper we use a simple "*old age security motive*" for raising children to show some of the major determinants of transitions. What causes a country to be trapped in a Malthusian economy? This question has resulted in an immense number of studies including North and Thomas (1973); Jones (1988); Mokyr (1990); Lee (1988, 1997); Kremer (1993); Goodfriend and McDermott (1995); Acemoglu and Zilibotti (1997); Tamura (2002); Lucas (2002); Galor and Weil (2000); Hansen and Prescott (1998); Jones (2001); Doepke (2004); Galor (2005), to quote just a few. These studies emphasize various factors that are often assigned a major role in the emergence of modern growth such as the relationship between demographic factors and changes in institutions that promote innovation, or the production of new ideas or the development of education or improvements in technology. Of course, the argument is not limited to the pre-industrial era, but the transition from Malthusian stagnation to modern growth has been the subject of intense development research. In this paper we examine a basic factor, the probability of child survival. The risk of premature death should affect fertility and is determined by fertility itself in certain contexts (technology, diseases, land exploitation). To this end the predictions of the literature are not homogeneous. In some of these models, infant and child mortality rates affect parent choices, raising parental demand for children, whereas in others, mortality and fertility are negatively related. Such models integrate precautionary motives with the marginal cost of offspring and education choices allowing for uncertainty over the number of surviving children.[1]

We set up a simple model where children are viewed as a capital good or, to be precise, as the only form of capital for parents to transfer income from their productive years to their old age. This should be not so far from the situation which characterized the European economy from the High Middle Ages to the 18th century, but this dismal condition is reported by modern data for less developed countries. When there is an alternative to children for transferring present to future consumption, parents will not invest in children if the return that they yield is lower than the return of investment in capital. Whenever improvements in income occur, households are prone to invest in new production technology or in new methods of exploiting and/or storing seed and wheat for future crops, or, further, they are ready to take this opportunity to introduce and disseminate

1. See LORENTZEN P. *et* AL. (2005) and DOEPKE M. (2005) for a survey of this literature.

new cereals (corn, *etc.*).[2] To investigate the effect of child mortality on demographic and economic growth we use a very simple overlapping-generation economy to emend the Malthusian model of Ashraf and Galor (2008) (A-G) with the old wage security motive assumption.

The paper is organized in the following way. In Section 2 we report the basic assumption of the model, stressing the role of the surviving parameter in determining fertility. This is essential in producing income for the old generation. The main hypothesis is that mortality affects production by inducing short-sighted behaviour. In Section 3 we present a set of simulations obtained through solving the model by shocking the benchmark parameters. Section 4 concludes.

2. - A Simple Model of Old Age Security

The overlapping generation model we present is a simple version of an old age security model. The main assumptions are related to the surviving probability and the cost of rising a child.

Production

We assume that each parent is endowed with an amount of income y_1 and brings up children during the first period, each endowed with an amount of labor capable of producing $y_2=n$. Parents view them as a capital good: children should provide for their parents' old age consumption in the second period of their life. However, the pre-industrial era was a time of gloom: for about 400 years the appearance of disease, plagues, warfare and famine had been the greatest agent of demographic dynamics (the real engine of this economy).[3] In order to include in the model the effects of the numerous epidemics and the continuous warfare which contributed to surging mortality during the early pre-industrial period, we use an "instantaneous surviving probability" ρ to model early childhood mortality and "discount" the labor input.

There is an alternative to children for transferring present to future consumption. Let k be capital, which captures such factors as the introduction and use of new seed, better soybean quality, and the use of new methods of cultivation and

2. See the surveys of RAZIN A. and SADKA E. (1995) and NERLOVE M. and RAUT L.K. (1997) amongst others.

3. See, for instance, ZIEGLER P. (1969); MCNEIL W.H. (1977); DEL PANTA L. (1980); BENEDICTOW O.J. (2004); VOIGTLANDER N. and VOTH H.-J. (2008).

irrigation. However, k is not governed, along with the number of children, by parents' decisions. In other words, k may bc an alternative to supporting children as capital, but to simplify the analysis we may imagine the parent's choice problem as the number of children with a fixed amount of k.

Thus, there is a single homogeneous good and the production function is a constant-returns-to scale technology, $\beta \in (0,1)$ with the output produced at time 2:

$$y_2 = (pn)^{\beta} k^{1-\beta} \tag{1}$$

In equation *(1)* pn stands for the expected surviving children. According to the standard literature, we assume that the survival probability follows a Poisson process:[4]

$$p = exp(-\rho \frac{n}{y_1}) \tag{2}$$

where ρ is the arrival rate or instantaneous probability. That is, the surviving probability decreases (the death rate increases) with the number of children, for a given endowment. This is due to the higher cost of raising a large number of offspring. Alternatively, p increases with the parents' income for a given number of children; rich people can afford more offspring. The arrival rate measures the velocity at which the surviving probability changes and, in our model, it may be a proxy of the causes (plagues, illness, malnutrition, *etc.*) of infant mortality in the *ancient régime.*

The economy's material conditions (income) and the capacity of reproduction, along with a given arrival rate, determine the expected surviving children. When income rises, *ceteris paribus*, the expected survival of children increases, whereas whenever the capacity of reproduction (for a given income) or the exogenous arrival rate (pestilence, war, famine, *etc.*) rises, the expected survival of offspring declines.

Preferences

The utility of the parents is assumed to depend on their first pcriod consumption C_1 and second period consumption C_2. We suppose that the utility function is of the Cobb-Douglas form:

4. See YAARI M.E. (1965) and BLANCHARD O. and FISCHER S. (1989).

(3) $$u(C_1, C_2) = C_1^{\alpha} C_2^{1-\alpha}$$

where the fraction α is the share of welfare accruing from present consumption and the remaining fraction 1-α from future consumption C_2.

Each parent is endowed with an amount of income y_1 and brings up children during the first period, each endowed with an amount of labor capable of producing y_2=n. We assume that parents provide a fixed bequest b.

Thus the parents face the following budget constraint in the first period:

(4) $$C_1 = y_1 - vn - k$$

where each child consumes v units in the first period. We further assume that the child-raising cost is a convex function of the parents' income:

(5) $$v = \omega\, y_1^2$$

Increasing the parent's endowment increases the unit cost per child and strongly reduces the optimal fertility choice. It should be noted that this intentional reduction of fertility might be related to educational motives (investment in child quality); as observed in the real world, families tend to substitute quantity of children with "quality" of parental care as income grows.

The parents' consumption in the second period is determined by altruism (parents care about their children):

(6) $$C_2 = (pn)^{\beta} k^{1-\beta} - b$$

The intergenerational (exogenous) gift b passes from parents to children, providing the latter with endowment. Parents allocate their income optimally between consumption and child rearing so as to maximize their intertemporal utility function *(3)* subject to the budget constraints *(4)* and *(6)* and the cost of raising children *(5)*. Notice that the effect of the exponential probability of survival is to increase the parent's rate of time preference:

(7) $$u(C_1, C_2) = C_1^{\alpha} C_2^{1-\alpha} = \left[y_1 - vn - k\right]^{\alpha} \left[(exp(-\rho \frac{n}{y_1} n)^{\beta} k^{1-\beta} - b\right]^{1-\alpha}$$

3. - The Workings of the Model: From the Pre-Industrial Era to Transition

The model previously described has been numerically solved and simulated in order to analyze the individual optimal fertility choice. The model has six parameters to be calibrated: the labor share in the production function β, fraction α of lifetime consumption spent on the present consumption, the instantaneous death rate ρ, the bequest b, the unit cost per child ω and the capital cost k. The labor share in the technology β (and the capital share parameter 1-β) is calibrated according to Hansen and Prescott (1999) whereas the death rate is defined following Livi-Bacci (1988). With regard to the consumption share we refer to Ashraf and Galor (2008). The remaining parameters were chosen in order to simulate the average offspring number of a typical pre-industrial family (see Graph 1).

GRAPH 1

BENCHMARK SIMULATION

(Parameters are in Graph)

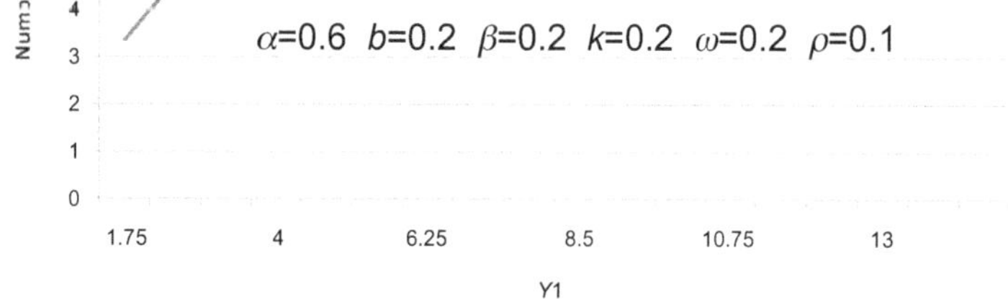

3.1 *The Benchmark Case*

The relationship between optimal offspring number n – along the vertical axis – and the initial income y_1 is illustrated in the benchmark simulation above (Graph 1). As the figure shows, there is a hump-shaped relationship between n and initial income y_1; for middle-low income levels, fertility is increasing in income and then decreasing. This provides a twofold point of view; if we look at the figure as a cross-section distribution, wealthier individuals give birth to fewer offspring than poorer ones. An alternative explanation emphasizes that whenever income increases (good crops, new seed, innovation in land use) households reduce fertility.[5]

The graph, however, can be exploited to investigate a given dynasty over time, with initial income growing over time. In this sense, the results indicate that in the pre-industrial era families had a higher fertility rate but, as time progressed, fertility in western countries decreased. According to the literature, birth rates fell due to increases in wages, urbanization, investment in education, access to contraception and several other social and cultural changes.[6] In this stage birth rates may drop to below the replacement level, leading to a shrinking population. In the next simulations we disentangle the model hypotheses which affect the result.

In the sections below, with this benchmark case, we carry out a series of counterfactual simulations, changing the cost of child-raising, the labor productivity parameter, the investment in alternative assets, time preferences and the stochastic probability of child survival.

3.2 *The Cost of Raising a Child*

In order to provide further theoretical evidence on the main factors which drive the transition, we perform some comparative dynamic simulations. In Graph 2, we let the consumption of child v change through parameter ω, ranging from 0.1 to 0.3, all other things being equal.

Increasing the unit cost per child reduces the optimal fertility choice, lowering the profile of the curves and shifting the peak leftward, consistently. It should be noted that this intentional reduction of fertility might occur by preventive checks: v is the consumption of a child and as population size grows beyond the capacity sustainable by available resources (as in the classical Malthusian hypothesis) its opportunity cost increases. However, also the positive check is at work: the cost of raising children may be related to malnutrition, disease and famine.

5. Chiarini B. (2010) stresses this non-Malthusian relationship for Italy from the 14th to the 19th century.

6. See Galor O. and Weil D.N. (2000); Boldrin M. and Jones L.E. (2002); Galor O. and Moav O. (2002); Doepke M. and Zilibotti F. (2005) and Doepke M. (2004) amongst others, who propose different causes which impinge on investment in child quality. See also Galor O. (2005). De Vries J. (1984); Malanima P. (2005); Bencivenga V.R. and Smith B.D. (1997); Sato Y. and Yamamoto K. (2005) and Zhang J. (2002) stress the role of urbanization.

GRAPH 2

INCREASING THE COST OF CHILD-RAISING

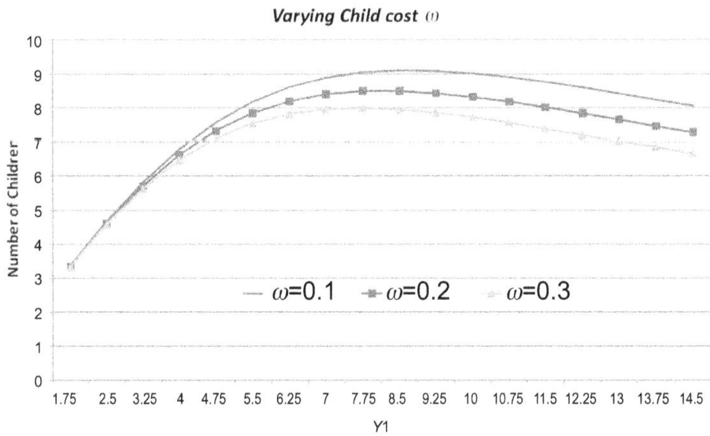

Two elements deserve emphasis. First, it should be noted that linking the cost of child survival to income may be considered as a proxy of introducing education choices into the model. Since the costs of children are proportional to income, we may conjecture that parents shift from child quantity to quality as their income rises, reducing fertility as shown in Graph 2. Secondly, the figure shows that rising costs do not effect fertility at lower income levels. The costs of child-raising in the pre-industrial era were very low, the marginal cost of an additional child for low-income parents was food, and was much lower than the marginal benefit, whereas these costs rose with schooling and hence with better income conditions. This parameter determines the model income-substitution effect. As shown in Graph 2, the increase in costs quickly leads the substitution effect to overcome the income effect.

3.3 *Labor Productivity*

As shown by Graph 3 below, the productivity parameter of child technology, $\beta \in (0,1)$, affects fertility: increasing β from 0.2 to 0.6 – hence, with a constant-returns-to scale technology production function, lowering the seed productivity $(1-\beta)$ – leads individuals to give birth to more offspring. In other words, children are a "better" asset than capital (they are an alternative investment): the return for a unit of investment in children is higher than the return for a unit of investment in seed.

GRAPH 3

INCREASING LABOR PRODUCTIVITY

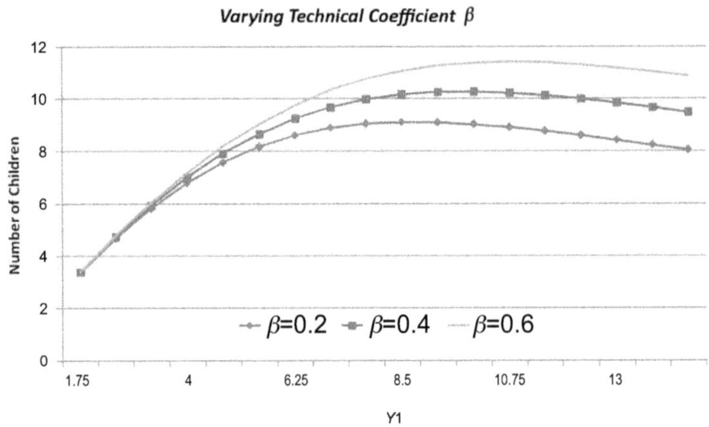

The fertility curve goes up as labor productivity increases. Notice that the fertility gap rises for medium and high income whereas it disappears for very low income. It follows, with a constant-returns-to-scale technology, that increasing β (decreasing the capital factor share) increases population. Hence total population must be higher with low (and less productive) capital, relative to offspring productivity, and *vice versa.* In other words, in this pre-industrial economy, a growing population may be sustained only with higher labor productivity.

3.4 *Raising the Capital Input* k

Fertility reacts to a variation in investment in seed k in the manner shown in Graph 4. Interestingly, higher investment in capital leads the individual to reduce the number of offspring as a reaction to lower first period income. The reason could lie in the income and substitution effect; evidently, for a given expected child survival, the increase in second period income accruing from a higher seed investment is stronger than those obtained from substitution between seed and children.[7]

---

7. It should be stressed that in this simple model k is not governed, along with the number of children, by the parent's decision. Thus, it cannot be an optimal alternative to support children as capital. Graph 4 shows that the "substitution effect" increases with income. We may hypothesize that a shock in rural wages may lead the family with primitive technology to increase its livestock and its storage of harvest and products. Saving reduces population and increases labor force quality. In any case this outcome should be depicted as an endogenous choice with an "old age security with physical capital" model.

GRAPH 4

INCREASING LIVESTOCK AND HARVEST STORAGE

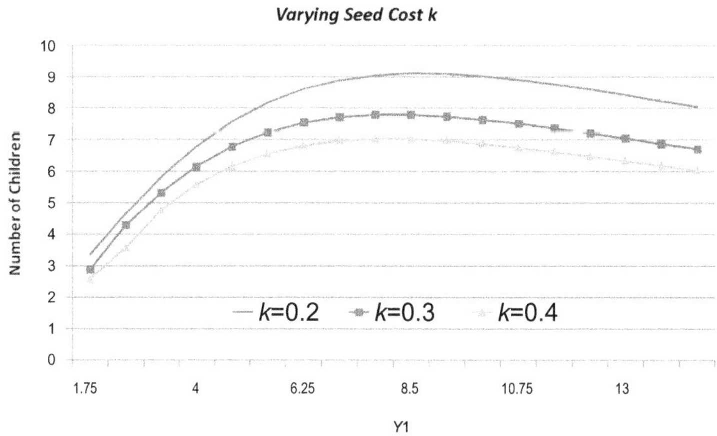

3.5 *Increasing the First Period Preference*

Graph 5 shows how results are affected by increasing α, the utility share from consuming during youth. An increase in the fraction of lifetime income α leads curves to shift down in the diagram. Increasing consumption in the first period requires a reduction in the income related to the asset of children in the second period and hence a drop in the birth rate.

GRAPH 5

CHANGING FIRST PERIOD PREFERENCES

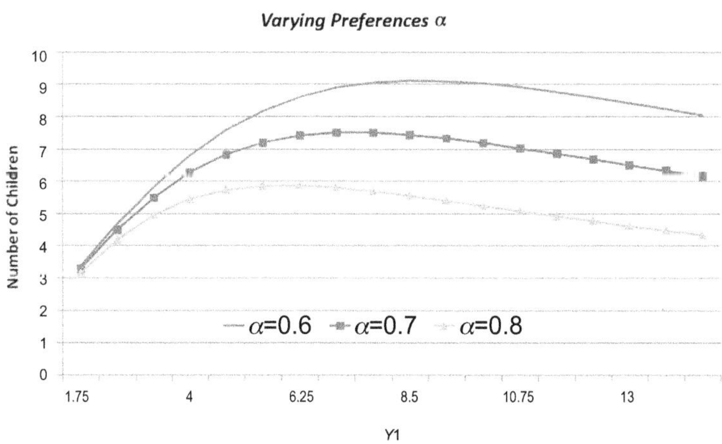

More impatient individuals lead to fewer children; individuals do not use children to foster consumption in the second period or, in other words, to transfer present to future consumption. The intensity of this outcome is important because in Europe the Black Death established a dramatic new regime of mortality that may have led not only to reduce birth rates (*via* the arrival rate ρ) but also to make individuals more impatient. We may imagine that for a family (adult parents) with a low probability of survival into old age and adulthood, it is not a rational behaviour to give birth to children for own consumption at the old age. Europe suffered numerous epidemics and almost continuous warfare. These "shocks" took several generations and limited population growth. In such a context people may well be more impatient or myopic even with a (Malthusian) substantial wage gain.[8]

3.6 *Increasing the Instantaneous Survival Probability*

Finally, the next figure shows what happens to the optimal fertility choice when the survival probability decreases due to an increase in the arrival rate ρ. As expected, a lower survival probability leads the individual to give birth to fewer offspring. Graph 6 shows the sharp reduction in the number of children produced by a change in the arrival rate. Moreover, the maximum peak of the hump-shaped curve tends to shift rightward, becoming quasi linear for higher arrival rates, meaning that a positive fertility choice requires higher income when ρ grows.

GRAPH 6

INCREASING THE ARRIVAL RATE

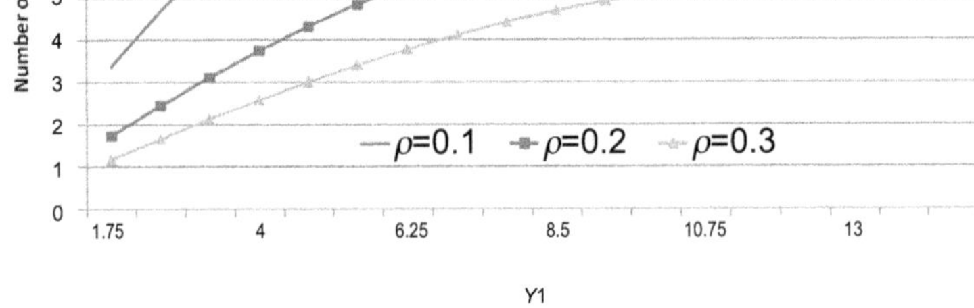

8. See VOIGTLANDER N. and VOTH H.-J. (2008; 2009). Moreover, poor health and disease generate a sort of poverty trap, making workers less productive and generating low income which reinforce poor health. See, for instance, DASGUPTA P. (2004).

The model may provide theoretical support to the dramatic reconstruction of the population data of the pre-industrial era in Europe rather than during the demographic transition. Large drops in population were caused by the Black Death which, along with wars (armies raised death rates through the epidemics that followed in their wake), the rise of urbanization (cities were death traps) and the development of trade (another vehicle to spread epidemics) created a new mortality regime with higher death rates but also with a change in the birth schedules.[9] These shocks were so large that population growth was curbed for centuries. In Italy, for instance, the pre-plague (Black Death) population level (1300) was to be reached only at the beginning of the 18th century.[10]

The model captures this new mortality regime with a rise in the arrival rate. Increasing ρ decreases the probability of surviving, bringing about lower investments in absolute and relative (children) terms. In this context people are much more likely to engage in short-sighted behavior, using the rise in income *per capita* to improve their own condition rather than invest in children. In other words, in these centuries of gloom and squalor, parents may not have been interested to define a precautionary demand for children, increasing fertility in response to expected future child mortality. This is the hording effect stressed by Sah (1991) and Kalemi-Ozcan (2003) during the demographic transition.

Thus, factors which spread epidemics had led to lower fertility and change marriage patterns[11] even with high real wages.[12] The result depicted in Graph 6

---

9. See, for instance, VOIGTLANDER N. and VOTH H.-J. (2008) and MALANIMA P. (2009) and the studies on the Black Death cited therein.

10. VOIGTLANDER N. and VOTH H.-J. (2009) emphasize that «After 1348-1349, the plague broke out again and again in Europe, before vanishing in the eighteenth century. Epidemics of other diseases, such as typhus and smallpox, were also common. Where they were not spread by troops on the march, they often arrived in the bottoms of merchant ships or on the wagons of traders» (page 250).

11. The tendency to marry late was one of the most influential constraints to population growth in pre-modern societies during the uncertainty periods. See VOIGTLANDER N. and VOTH H.-J. (2009) and MALANIMA P. (2009) and the works quoted therein.

12. This result lends theoretical support to a recent empirical analysis by CHIARINI B. (2010) who shows, by estimating and simulating a vector error correction model for the pre-industrial era in Italy, that the rise in income *per capita* may not generate an increase in population. The positive check is strong and statistically significant and it explains an important part of the dynamics of mortality. However, the other equilibrating mechanism in the Malthus model, the preventive check, based on the positive relationship between fertility and real wages, did not operate in Italy: the population shows a negative and statistically significant response to an increase in real wage.

is, however, discussed in demographic transition models. Barro and Becker (1989), shows that infant and child mortality rates affect choices because they affect the overall cost of a surviving child. Falling mortality rates lower the cost of having a surviving child, hence net fertility (number of surviving children) actually increases, not decreases, as mortality declines. Models by Ehrlich and Lui (1991); Boldrin and Jones (2002); Galor (2004) and Doepke (2005) predict that child mortality and net fertility may be inversely and/or positively correlated in demographic transition.

The model simulation depicted in Graph 6 does not lend support to the model of Eckstein, Mira and Wolpin (1999), who predict that a child mortality decline amplifies the effect of rising wages on fertility. The figure shows that such an amplification effect does indeed occur, but with an opposite sign with respect to the Eckstein-Mira-Wolpin model: as the arrival rate ρ declines (the probability of surviving increases), fertility rises with income.[13]

Moreover, it should be borne in mind that our model, though linking the cost of raising a child to income, does not take explicitly into account the quantity-quality children tradeoff (endogenous education choice). If the latter is the driving force behind fertility decline, rising wages may increase the role of human capital, which induces parents to lower fertility and invest more in the education of their children.[14]

From the 14th to the 18th centuries, parents was not able to determine their own consumption at adulthood and old age, because their life expectancy was very short or extremely uncertain. In that case the effect depicted in Graph 6 should be combined with that reported in Graph 5 which shows an increase in the fraction of the lifetime income α. A low probability of their surviving into old age, and of their children, into adulthood, would limit their propensity to have children. In this context, fertility decline is interpreted as a substitution of child quantity by child quality, but not in the usual human capital sense: fewer children in whom parents invest in terms of education or human capital. Graph

13. Eckstein Z., Mira M. and Wolpin K.I. (1999), fit a theoretical model of fertility choice to Swedish data. Their counterfactual simulations aim to disentangle the contributions of child mortality decline and wage increases to fertility decline over the period 1856 to 1946. *Ceteris paribus,* the effect of mortality decline would reduce the overall fertility rate by 0.62. A wage increase produces a decrease in total fertility of 0.85. The combined effect of both mortality and wage change is a decline of 1.81 in total fertility.

14. See amongst others, Doepke M. (2005).

6 shows a gloomy situation where a high infant mortality rate may generate a higher fertility rate only for wealthy families.

Our model, however, allows for investments in children and other assets. The level of income affects fertility through an income and a substitution effect. Fertility falls as incomes rise because the substitution effect is stronger than the income effect. If child mortality is high, the cost of children amplifies the substitution effect and leads to a fertility decline in response to income.[15]

3.7 *How Bequest Affects Results*

In this last simulation we show how the bequest can affect fertility choice, by letting *b* increase from 0.1 to 0.3. In order to leave a higher bequest, individuals must be richer (the peak tends to shift rightward) and consequently have more offspring, second period income being strictly related to such a choice. Consistent with such assumptions, individuals who wish to provide children with a higher

GRAPH 7

PROVIDING CHILDREN WITH HIGHER ENDOWMENT
Varying bequest b

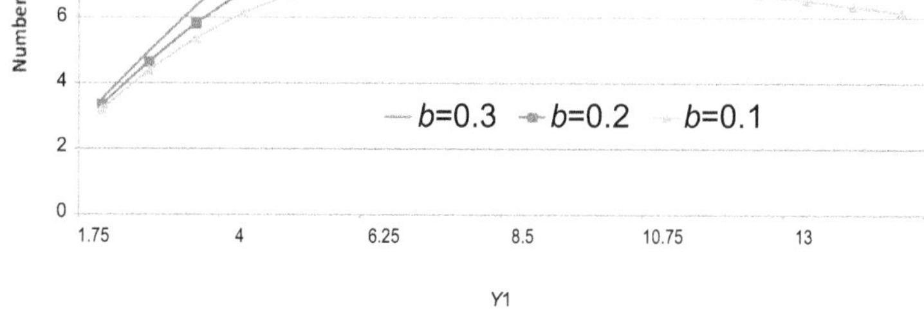

15. This result may be achieved with models determined by an optimal choice of child quality *versus* child quantity as in the Barro-Becker model. As income increases, child quality becomes more attractive, which raises education and lowers fertility.

endowment must invest in children, increasing the number of offspring. But such an effect, in turn, is related to a higher initial income.

4. - Concluding Remarks

We set out a very simple model for analyzing the dynamic relationship between birth rate and several major determinants in the pre-industrial world. The hypothesis is that the economy may be represented by an "old age security motive" model, where children are viewed as a capital good for parents to transfer income from their productive years to their old age.

Papers in economic growth that have explicitly related demographic regarding fertility rate and growth are based on Malthusian theory. Amongst them, the models of Galor and Weil (1966; 2000); Doepke and Zilibotti (2005); Doepke (2004); Dahan and Tsiddon (1998) and many others emphasize the role of education, human capital and parent altruism in decisions about fertility. In this paper we emphasized the role of several factors which impinge on fertility, such as labor productivity, the cost of raising children and the possibility to invest in other assets (for instance introduction and use of new seed, better soybean quality, the use of new farming and irrigation methods).

In particular we stress the preponderant role of infant mortality in decisions about fertility. In pre-industrial European economies, both death rates and birth rates were highly influenced by many natural and human-induced events such as disease, drought, famine, wars, and the development of unhealthy cities and trade. All these events and developments have spread epidemics and death, although cities and trade have also been crucial determinants for the transition to modern economies.

Our model shows that the survival probability of children strongly affects birth rates. Raising the arrival rate (reducing the survival probability) changes the canonical hump-shaped curve which describes the relationship between income and birth rate, pushing down the number of children per woman. A decline in the arrival rate (which may be related to improvements in agricultural production and techniques and in public health) and a rapid rise in birth and population have driven the demographic transition.

BIBLIOGRAPHY

ACEMOGLU D. - ZILIBOTTI F., «Was Prometheus Unbound by Chance? Risk, Diversification, and Growth», *Journal of Political Economy*, no. 105, 1997, pages 709-751.

ASHRAF Q. - GALOR O., «Dynamic and Stagnation in the Malthusian Epoch: Theory and Evidence», Brown University Department of Economics, *Woerking Papers*, no. 14, 2008.

BARRO R. - BECKER G., «Fertility Choice in a Model of Economic Growth», *Econometrica*, no. 57, 1989, pages 481-501.

BENCIVENGA V.R. - SMITH B.D., «Unemployment, Migration, and Growth», *Journal of Political Economy*, no. 105, 1997, pages 582-608.

BENEDICTOW O.J., *The Black Death 1346-1353. The Complete History*, Woodbridge, The Boydel Press, 2004.

BLANCHARD O. - FISCHER S., *Lectures on Macroeconomics*, The MIT Press, 1989.

BOLDRIN M. - JONES L.E., «Mortality, Fertility, and Saving in a Malthusian Economy», *Review of Economic Dynamics*, no. 5, 2002, pages 775-814.

CHIARINI B., «Was Malthus Right? The Relationship between Population and Real Wages in Italian History, 1320 to 1870», *Explorations in Economic History*, no. 47, 2010, pages 460-475.

CRAFTS N. - MILLS T.C., *From Malthus to Solow: How did the Malthusian Economy Really Evolve?*, mimeo, 2007.

DAHAN M. - TSIDDON D., « Demographic Transition, Income Distribution, and Economic Growth», *Journal of Economic Growth*, no. 3, 1998, pages 29-52.

DASGUPTA P., «World Poverty: Causes and Pathways», in BOURGUIGNON F. - PLESKOVIC B. (eds.), *Annual World Bank Conference on Development Economics*, Oxford, Oxford University Press, 2004.

DE VRIES J., *European Urbanization 1500-1800*, Harvard University Press, Cambridge MA, 1984.

DEL PANTA L., *Le epidemie nella storia demografica italiana (secoli XIV-XIX)*, Loescher Editore, Torino, 1980.

DOEPKE M., «Child Mortality and Fertility Decline: Does the Barro-Becker Model Fit the Facts?», *Journal of Population Economics*, no. 18, 2005, pages 337-366.

-.-, «Accounting for Fertility Decline During the Transition to Growth», *Journal of Economic Growth*, no. 9, 2004, pages 347-383.

-.-, «Growth Takeoffs», *New Palgrave Dictionary of Economics,* 2nd edition, 2006.

DOEPKE M. - ZILIBOTTI F., «The Macroeconomic of Child Labor Regulation», *American Economic Review*, no. 95, 2005, pages 1492-1524.

EHRICH L. - LUI F.T., «Intergenerational Trade, Longevity, and Economic Growth», *Journal of Political Economy*, no. 99, 1991, pages 1029-1059.

ECKSTEIN Z. - PEDRO M. - WOLPIN K.I., «A Quantitative Analysis of Swedish Fertility Dynamics: 1751-1990», *Review of Economic Dynamics*, no. 2, 1999, pages 137-165.

GALOR O., «The Demographic Transition and the Emergence of Sustained Economic Growth», *CPER Discussion Paper*, no. 4714, 2004.

-.-, From Stagnation to Growth: Unified Growth Theory», in AGHION P. - DURLAUF S.N. (eds.), *Handbook of Economic Growth*, vol. 1A, North-Holland, Elsevier Science, Amsterdam, 2005.

GALOR O. - MOAV O., «Natural Selection and the Origin of Economic Growth», *Quarterly Journal of Economics*, no. 117, 2002, pages 1133-91.

GALOR O. - WEIL D.N., «Population, Technology, and Growth: From Malthusian Stagnation to the Demographic Transition and Beyond», *American Economic Review*, no. 90, 2000, pages 806-828.

-.-, -.-, «The Gender Gap, Fertility, and Growth», *American Economic Review*, no. 86, 1996, pages 374-387.

GOODFRIEND M. - MCDERMOTT J., «Early Development», *American Economic Review*, no. 85, 1995, pages 116-133.

HANSEN G. - PRESCOTT E., «Malthus to Solow», Federal Reserve Bank of Minneapolis, *Research Department Staff Report*, no. 257, 1999.

KALEMI-OZCAN S., «Does the Mortality Decline Promote Economic Growth?», *Journal of Development Economics*, no. 70, 2002, pages 411-439.

KREMER M., «Population Growth and Technological Change: One Million B.C. to 1990», *Quarterly Journal of Economics*, no. 108, 1993, pages 681-716.

JONES C., *Growth Recurring: Economic Change in World History*, Oxford University Press, Oxford, 1988.

-.-, «Was an Industrial Revolution Inevitable? Economic Growth over the Very Long-Run», in *Advances in Macroeconomics*, no. 1(2), article 1, 2001.

LEE R.D., «Induced Population Growth and Induced Technological Progress: Their Interaction in the Accelerating Stage», *Mathematical Population Studies*, no. 1, 1988, pages 265-288.

-.-, «Population Dynamics: Equilibrium, Disequilibrium, and Consequences of Fluctuations», in ROSENZWEIG M.R. - STARK O. (eds.), *Handbook of Population and Family Economics*, vol. IB, Elsevier North-Holland, Amsterdam, 1997.

LIVI-BACCI M., *A Coincise History of World Population*, 2nd ed., Blackwell, Oxford, 1997.

LORENTZEN P. - MCMILLAN J. - WACZIARG R., «Death and Development», *NBER Working Paper*, no. 11620, September, 2005.

LUCAS R.E. JR., «The Industrial Revolution: Past and Future», in LUCAS R.E. JR. (ed.), *Lectures on Economic Growth*, Harvard University Press, Cambridge, MA, 2002.

MALANIMA P. «Urbanisation and the Italian Economy During the Last Millennium», *European Review of Economic History*, no. 9, 2005, pages 97-122.

MALANIMA P., *Pre-Modern European Economy*, Brill, The Netherlands, 2009.

MCNEILL W.H., *Plagues and People*, New York, Anchor, 1977.

MOKYR J., *The Lever of Riches*, Oxford University Press, Oxford, 1990.

NERLOVE M. - RAUT L.K., «Growth Models with Endogenous Population: A General Framework», in ROSENZWEIG M.R. - STARK O. (eds.), *Handbook of Population and Family Economics*, North-Holland, Elsevier Science, Amsterdam, 1997.

NORTH D.C. - THOMAS R.P., *The Rise of the Western World: A New Economic History*, Cambridge, Cambridge University Press, 1973.

RAZIN A. - SADKA E. (eds.), *Population Economics*, MIT Press, Cambridge Mass, 1995.

SAH R.K., «The Effects of Child Mortality Changes on Fertility Choice and Parental Welfare», *Journal of Political Economy*, no. 99, 1991, pages 582-606.

SATO Y. - YAMAMOTO K., «Population Concentration, Urbanization, and Demographic Transition», *Journal of Urban Economics*, no. 58, 2005, pages 45-61.

TAMURA R., «Human Capital and the Switch from Agriculture to Industry», *Journal of Economic Dynamics and Control*, no. 27, 2002, pages 207-242.

VOIGTLANDER N. - VOTH H.-J., *The Three Horsemen of Riches: Plague, War and Urbanization in Early Modern Europe*, mimeo, University of Pompeu Fabra, 2009.

-.-, -.-, «Malthusian Dynamism and the Rise of Europe: Make War, Not Love», *American Economic Review, Papers & Proceedings*, 2009, pages 248-254.

YAARI M.E., «Uncertain Lifetime, Life Insurance and the Theory of the Consumer», *Review of Economic Studies*, no. 32, 1965, pages 137-1350.

ZHANG J., *Urbanization, Population Transition, and Growth*, Oxford University Press, no. 54, 2002, pages 91-117.

ZIEGLER P., *The Black Death*, Collins, London, 1969.

A Basic Model of Take-Off and Fertility Choices in the Economic Development Process

Edgardo Bucciarelli - Gianfranco Giulioni*
University of Chieti-Pescara,
Department of Quantitative Methods and Economic Theory

We present a simple model in which the transition from Malthusian stagnation to modern growth can occur. Agents are endowed with full control over their fertility but, differently from other studies, the degree of agents' altruism which mainly affects fertility choices is allowed to change with the standard of living. We relate agents' altruism to the marginal utility of consumption. The occurrence of take-off and the balanced growth path of the model are analyzed. Our model also provides for a potential explanation to the J-shaped relationship between natality rates and standard of living found by recent empirical studies.
[JEL Classification: J13, O11, O12, I25].

Keywords: malthusian stagnation, modern growth, increasing marginal utility, development process, fertility choices.

* *<e.bucciarelli@unich.it>*; *<ggiulioni@unich.it>*.

1. - Introduction

The topic of this paper arose out of the aim to contribute to the historical Malthusian controversy which, in recent times, has found renewed interest. The historical evolution of the relationship between population growth, technological change and the standard of living has motivated a few scholars to develop "unified models". The effort is that to build models the dynamics of which pass through the three distinct regimes which have characterized the entire process of economic development: the "Malthusian regime" observed in early stages of development, in which output *per capita* is kept at the survival level by a high fertility rate in a limited resources context; the subsequent "post-Malthusian regime", in which the intensified rhythm of technological change and the improved trust on education as a mean to rise earnings allow the economic system to have a start and to take off; and the "modern growth regime" characterized by steady growth in both income *per capita* and the level of technology, and a low level of the growth rate of population (Galor and Weil, 2000).[1]

The literature on this topic is very wide. We briefly discuss hereafter that which focuses on the relationship between the level of standard of living and the population growth rate, which is relevant for this paper.

Most of theoretical literature has been oriented toward the so called "modern growth regime", trying to take the negative relation between income and population growth into consideration from both a cross-sectional and a time series perspectives (Barro and Becker, 1989). Several mechanisms have been identified. We sketch some of them hereafter. First, in developed economies, a substitution of quality for quantity of children is caused by higher returns to child quality (Becker *et* al., 1990). Secondly, women have a higher potential income in developed territories, so that the opportunity cost of children is greater (Galor and Weil, 1996). Thirdly, the development of countries determines a rise in the net flow of transfers from parents to children (Caldwell, 1976; Morand, 1999). A strand of this literature has highlighted how the aforementioned mechanisms affect human capital accumulation, and how the key role is now played by human capital rather than by physical capital or land. For example, Lucas (2002), which is based on Becker *et* al. (1990), gives much importance to both human capital accumulation and fertility choices. Lucas' model can be characterized by either Malthusian or modern properties because of the value of the parameter which

---

[1] Interestingly, the phases of the development process can be also gathered from a book by KULA E. (1998) on the history of environmental economic thought.

controls the private return to human capital accumulation. Therefore, an exogenous change in the return to human capital accumulation is required in order to have a transition from stable to growing living standards.

Galor and Weil (2000), and Jones (2001) study models where the transition from Malthusian stagnation to modern growth is a feature of the equilibrium growth path. In these models, standards of living are initially invariable due to the presence of a fixed input in production, and because population growth raises with living standards in the initial stage of development. The factor which captures a particular attention is the long-run impact of a new technology. Indeed, in the long run, technologies may be "skill biased" or else "skill saving" (Galor and Weil, 2000). But the introduction of new technologies is mostly skill biased (for micro estimates of technology-skill complementarity, see among others Galor and Tsiddon, 1997; Goldin and Katz, 1998). If technological changes are skill biased in the long run, the factor on which the research focuses will be improved; while, if technology is skill saving, it will be blunt. In this direction, some authors have considered and tested growth models which can match several key evidences of economic history. In Jones (2001), increasing returns to scale cause growth rates of population and technological progress to accelerate over time and, eventually, this permits a shift from Malthusian stagnation. Jones, in his quantitative analysis, highlights two factors which mainly affect these dynamics. The two factors are the improvement in institutions and the virtuous circle of knowledge. The former plays a key role in developing innovations so that, for example, inventors can obtain a reward for their labor thanks to property rights. The latter is related to the promotion of potential ways of thinking, which consequently encourage an additional population growth.

The empirical literature is also wide. Here, we just report on a recent article by Myrskylä *et* al. (2009) where authors perform cross sectional and longitudinal analyses to examine the correlation between the total fertility rate and the human development index (HDI). Their main finding is that in highly developed countries with HDI above 0.9, further development halts the declining fertility rates. In other words, there has occurred a fundamental change in the well-established negative relationship between fertility and development. In fact, the relationship is reverted in the data recorded in the last few decades, and the previously observed negative development-fertility association becomes *J*-shaped. This change, not only challenges conventional knowledge, but also would require that policy makers re-evaluate their present assumptions regarding the fertility-development relationship when they hammer out future policies.

In line with the sketched literature, this paper focuses on building a single economic model which could explain the dynamics both of income per worker and of population in order to interpret the transition from the Malthusian stagnation to sustained modern growth. As standard in contemporary macroeconomics, households' behavior is governed by utility maximization. We attempt to improve the existing literature by integrating the standard microeconomic analysis with new elements. In particular, we elaborate on the recent idea put forward by Karelis (2007) according to which the marginal utility is increasing at low levels of consumption. Karelis' main result is that under increasing marginal utility of consumption, the choice of making no effort to improve the standard of living is rational. This provides a potential explanation for poverty traps. We use a simplified version of the utility function introduced by Becker and Barro (1986) where we let the marginal utility of consumption increase at low levels of income per worker (which is taken as a proxy for the standard of living). By using insights from the solution of the agents' utility maximization problem, we show how the model can generate different types of dynamics: the Malthusian trap, a high standard of living situation where the growth rate of income per worker fades out, and one where the latter variable increases.

The paper is organized as follows. In section 2, we set out the model and analyze the individual solutions for education and fertility. In section 3, we explain how the levels of education and technological progress co-evolve and how the take-off is obtained in the model. Section 4 explores the relationships among fertility, education and income. These results are used to analyze the joint evolution of fertility and per-worker income in section 5. Section 6 contains concluding remarks.

2. - The Model

As stressed above, recent contributions endow people with full control over their fertility. The study of the relationships between fertility choices and economic aspects is an interesting and stimulating field because it encourages economists to work under unusual and new assumptions. The ones we will use in this work are altruism (Collard, 1978; Margolis, 1982; Becker and Barro, 1986, among others) and the more recent topic of increasing marginal utility of consumption (Karelis, 2007). It is convenient to shortly summarize the content of Karelis' book because it inspired us in starting this work. The aim of the book is to find a rational explanation to «Five patterns that have been common among the poor in may times and places [...] 1. not working much for pay; 2. not getting much education; 3. not saving for a rainy day; 4. abusing alcohol; and 5. taking risk with the law» (page 13). Two broader questions beneath the five listed points are the following. First, why poor people do not make effort to improve their situation? Secondly, why poor people do not fear (consumption) volatility and risk? We voluntarily commit the "sin" of oversimplification to give an intuitive understanding. Concerning the first question, imagine a hungry person which has ten grams of food and could obtain fifteen grams by working more. Imagine further that at least 100 grams of food is needed to decrease a person's hunger. It is highly probable that the effort to get five more grams of food overcompensates the relief given by eating the additional food. This is a potential explanation for why poor people do not make effort. The behavior toward risk is easily understood by using expected utility theory which shows how concave utility functions (which have increasing marginal utility) are associated with risk loving agents. Let us further point out, because it will be used below, that the constrained maximization of a concave function delivers a corner solution. In Karelis' book a number of examples supporting the change of the marginal utility behavior are provided.

We now analyze the agent's choice.

2.1 *Utility Function*

As in other models we assume that each individual has one parent[2] and her relevant life (for the analysis) is divided into two parts. In the first part of the life, she has no decision to take, and this time span is dedicated to follow the parent's guidelines. In the second part of the life, she earns an income which is allocated in consumption and expenditure for children. The parent's problem is that of maximizing utility under the balance sheet constraint. Quantity and quality of children are the subject's choice variables beside the level of consumption.

Parent's utility depends positively on her own consumption ($u_t(c_t)$) and the benefit from having offspring ($k(n_t)$). Moreover, the utility is positively affected by children's utility ($u_{t+1}(.)$). The functional form we use is a simplified version of that used by Becker and Barro in a number of papers (Becker and Barro, 1986;

2. Alternatively one can think of modeling the dynamics of one of the genders, and to obtain the evolution of the work force doubling the values. Since it is unnatural to think of a male expecting a child, we will use the feminine when referring to an agent.

Barro and Becker, 1989; Becker *et* al., 1990). Differently from them, we assume parent's utility to be only affected by the income available to their children (the number of grandsons is not relevant for an adult):

$$U_t = u_t(c_t) + ak(n_t)\, u_{t+1}(y_{t+1})$$

where a is a parameter which regulates the level of altruism.

We will use the following functional form for an adult's utility:[3]

$$U_t = c_t^\alpha + a\,(n_t y_{t+1})^\beta \tag{1}$$

with $0 < \beta < 1$, and α is allowed to change to permit both increasing and decreasing marginal utility (more on this below).

2.2 *Budget Constraint*

Utility is maximized under the constraint

$$y_t = c_t + n_t p_n y_t + n_t p_e y_t e_t \tag{2}$$

where y_t is the parent's available income, c_t is her consumption, e_t is the level of education given to each child, p_e is the cost of an unit of education and p_n collects the other costs to grow a child (these costs are expressed as shares of income).

We now formalize the income of an individual. Let us start from the aggregate production function

$$Y_t = h_t^\gamma\ A_t^\tau\ L_t^\psi$$

where h_t is human capital, A_t the available technology and L_t the workforce.

This formulation of the production function is general and can be specialized by making assumptions on the value of the parameters γ, τ and ψ. As an example, a labor augmenting technological progress can be obtained by putting $\tau=\psi$.

Concerning the value of these parameters, we require $0 < \psi < 1$ and we exclude increasing return to scale. Under decreasing and constant return to scale, the production factors income shares can be computed in a way which is coherent with

3. We use here power functions for $k()$ and $u_{t+1}()$ and we let their exponents to be the same. The results are robust to alternative assumptions on the value of these exponents.

perfect competition markets. The most important observation concerning the purpose of obtaining the per worker income is that workers, in this model, are the owners of all the production factors. This implies[4]

$$(3) \qquad y_t = \frac{Y_t}{L_t} = h_t^{\gamma} A_t^{\tau} L_t^{\psi-1}$$

Let us spend some more words for technology and human capital. Technologies need a number of circumstances to be optimally exploited. In particular, we refer to the level of education of the utilizer (which will be denoted by e) and the availability of infrastructures (which will be denoted by ϕ). For example, the productivity of a person endowed with the latest generation laptop depends on the effort she made in learning softwares and computational techniques (this is e in our context). The productivity of two individuals having the same education and the same laptop depends, among other factors, on the availability of electricity power and network connection during the working hours (ϕ summarizes the effects of these factors). The role of ϕ is important in our model, so that we discuss it in more details. This parameter aims to grasp the relationship between technological advancement and the socio-economic environment which is reflected in the fact that new technologies require a modified environment to be fully exploited (environments which do not adapt loose efficiency). In the literature this phenomenon is referred to as the "erosion effect" of technological progress (Galor and Weil, 2000; Ahituv and Zeira, 2002). Consequently, ϕ depends on the growth rate of technological progress. More formally $\phi = f(g_A)$ with $\phi'' < 0$ and $\phi'' < 0$.[5]

4. In the case of constant return to scale, an agent gets a reward because she sells her unit amount of work (this is the wage) and two additional rewards: the first one because she uses the technology and the second one because she owns human capital. If, as happens in perfect competition markets, factors are rewarded at their marginal product, the aggregate income collected by h_t, A_t and L_t is respectively $(\partial Y_t/\partial h_t)h_t = \tau Y_t$, $(\partial Y_t/\partial A_t)A_t = \gamma Y_t$ and $(\partial Y_t/\partial A_t)L_t = \psi Y_t$. These amounts have to be divided by the number of workers to obtain the individual reward. Summing over the three sources of income one obtains equation *(3)*. The same result is obtained under decreasing return to scale, where in addition to the three mentioned sources of income, workers also share what is called the "real economic profit" (see for example Mankiw N. G., 2010, chapter 3). This fourth element is the reward of the non producible factor not included in the production function (say land) which justifies the decreasing return to scale assumption.

5. Here and below in the text we use the common notation: given a function $x = x(z)$, x' denotes dx/dz and x'' denotes d^2x/dz^2.

Both education and erosion affect human capital. In the present model we formalize human capital as

$$h_t = e_{t-1}^{\phi}$$

We will show later that $0 \leq \phi < \psi\beta/\gamma$. We require ψ, β and γ to be such that the function is strictly increasing and concave (a function having these features is used in Fernàndez-Villaverde, 2001).

After these considerations, the individual income can be written as follows:

$$y_{t+1} = e_t^{\phi\gamma} A_{t+1}^{\tau} L_{t+1}^{\psi-1} \tag{4}$$

2.3 *Maximization*

By substituing *(4)* in *(1)* we have

$$U_t = c_t^{\alpha} + a n_t^{\beta} e_t^{\phi\gamma\beta} A_{t+1}^{\tau\beta} L_{t+1}^{(\psi-1)\beta}$$

In our context we have $L_{t+1} = L_t n_t$. Furthermore, we put $\delta_t = 1 + g_{A,t}$, where $g_{A,t}$ denotes the growth rate of technology, so that we can write $A_{t+1} = A_t \delta_t$. Using these definitions we can express the utility function as

$$U_t = c_t^{\alpha} + a n_t^{\psi\beta} e_t^{\phi\gamma\beta} (A_t^{\tau} \delta_t^{\tau} L_t^{\psi-1})^{\beta} \tag{5}$$

For convenience in writing equations, we pose $D_t = a\,(A_t^{\tau} \delta_t^{\tau}\ L_t^{\psi-1})^{\beta}$, and, substituting the consumption obtained from the constraint *(2)*, the utility function can be now written as

$$U_t = (y_t - n_t p_n y_t - n_t p_e y_t e_t)^{\alpha} + D_t n_t^{\psi\beta} e_t^{\phi\gamma\beta}$$

The choice variables (c_t, n_t and e_t) can be in principle determined by solving the system of equations made up of two first order conditions (these for e_t and n_t) and the constraint.

The FOCs are

$$\frac{dU_t}{de_t} = -\alpha c_t^{\alpha-1}\ n_t p_e y_t + D_t n_t^{\psi\beta} \phi\gamma\beta e_t^{\phi\gamma\beta-1} = 0$$

$$\frac{dU_t}{dn_t} = -\alpha c_t^{\alpha-1}(p_n + p_e e_t)y_t + D_t \psi\beta n_t^{\psi\beta-1} e_t^{\phi\gamma\beta} = 0$$

It is not possible to obtain analytically the complete solution. However, from the FOCs above, after algebraic manipulations, we obtain the following solution for the level of education

$$e_t = \frac{\phi\gamma}{\psi\beta - \phi\gamma}\frac{p_n}{p_e} \tag{6}$$

The result obtained for e_t allows us to deal with the dynamics of education and technological progress separately from the other elements of the model as happens in Galor and Weil (2000). We will elaborate on this topic in the next section and we delay the problem of finding the solution for n_t to section 4.

3. - The Dynamics of Education and Technological Progress

3.1 *The Dynamical System*

The solution obtained for education in the previous section makes sense if $0 \le \phi < \psi\beta/\gamma$. As a consequence, we formalize the parameter ϕ as follows:

$$\phi = \frac{\psi\beta}{\gamma} f(g_{A,t})$$

with $f(0) = 0, f' > 0, f'' < 0$ and $\lim_{g_{A,t} \to \infty} f = 1$, so that equation *(6)* can be written as

$$e_t = \frac{f}{1-f}\frac{p_n}{p_e}$$

Note how the *ratio* $f/(1-f)$ is a function of g_A only, and we can write

$$e_t = e(g_{A,t})\frac{p_n}{p_e} \tag{7}$$

Using the assumptions we have made on f, it is possible to show that equation *(7)* has the following features: $e(0) = 0$, $\lim_{g_{A,t} \to \infty} e = \infty$,

$$\frac{de}{dg_{A,t}} = \frac{f'}{(1-f)^2} > 0, \quad \text{and} \quad \frac{d^2e}{d(g_{A,t})^2} = \frac{f''(1-f)+2(f')^2}{(1-f)^3} \lesseqgtr 0$$

To obtain a dynamical system, we need to formalize the dynamics of technological progress. As in Prskawetz *et* al. (2000), we identify the level of education as the main determinant of technological progress, and we formalize the relationship between the two variables by a function

$$g_{A,t+1} = g(e_t) \tag{8}$$

having the following features: $g(0) > 0$, $g' > 0$ and $g'' > 0$ for low levels of e and $g'' < 0$ for high levels.[6]

Equations *(7)* and *(8)* determine the dynamics of education and technological progress. When $g(e_t)$ is bounded (as in Prskawetz *et* al., 2000) the system has at least one steady state. In the general case in which the just mentioned condition does not hold, we require the inverse of the $e(g_{A,t})$ function which appears in equation *(7)* to be an infinity of higher order with respect to $g(e_t)$ for $e_t \rightarrow \infty$.

A simple example can be obtained by putting $\gamma = \beta$ and formalizing ϕ as follows:

$$\phi = \psi\left(1 - \frac{z}{g_{A,t}+z}\right) \tag{9}$$

Note that $\phi' > 0$ and $\phi'' < 0$ as required above. z is a parameter which signal an "average" level of efficiency (in fact $g_{A,t} = z$ implies $\psi/2$).

Substituting *(9)* in *(6)* and solving $g_{A,t}$, we obtain the linear relationship

$$g_{A,t} = e_t z \frac{p_e}{p_n} \tag{10}$$

which will be used in our graphical representations.

Graph 1 shows a situation where the system made up of equations *(8)* and

6. Indeed, PRSKAWETZ A. *et* AL. (2000) make a more restrictive assumption because they use a logistic function (see their equation (*10*)). More generally, functions with a flex point are normally used in the literature (BECKER G. *et* AL., 1990; STRULIK H., 1999, are examples).

(10) has two stable stationary points $\left(e^{a}, g_{A}^{a}\right)$ and $\left(e^{b}, g_{A}^{b}\right)$. The main problem concerning this kind of situations is to explain how an economy trapped into the "low" equilibrium can reach the basin of attraction of the "high" equilibrium.

In other words, the problem is to find out what triggers the take-off.

Graph 1

THE DYNAMICS OF e_t AND $g_{A,t}$

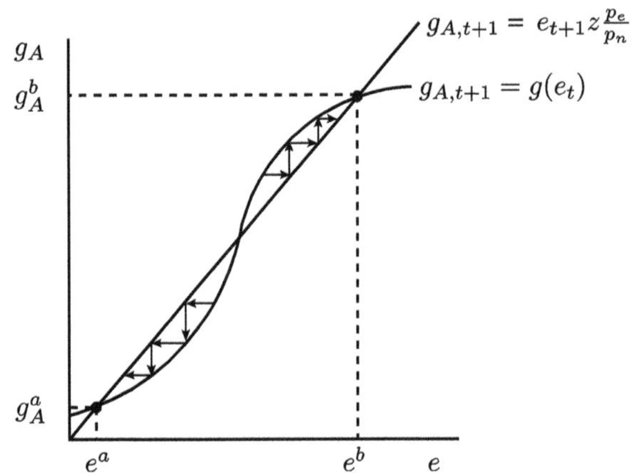

3.2 *Take-Off*

Explanations for the take-off are obtained in the literature by using a more rich version of equation *(8)*. In section 1, we reported on papers where the rate of growth of technology is positively affected by education and some other variable. For example, in Galor and Weil (2000) the *g*(.) function, which appears in equation *(8)*, also depends on work force (*L*) (see equation *(12)*, page 816 of their article). An increase in this variable shifts the curve upward, so that economies can take off.

The model presented here suggests a different mechanism which is able to trigger the take-off. In fact, here the dynamics crucially depend on the p_e/p_n *ratio.* Some comments on these two costs can be useful.

In our model the two phases of an agent's life (childhood and adulthood) are of fixed length. In the early phases of development, children learn the available stock of technologies rather quickly and could in principle provide for their needs in a relevant part of what in our model is classified as childhood. This is to say that

p_n increases with the stock of knowledge. Other arguments can be alleged for the cost of education p_e: it could be expected to decrease at the beginning of the development process, and then to stabilize or grow slowly with time, because, for example, instructors gain efficiency in teaching the available stock of knowledge.

So, starting from a situation where technologies are not available, the cost of education is infinite while p_n is low but positive. In Graph 2, point E_0 identifies an economy in which these conditions are satisfied. When knowledge increases, countries on or close to the technological frontier eventually have a gradual reduction of the p_e/p_n *ratio* and the economy smoothly moves from E_0 towards E_1. Eventually, the *ratio* reaches the level $(p_e/p_n)_2$ where a further reduction triggers the take-off.[7]

GRAPH 2

THE EFFECT OF COST OF INSTRUCTION

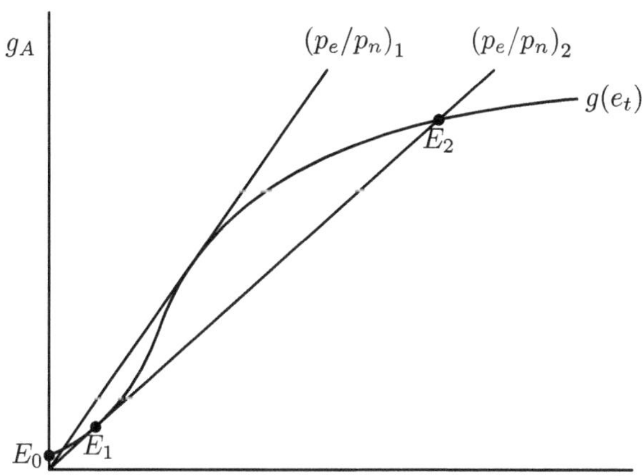

It is often maintained (see Jones, 2001, for example) that a number of socioeconomic conditions should be present at the same time to trigger the take-off. From a policy point of view all of them should be improved. The costs highlighted in our model can be viewed as two of them. This consideration gives us the occasion to comment on the effectiveness of helping countries far from the technological frontier. Indeed, even in our simplified model, making education cheaper by building schools could not be sufficient because the underlying production structure uses low level technologies which can be learned in a fast way.

7. In the presented framework, an economy which is in the high equilibrium switches to the low one if its p_e/p_n *ratio* increases above $(p_e/p_n)_1$.

This keeps the cost of children low so that the p_e/p_n *ratio* could be still high for the take-off.

4. - Fertility, Education and Income

In section 2, we left the parent's maximization problem partially unsolved to discuss the dynamics of education and technology. In order to arrive at a complete solution, we will investigate, in the first part of this section, the fertility choice at different levels of education (other things being equal). Then, we will evaluate the effect of income on fertility. The results obtained from these investigations will be used in the analysis of the long run dynamics of the model performed in section 5.

Before going on, let us recall what has been told above about the parameters of our model. β represents the satisfaction an individual has from having offspring. We have assumed $0 < \beta < 1$ and it does not change over time. α determines the marginal utility behavior of the adult's consumption. Standard economic theory is based on decreasing marginal utility of consumption, but it does not exclude the possibility of an increasing marginal utility at low levels of consumption. We have also discussed about the importance of an increasing marginal utility of consumption in explaining the behavior of agents in low income situations which has been stressed in the recent book by Karelis (2007).

We formalize the change in marginal utility behavior by letting α to depend inversely on the level of the individual income, in such a way that $\alpha > 1$ for low levels of y_t and $\alpha < 1$ for high levels.

4.1 *Numerical Insights*

The need for a general knowledge of the solution gives us motivations to investigate the household's problem numerically. First, due to the non-convexity of the utility function, the critical point found by the analytic solution could not be the global maximum; in these cases the corner solution is to be taken into account, and it is easy to detected it numerically. Secondly, in a numeric context, the decision on education, fertility and consumption can be obtained under the assumption of a smooth change in the parameter α.

Our aim is here to find out the shape of the relationship between n_t and the stationary state level of education, and to get insight into how this relationship is affected by income.

To this aim let us take up equation *(5)*

$$U_t = c_t^{\alpha} + a n_t^{\psi\beta} e_t^{\phi\gamma\beta}\left(A_t^{\tau}\delta_t^{\tau}L_t^{\psi-1}\right)^{\beta}$$

First, we use the balance sheet constraint to substitute consumption; secondly, we compute it at steady state levels so that we remove the t lower-script to the level of education and we use $\delta = 1+g(e)$; lastly, we substitute $e^{\phi\gamma}A_t^{\tau}L_t^{\psi-1}$ with y_t in the second term of the right hand side. After these expedients, we obtain

$$(11)\qquad U_t = \left(y_t - n_t p_n y_t - n_t p_e y_t e\right)^{\alpha} + a n_t^{\psi\beta} y_t^{\beta}\left(1+g(e)\right)^{\beta\tau}$$

Our exercise consists in finding numerically the level of n_t which maximizes this function given the levels of y_t and e. We constrain the search to be performed in the $[0,\bar{n}]$ interval, where $\bar{n}$ denotes the maximum number of children allowed by nature. By keeping income fixed and performing the aforementioned search for different levels of e, we are able to find out how the number of children which maximizes utility changes with the level of education at a given level of income. Then, we evaluate the effect of income by computing this relationship at different levels of income.

Graph 3 reports the results obtained by using the following parameterization: $\bar{n} = 4$, $a = 1$, $\beta = 0.5$, $\psi = 0.72$, $\tau = 1$, $p_n = 0.05$, $p_e = 0.05$, $g(e) = 0.05[1 + \exp(4 - 0.2e)]^{-1}$ and $\alpha = 0.5 + 1/y$. The figure shows how fertility negatively depends on education, while the dependence on the level of income is more complicate.

Let us now focus on the relationship between fertility and education at a low level of income. Refer to the case $y = 1$ in Graph 3. In this case, α is greater than one, and consequently the marginal utility of consumption is increasing. Beside the decreasing relationship between fertility and education, this case also shows how the corner solution, which prevails at low levels of education (see Graph 4A), is relevant.[8] As e increases, a local minimum appears, but its level of utility is lower than that of the highest admitted value of n.[9] As the level of education increases, the utility of the internal critical point increases and overcomes that re-

8. In our parametrization the phenomenon is more evident for $\psi \geq 0.72$. It is why we set $\psi = 0.72$ to obtain the graphs.

9. It could be useful to precise that the minimum admitted value of n is equal to the minimum between $\bar{n}$ and the value obtained from the balance sheet constraint. The latter has an increasing importance when ψ increases while its values is above 0.72.

Graph 3

THE RELATIONSHIP BETWEEN FERTILITY AND EDUCATION AT THREE DIFFERENT LEVELS OF INCOME

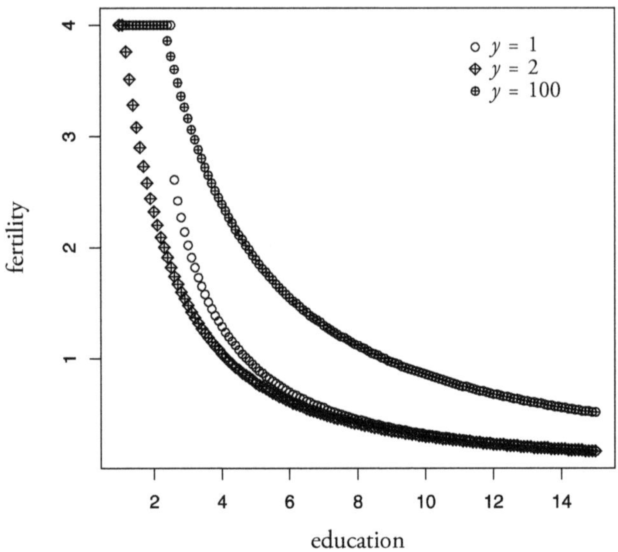

Graph 4

THE UTILITY FUNCTION AT TWO DIFFERENT LEVELS OF EDUCATION

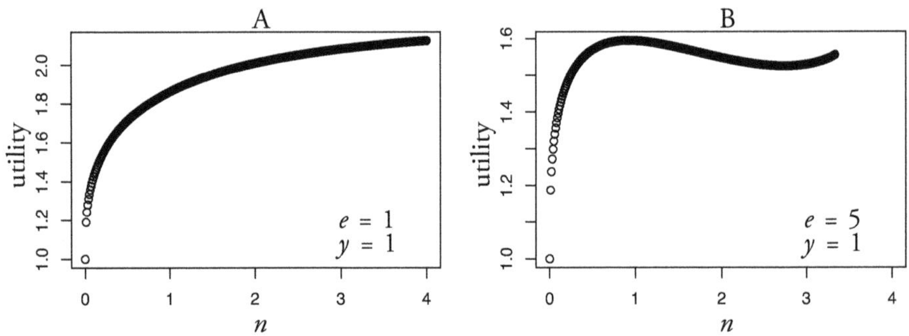

alized by the corner solution. The local minimum becomes global when *e* crosses a threshold (Graph 4B shows the shape of the utility function when the level of *e* is beyond the threshold). In Graph 3, at $y = 1$, a discontinuity in the solution can be observed. Although the sudden trough in the chosen number of children is a potential explanation for the fast reduction in natality rates observed in the data of several countries, we leave the study of this result for the future and we focus on the negative relationship between fertility and education.

Graph 3 also shows in what way the fertility-education relationship is affected by income. An increase of income starting from low levels of the latter (that is going from $y = 1$ to $y = 2$ as the figure depicts) makes fertility decrease.

The effect is reverted at high level of income ($y = 100$ in Graph 3).

4.2 *Analytical Insights*

This section contains an attempt to verify if the relationships among fertility, education and income found in the numerical investigation of the previous section can be supported by analytical considerations. Let us first say that these insights are valid if the mathematical problem is concave, that is for $\alpha < 1$.

Let us take up the utility function *(11)* and express it as

$$U_t = y_t^\alpha \left(1 - n_t p_n - n_t p_e e\right)^\alpha + a n_t^{\psi\beta} y_t^\beta \left(1 + g(e)\right)^{\beta\tau}$$

The FOC for n_t is

$$-y_t^\alpha \alpha \left(1 - n_t p_n - n_t p_e e\right)^{\alpha-1} \left(p_n + p_e e\right) + a\psi\beta n_t^{\psi\beta-1} y_t^\beta \left(1 + g(e)\right)^{\beta\tau} = 0$$

Dividing by y_t^α we can write it as

$$H = 0$$

where

$$H := -\alpha \left(1 - n_t p_n - n_t p_e e\right)^{\alpha-1} \left(p_n + p_e e\right) + a\psi\beta n_t^{\psi\beta-1} y_t^{\beta-\alpha} \left(1 + g(e)\right)^{\beta\tau}$$

According to the implicit function derivation theorem one can recover derivatives in the following way

$$\frac{dn_t}{de} = -\frac{\frac{\partial H}{\partial e}}{\frac{\partial H}{\partial n_t}} \quad \text{and} \quad \frac{dn_t}{dy_t} = -\frac{\frac{\partial H}{\partial y_t}}{\frac{\partial H}{\partial n_t}}$$

Partial derivatives with respect to education and fertility are

$$\frac{\partial H}{\partial e} = -\left[\alpha(1-\alpha)\left(1 - n_t p_n - n_t p_e e\right)^{\alpha-2} n_t p_e \left(p_n + p_e e\right) + \alpha \left(1 - n_t p_n - n_t p_e e\right)^{\alpha-1} p_e\right] + \\ + a\psi\beta^2 \tau n_t^{\psi\beta-1} y_t^{\beta-\alpha} \delta^{\beta\tau-1} g'$$

and

$$\frac{\partial H}{\partial n_t} = -\left[\alpha(1-\alpha)(1-n_t p_n - n_t p_e e)^{\alpha-2}(p_n + p_e e)^2 + a\psi\beta(1-\psi\beta)n_t^{\psi\beta-2}y_t^{\beta-\alpha}\delta^{\beta\tau}\right]$$

Obtaining the partial derivative with respect to income is more plodding because α also depends on income:

$$\frac{\partial H}{\partial y_t} = -(p_n + p_e e)(1-n_t p_n - n_t p_e e)^{\alpha-1}\left[1+\alpha \ln(1-n_t p_n - n_t p_e e)\right]+$$
$$+a\psi\beta n_t^{\psi\beta-1}\delta^{\beta\tau}\left[(\beta-\alpha)y_t^{\beta-\alpha-1} - y_t^{\beta-\alpha}\ln y_t \alpha'\right]$$

We are interested in the signs of these partial derivatives which can be used to establish how fertility depends on education and income.

Under our assumptions ($0 < \alpha < 1$, $0 < \phi < 1$ and $0 < \beta < 1$), the sign of $\partial H/\partial n_t$ can be established as negative.

$\partial H/\partial e$ has two components: the first is negative while the second is positive.

The latter depends on g'. The partial derivative is negative if $g(e)$ increases moderately with e. Recalling the shape of the $g(e)$ function, we know this is the case for low and high levels of education; when the increase of $g(e)$ is moderate also for intermediate levels of e, we obtain a result which is compatible with what we found in the previous section: $dn_t/de < 0$.[10]

Concerning $\partial H/\partial y_t$, we can observe that an important term for the sign of this derivative is $\beta-\alpha$ which appears in the second addend of the derivative.

This addend increases as α decreases, and eventually the sign of the partial derivative becomes positive. In other words we can identify a level of α, say $\hat{\alpha}$, which represents a threshold where the partial derivative changes its sign:

$$sign\left(\frac{dn_t}{dy_t}\right) = sign\left(\hat{\alpha}-\alpha\right)$$

Being α a negative function of y_t one can find the level of income $\hat{y}_t$ which makes the sign of $\partial H/\partial y_t$ switch from negative (for $y < \hat{y}_t$) to positive (for $y > \hat{y}_t$).

10. The case in which g' is such that $\partial H/\partial e > 0$ for intermediate levels of education opens the way to an extension of the model because it generates an increase in the fertility rate, which is a phenomenon known as "baby boom". We leave this eventual development for the future.

Consequently, the implicit function derivation argument implies

$$sign\left(\frac{dn_t}{dy_t}\right) = sign\left(y - \hat{y}\right)$$

which is the result obtained with the numerical exercise.

5. - The Long Run Dynamics of the Economy

This section is aimed at using the results obtained above to evaluate how technology, fertility and income affect each other and how these mutual interactions affect the long run dynamics of the economic system.

Consider the growth rate (g_x) of a variable x. As it is well known, a growth rate is approximated by the difference of the logarithms of the variable taken at two consecutive time steps.

We are here interested in the income per worker $y_t = e_{t-1}^{\phi\gamma} A_t^{\tau} L_t^{\psi-1}$. It can be expressed as

$$g_{yt} := \frac{y_t - y_{t-1}}{y_{t-1}} \approx log\left(y_t\right) - log\left(y_{t-1}\right) = \psi\gamma g_e + \tau g_A - \left(1-\psi\right) g_L$$

GRAPH 5

THE DETERMINANTS OF THE GROWTH RATE OF INCOME PER WORKER ($g_{A,t}$ and $g_{L,t}$)

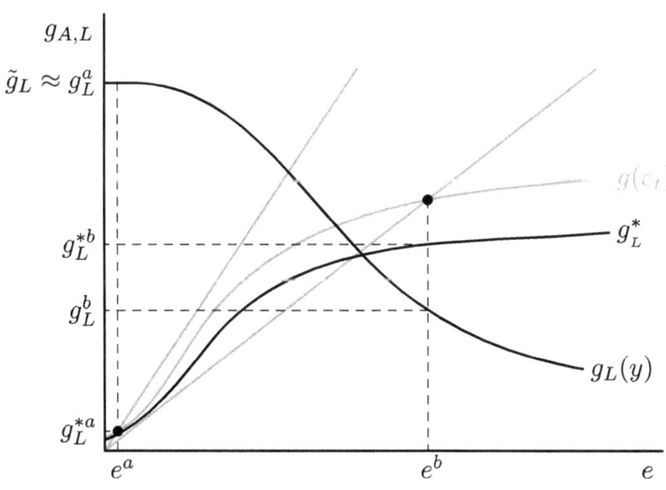

From sections 3.1 and 3.2 we know that education converges to a constant value, which implies $g_e = 0$; the behavior of g_A is also known from these sections.

Section 4 gives hints on how the growth rate of the work force, which is the remaining variable affecting g_y, is a decreasing function of the steady state level of education.[11] This implies that the growth rate of the work force ($g_L := n_t - 1$) can be represented as the decreasing line in the (e_t, g_A) plane visible in Graph 5.

To evaluate the growth rate of the income per worker we compute the growth rate of the work force which keeps the income per worker constant (g_L^*). It can be determined by requiring the right hand side of equation *(12)* to be equal to zero. Remembering that $g_e = 0$, we obtain

$$g_L^* = \frac{\tau}{1-\psi} g_A$$

and finally, by using equation *(8)*

$$g_L^* = \frac{\tau}{1-\psi} g(e)$$

according to which g_L^* is a rescaled version of $g(e_t)$. This locus lies above $g(e_t)$if $\tau > 1 - \psi$, below if $\tau < 1 - \psi$ and it overlaps $g(e_t)$ if the equality sign holds.

As an example, in figure 5 we show g_L^* in the case $\tau < 1 - \psi$.

Graph 5 can be used to understand the dynamic properties of the two steady states.

In the "low" steady state, the growth rate of the workforce is higher than the one which ensures a constant income per worker. In fact, the left vertical dashed line crosses the two black lines at different levels of the workforce growth rate.

Being $g_L^a > g_L^{*a}$, the growth rate of the income per worker is negative. Thus, the low steady state has the Malthusian properties: due to the fact that poor people choose to have a high number of low educated children, the workforce grows at an higher rate than technological progress, and consequently the income per worker decreases. This keeps people poor, and the situation of a large number of low educated children prevails. Furthermore, in this context, a positive relationship between income and fertility should be observed. In fact the "chosen" fertility

11. The eventual discontinuity at the individual level are smoothed out (if enough heterogeneity among agents exists) when computing the average fertility rate.

GRAPH 6

CONVERGENCE TO A BALANCED GROWTH PATH

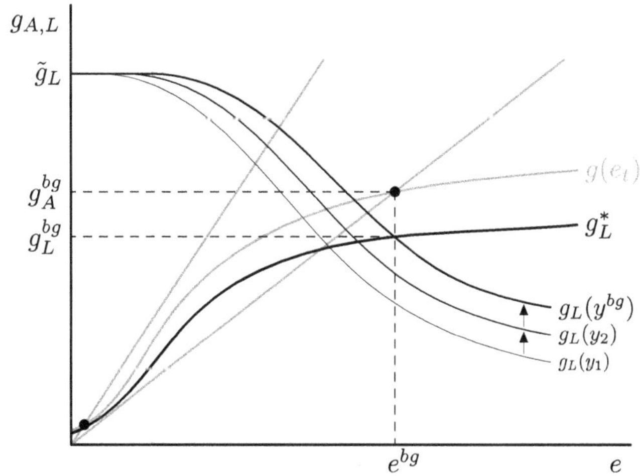

(the one resulting from the utility maximization) cannot be realized because of income shortage and the "observed" fertility is bounded by income. An increase in income implies a rise in "observed" fertility as long as the latter is smaller than the "chosen" one.

The situation in the "high" state is depicted in Graph 5 by the intersection points of the vertical dashed line on the right with the g_L^* and $g_L(y)$ lines. Contrary to the previous case, now $g^{*h}_L > g^h_L$. Thus, a low number of high educated children is chosen. This causes the growth rate of income per worker to be positive, and consequently an increasing income per worker is observed. A situation which can be associated to the "modern growth regime".

To complete our reasoning, the effect of income on the $g_L(y)$ curve is to be taken into account. This issue is relevant for economies in the "high" steady state. In fact, in the low steady state $g^a{}_L$ is close to $\tilde{g}_L := \tilde{n}-1$ regardless of the y level, and closing the gap between $g^a{}_L$ and $g^{*a}{}_L$ by changes in the income per worker is improbable. In section 4.2, the sign of the *dn/dy* has been studied. It comes out that the sign of the derivative is the same of $\hat{\alpha}$ - α. Thus, the $g_L(y)$ locus moves downward if $\alpha > \hat{\alpha}$, and upward otherwise. In the latter case the economy could approach in the long run a balanced growth path with a constant level of the income per worker. These movements of the $g_L(y)$ locus and the final stationary situation for the case $\alpha < \hat{\alpha}$ is depicted in Graph 6. From this figure it is possible to see how g_L^b grows and gradually approaches g_L^{*b} leading to a situation where $g_y = 0$. In the alternative case ($\alpha > \hat{\alpha}$) the gap between g_L^a and g_L^{*a} increases, and consequently, the growth rate of the income per worker also rises.

To summarize, in our model, underdeveloped realities are subjected to forces which keep them in that state. They can escape this trap if a sufficiently low level of the p_e/p_n *ratio* is realized. The long run behavior of developed realities depends on the levels of the parameter α. If the value of α is lower than $\hat{\alpha}$, the relationship between income and fertility is positive; as a consequence, the increase in the income per worker gradually slows down due to the increase of the fertility rate. The model generates a negative relationship between income per worker and fertility, and an increasing growth rate of the income per worker if $\alpha > \hat{\alpha}$. Note that if the α parameter decreases with income as we have assumed above on the basis of Karelis' argument, our model can generate the J-shaped relationship between level of development and fertility recently found in real world data by Myrskylä *et* al. (2009).

6. - Conclusions

One of the puzzles faced by economists is to explain abrupt changes in the dynamical behavior of economic systems. Perhaps, the most evident of such phenomena is the transition from the Malthusian stagnation to modern economic growth. About this particular topic the challenge is to build a unified model which could account for such transition (Galor, 2005). In the introduction of this paper we report on a number of attempts which try to achieve this aim. As required by contemporary economic theory, the result comes out from a rigorous micro foundation that accounts for, among other factors, the agents' decision about quantity and quality of children, and human capital formation.

This paper contains a further attempt in this direction. We keep the model simple to avoid the overshadowing of the mechanisms at work in the model by technicalities. The main concepts highlighted by our analysis are basically two. The first one fosters the idea that several conditions must be present at the same time to take off. The model highlights two of these conditions: the costs for education and those for growing children. Our result suggests that a low level of the former and a high level of the latter is the necessary condition to take off. The two requirements end up to be fulfilled by countries pushing the technological frontier, while with more difficulties they are both satisfied by low developed countries. The second point stressed by our model is that the behavior of an agent towards her own consumption and the consumption of the offspring changes according to the standard of living. This has consequences on the value given by parents to children, and, consequently, on fertility. At the beginning of the development process, when the stock of knowledge is small, all the available technologies can be learned in a small time interval, and in the remaining part of the childhood an individual can earn an income for her own or her family maintenance. When the stock of knowledge is big, the probability to get an income (even in adulthood) is low unless one has accumulated a significant level of education during childhood. From this perspective, the parent's evaluation of children changes: they are useful at the beginning of the development process, and they become priceless in the "modern growth regime" (Zelizer, 1985). Finally, we have also highlighted that the selfishness (build into the model by increasing marginal utility of consumption) of poor individuals could have a role in explaining the fast reduction of natality rates observed during a demographic transition.

BIBLIOGRAPHY

AHITUV A. - ZEIRA J., «Technical Progress and Early Retirement», *Working Paper*, Series rwp 02-007, Harvard University, John F. Kennedy School of Government, February, 2002.

BARRO R.J. - BECKER G.S., «Fertility Choice in a Model of Economic Growth», *Econometrica*, no. 57(2), 1989, pages 481-501.

BECKER G.S. - BARRO R.J., «Altruism and the Economic Theory of Fertility», *Population and Development Review*, no. 12, 1986, pages 69-76.

BECKER G.S. - MURPHY K.M. - TAMURA R., «Human Capital, Fertility and Economic Growth», *Journal of Political Economy*, no. 98, 1990, pages S12-S37.

CALDWELL J.C., «Toward a Restatement of Demographic Transition Theory», *Population and Development Review*, no. 2 (3/4), 1976, pages 321-366.

COLLARD D., *Altruism and Economy: A Study in Non-Selfish Economics*, Oxford University Press, 1978.

FERNÀNDEZ-VILLAVERDE J., *Was Malthus Right? Economic Growth and Population Dynamics*, University of Pennsylvania, 2001.

GALOR O., «From Stagnation to Growth: Unified Growth Theory», in AGHION P. - DURLAUF S. (eds.), *Handbook of Economic Growth*, 1st edition, vol. 1, Part A, Chapter 04, Elsevier, 2005, pages 171-293.

GALOR O. - TSIDDON D., «Technological Progress, Mobility, and Growth», *American Economic Review*, no. 87(3), 1997, pages 363-382.

GALOR O. - WEIL D.N., «The Gender Gap, Fertility, and Growth», *American Economic Review*, no. 86 (3), 1996, pages 374-387.

-.-,-.-, «Population, Technology, and Growth: From Malthusian Stagnation to the Demographic Transition and Beyond», *American Economic Review*, no. 90(4), 2000, pages 806-828.

GOLDIN C. - KATZ L.F., «The Origins of Technology-Skill Complementary», *Quarterly Journal of Economics*, no. 13(3), 1998, pages 693-732.

JONES C.I., «Was an Industrial Revolution Inevitable? Economic Growth Over the Very Long Run», *Advances in Macroeconomics*, Berkeley Electronic Press, no. 1(02), 2001, pages 1-45.

KARELIS C., *The Persistence of Poverty: Why the Economics of the Well-off Can't Help the Poor*, Yale University Press, 2007.

KULA E., *History of Environmental Economic Thought. Routledge Studies in the History of Economics*, London and New York, Routledge, 1998.

LUCAS R.E., «The Industrial Revolution: Past and Future», in *Lectures on Economic Growth*, Harvard University Press, 2002.

MANKIW N.G., *Macroeconomics*, 7th ed., Worth Publishers, 2010.

MARGOLIS H., *Selfishness, Altruism, and Rationality: A Theory of Social Choice*, The University of Chicago Press, 1982.

MORAND O.F., «Endogenous Fertility, Income Distribution, and Growth», *Journal of Economic Growth*, no. 4(3), 1999, pages 331-349.

MYRSKYLÄ M. - KOHLER H.-P. - BILLARI F.C., «Advances in Development Reverse Fertility Declines», *Nature*, no. 460, 2009, pages 741-743.

PRSKAWETZ A. - STEINMANN G. - FEICHTINGER G., «Human Capital, Technological Progress and the Demographic Transition», *Mathematical Population Studies*, no. 7(4), 2000, pages 343-363.

STRULIK H., «Demographic Transition, Stagnation, and Demoeconomic Cycles in a Model for the Less Developed Economy», *Journal of Macroeconomics*, no. 21(2), April, 1999, pages 397-413.

ZELIZER V.A., *Pricing the Priceless Child: The Changing Social Value of Children*, Princeton University Press, 1985.

Population, Earth Carrying Capacity and Economic Growth

Giovanni Scarano*
University of Rome "Roma Tre"

This paper deals with the interaction between population growth and capital accumulation in an ecological perspective. Some demographic behaviours are modelled taking an ecological economics approach and combining the effects of technical progress geared to prevent decline in the marginal productivity of capital with the logistic growth model. Connection between the biological side and the economic side of the model is achieved by connecting the ecological concept of carrying capacity with that of subsistence, a very "classical" economic concept, strictly consistent with Malthus' original approach. The economic analysis of the model is implemented with a growth accounting approach.
[JEL Classification: Q56, Q57, O41, J10].

Keywords: population growth, carrying capacity, economic growth, subsistence.

* *<scarano@uniroma3.it.>*. The author wishes to thank the anonymous referees for very useful comments and suggestions. The usual disclaimer applies.

1. - Introduction

This paper deals with the relation between economic growth and the earth's carrying capacity for mankind.

During the last few decades economists have almost totally neglected the relation between population and economic growth in a truly Malthusian perspective, that is, focusing on the problem of the population pressure on finite natural resources. Many endogenous growth models have dealt with human capital accumulation, but this is a topic which, even though partially related to such demographic dynamics as that of fertility, concerns above all the supply side of the models and the technical change it entails. Thus, it is quite different from the classical demographic issues, such as population pressure on natural resources and the con-sequent repressive feedbacks.

In the Solow-Swan growth model, an increase in the population growth rate has effects analogous to those deriving from a decrease in the saving rate, reducing the steady state level of output per effective worker, but the fertility and death rates are exogenous, and the population follows an exponential path over time that is not accounted for by the model.

In this context, the principal exceptions can be found in certain empirical studies in development economics and theoretical approaches in environment economics. In both fields, the prevailing approach has substantially been full of doom and gloom. The apparently exponential growth of the world population over the last two centuries has in fact frequently raised neo-Malthusian fears of a near excessive human pressure on the natural resources of the planet (Becker *et* al., 1999).

In 1973, for example, Robert S. McNamara, former World Bank President, declared that «the threat of unmanageable population pressures is very much like the threat of nuclear war. Both threats are undervalued. Both threats are misunderstood. Both threats can and will have catastrophic consequences unless they are dealt rapidly and rationally». This doomster vision is the same we can find associated with the Ehrlich concept of "population bomb". In an ecological perspective, that would mean that the world population is hurtling blindly beyond the earth's *carrying capacity* for mankind, unleashing repressive and possibly catastrophic ecological brakes, such as mass starvation, political chaos and wars. The only survival possibility seemed to be a more reasonable population growth through public population planning, imposed against natural demographic tendencies.

In fact, this reading of the recent demographic trends presents the same faults of the original Malthus theory. Malthus, in fact, set out to utilise a hypothetical natural law to demonstrate, against Godwin and Condorcet, that social progress was unsustainable. Consequently he postulated an intrinsic opposition between a geometrical progression of the population and an arithmetic progression of human subsistence, but neither phenomena were really accounted for, either on the logical or the empirical side. And the contemporary neo-Malthusian authors continue to do so. In fact, their predictions, like Malthus's, have not so far come out in most the countries. As Kuznets observed in 1960, a few years before the explosion of neo-Malthusian literature, «we have not tested, or even approximated, empirical coefficients with which to weigh the various positive or negative aspects of population growth». But the doomster vision still persists despite an ample literature that should induce more cautious positions (Kelley, 1985).

Moreover, in the modern environmentalist literature the relation between human population growth and natural resources has always been analysed only with regard to the impact of the former on the latter. Thus, consideration has frequently been limited only to the repressive effects of finite natural production factors on human population.

In this paper, instead, in line with the results of the endogenous growth literature (Romer, 1986; King and Rebelo, 1990, 1993; Rebelo, 1991; Barro and Sala-i-Martin, 1995), we reaffirm an optimistic technological vision, analyzing the conditions for social material improvements. We propose a way to model how the carrying capacity for mankind can be raised by capital accumulation and technological progress.

The model presented in the following pages thus formalizes some demographic behaviours in biological and ecological terms. Thus, it is not a typical fertility model, like those utilized in the more famous endogenous growth models. With it we only present anew some well-known results of endogenous growth theory in a different theoretical framework, following an ecological economics approach (Costanza, 1989). This means that we set out a basis upon which to combine the effects of technical progress geared to prevent decline in the marginal productivity of capital with a typical model of the ecological sciences, like the logistic growth model. The aim of this operation is to analyse the interaction between population growth and capital accumulation taking an approach consistent with ecological analysis of the relationships between economic growth and the stationary equilibria of the ecosphere. Connection between the biological side and the economic side of the model is achieved simply by connecting the ecological concept of *carrying capacity* with that of *subsistence*, a very "classical" economic concept, strictly consistent with Malthus' original approach. Economic analysis of the model will then be implemented with a simple growth accounting approach.

2. - Population Growth and Earth's Carrying Capacity

The *carrying capacity* of an ecosystem for a living species is normally defined as the maximum number of individuals which the ecosystem can support by means of the resources it generates for them. Indeed, it is a very "Malthusian" concept, even though Malthus never used it explicitly.

Malthus recognised geometric progression as the natural trend of human population growth when it is not braked by land fertility, that is the power of land to generate subsistence for human beings (Malthus, 1970). This concept of "subsistence" is really strictly connected with that of carrying capacity used in modern ecological sciences, because it is related to all the resources necessary for the survival of a given human population.

Without technological progress, in Malthus' analysis there is a limit to the human population level determined by the land productivity or, in a more general sense, by the potential flow of goods and services produced by the ecosystem in each period of time. Human beings can increase the land product by means of their labour, but only with decreasing returns (Malthus, 1970). When the population grows, the product does not grow proportionally, so that *per capita* incomes decrease, cutting down the birthrate and raising the death rate until the growth rate falls to zero. Even though not formalised, the original Malthusian model had a more complex dynamics than its successive mathematical "vulgate".

Today, Malthus's original intuition is always formalised by means of the following differential equation:

$$\frac{dN}{dt} = (b - d)N(t) = nN(t) \tag{1}$$

where:

$N(t)$ is the number of human individuals at time t;
b is birthrate;
d is death rate;
n is population growth rate;

Thus, the time path of population is an exponential function, as follows:

$$N(t) = N(0)e^{nt} \tag{2}$$

The concept of *carrying capacity* was originally introduced by Pierre-François Verhulst, a Belgian mathematician, in 1838, eight years after the last demographic essay by Malthus, to endogenously correct the "Malthusian" exponential model of population growth (Verhlust, 1838). The Verhlust model, also known as *logistic growth model*, shows a positive constant K, referred to as the environmental carrying capacity, which enters into the new function that determines the values of n over time (Clark, 1990):

(3) $$n(t) = n_i\left(1 - \frac{N(t)}{K}\right)$$

where n_i is the *intrinsic growth rate*, that is, the balance of birthrate and death rate, as they are genetically determined, excluding death causes produced by the environment, such as predation, illness, famine, and so on. K is exactly the maximum number of individuals that can survive at each time, given the yearly flows of natural resources, such as food, water, air and so on, provided by the ecosystem in which the population lives.

Thus, the motion equation for population becomes:

(4) $$\frac{dN}{dt} = n_i\left(1 - \frac{N(t)}{K}\right)N(t)$$

The population time path is consequently modified as follows:

(5) $$N(t) = \frac{K}{1 + ce^{-n_i t}}$$

where c is the initial condition:

(6) $$c = \frac{K - N(0)}{N(0)}$$

that is, the potential maximum rate of variation of the population.

From equation *(5)* it follows that:

(7) $$\lim_{t\to\infty} N(t) = K \quad \text{provided that} \quad N(0) > 0$$

This means that K is a stable dynamic equilibrium for the population.

But humanity is a very particular species, because it utilises *production*, which is in fact a specific human way to transform useless things into goods, *i.e.* new objects able to satisfy human needs. Thus, the earth carrying capacity for the human species depends on the features of the production process and consequently on the productivity of labour. The stocks of natural resources can obviously play a role as inputs in the production function, but, within certain limits, they are generally substitutable with other kinds of resources (Solow, 1974*a*, 1974*b*; Romer, 2001).

Most estimations of how many people the earth could support have always undervalued this limit, normally ignoring the extent to which techniques of production can change. Indeed, the production process changes continuously over time, thanks to technological progress, and the necessary resources for human individuals change with it.

In a part of contemporary economic literature – the more environmentalist part – population growth has been always seen as an exponential engine of the human pressure on the environment (Meadows *et* al., 1972; 1992; 2004) and the human population has simply been dealt with like a population of bacteria in a jar with an ample supply of nutrients (Lomborg, 2001). This view simply echoes some of the classical topics treated by Malthus, even though masking them behind the instruments and concepts of the modern theory of dynamic systems. The approach was effectively encapsulated in the famous aggregate index of environmental impact, conceived by Ehrlich in early 1970's (Ehrlich, Holdren, 1970, 1971, 1972), referred to as the IPAT index, an acronym based on the following formula:

$$I = P \times A \times T \qquad (8)$$

where:

I is the value of the impact;

P is the number of individuals of the human population;

A is the *per capita* affluence, measured by the average *per capita* GDP;

T is the total quantity of material and energy needed for the production of each unit of the GDP.

Associated with a Malthusian exponential model of population growth, in the early 1970's this impact index underlay neo-Malthusian fears of a "population bomb" that could only unleash catastrophic ecological brakes. This conclusion rested on two pessimistic assumptions: non operating sociological preventive mechanisms of demographic control and technological pessimism. In this index, indeed, the letter *T* represents *technology*, but, while this word generally means the knowledge existing and utilized in the production process at a certain time, in this equation it is only meant to capture the fact that technological progress often produces new kinds of increasingly complex products, embodying ever more materials and energy, and thereby increasing the human pressure on the natural environment. The fact is ignored that, so far, progress in technology has gone hand in hand with increasing efficiency in using materials and energy, which offsets environmental depletion.

But an enduring exponential population growth, associated with growing *per capita* incomes, only appeared on the stage of history with the industrial revolution, while throughout almost all historical time the world population had only shown minimal increases (Becker *et* al., 1999). Moreover, much of what has occurred since the industrial revolution is substantially inconsistent with the fundamental previsions of Malthusian analysis. So far, indeed, fertility has not continuously increased with *per capita* incomes, but has eventually begun to fall in the most developed countries. Malthusian schemes have been only verified under conditions prevailing in poor and mainly agricultural countries, with limited technical and human capital and rudimentary technology. In other words, the Malthusian model seems to be typical of precapitalistic economies out of equilibrium because of their connections with the world capitalistic market.

Today demographers often explain declining fertility with *demographic transitions*, *i.e.* changes in demographic behaviours associated with social changes in family organization, the labour market, and production structure, ultimately driven by income growth and economic development. But in the basic neoclassical growth model, population is still dealt with as an exogenous engine that produces workers at a given growth rate (Becker *et* al., 1990). So, in the original version of this model, the growth of output per worker will ultimately cease as the economic system reaches a steady state.

In historical experience, on the other hand, this point has been reached by no advanced industrialised country, and, beginning from the industrial revolution, an apparently continuous flow of innovations has increasingly improved the exploitation of natural resources, so that environmental and resource constraints have not so far produced stagnation (Smulders, 1999). According to the Solow-Swan model, this result can only be justified by growing exogenous technical progress.

But there is quite strong historical evidence of a close link between investments in technical capital and technological progress, because new capital goods frequently embody technical change. Since enduring economic growth depends on advances in technological and scientific knowledge, and technical capital embodies both of them, then it is very probable that the former depends mainly on accumulation of the latter.

So as not to converge on a steady state, the neoclassical growth model needs a *Hicks-neutral technical change*, with proportional saving effects on capital and labour for each technique, or a Cobb-Douglas production function with *Harrod-neutral technical change*, which is purely labour augmenting, as in the Solow-Swan model (Foley, Michl, 1999). While the former technical change does not play an important role in most of theoretical models, Harrod-neutrality is equivalent to it only in the Cobb-Douglas family of production functions.

The Classical model of economic growth, albeit not accurately formalised, worked in a different way, illustrating the evident historical tendency of developed economies toward greater mechanization by means the bias of technical change toward labour saving.

But, in every case, the real problem is: what generates technical change? This question has obsessed economists for almost two centuries and is still the source of intellectually stimulating controversies; it is in fact very hard to say anything new about it. In this paper we shall simply select some existing hypothesises which we think can help explain the stylised facts of world population growth.

Usually, the growth of the stock of physical capital stimulates changes in the organization of production and in the productivity of labour. Competing firms have continuously either to invent new products or to introduce new processes and new methods of organizing production to achieve, or at least not lose, advantages over their rivals. Thus, the competition mechanism generates increasing labour productivity as its by-product.

There are two ways to formalise this kind of technical progress in growth models. One deals with it as an externality; that is, as an involuntary by-product of ordinary economic activity. This, for example, is the case of the Arrow model of *learning by doing*. The other way is to consider technical progress as the result of an intentional and financed activity of Research and Development (R&D).

In accordance with this interpretation of technical progress, let us henceforth assume that the increasing efficiency of labour in our growth model is an increasing function of the stock of technical capital.

3. - The Model

If we consider the whole planet as a single ecosystem, we can deal with its *carrying capacity* with reference to the whole of mankind.

For the sake of simplicity, let us adopt an aggregate model of the economy with a single product to describe the worldwide economic system. We can also assume that there is a historically determined level of consumption, which we will call "social subsistence", that grants the reproduction of each individual over time with all his/her social and productive features. Of course, social subsistence does not have to be constant over time. It can in fact vary in accordance with a time function, which we will return to later on.

Then the carrying capacity, understood as the maximum number of social individuals for which social subsistence can be granted, depends on the total quantity of subsistence consumption that production can implement in each period of time, as follows (Scarano, 2008):

$$N_{max} = \frac{C(t)}{c(t)} \tag{9}$$

where:

N_{max} is the *carrying capacity*;
$C(t)$ is the aggregate potential consumption at time t;
$c(t)$ is the function of *per capita* social subsistence at the same moment;

The aggregate potential consumption, in turn, depends on the difference between the aggregate economic output and the aggregate saving:

$$C(t) = Y(t) - S(t) \tag{10}$$

where:

$Y(t)$ is the aggregate economic output at time t;
$S(t)$ is the aggregate saving.

Of course, as usual in aggregate growth models, here we ignore all the problems of coordination, supposing perfect identity between saving and investment.

At each time, given investment decisions and the level of *per capita* social subsistence, the potential consumption function is then a residual flow that determines the potential number of individuals the social system can support with its production capacity and investment plans.

Let us assume that worldwide economic output grows over time because of these investment plans, in accordance with a Solow-Swann growth model.

This kind of growth model is generally assumed to be based on a general-equilibrium structure (Barro, Sala-i-Martin, 1995). But for our task, in a simpler way, the model can also be interpreted as an aggregate representation of a human society with some form of social coordination with regard to different uses of its social product and, in particular, its sharing into consumption and investment. What this form of social coordination might be, whether market clearing or something else, does not matter here.

Now, we can assume that the aggregate economic output is determined by means of a classical Cobb-Douglas production function, as follows:

$$Y(t) = [K(t)]^{\alpha}[A(t)L(t)]^{1-\alpha} \qquad 0 < \alpha < 1 \tag{11}$$

where:

$K(t)$ is the stock of physical capital running at time t;

$A(t)$ is purely labour-augmenting technical progress or the "effectiveness of labour".

$L(t)$ is labour force or the number of workers utilised at time t;

Moreover, we adopt a behavioural approach to specify savings, assuming that a behavioural function exists and has the following standard form:

$$S(t) = sY(t) \tag{12}$$

where s is the average and marginal propensity to save.

Consequently, the equation of motion for capital is:

$$\dot{K}(t) = sY(t) - \delta K(t) \tag{13}$$

where δ is the amortization rate of physical capital.

For the sake of simplicity, henceforth the labour force is assumed to be equal to the world human population:

$$L(t) = N(t) \tag{14}$$

On the basis of the considerations on technical change made in section 2, and in accordance with Kaldor (1957); Arrow (1962) and Romer (1990), we assume that:

- the technical change is a function of accumulation of capital, that is: $A(t)=A[K(t)]$;
- the changing rate of A depends on the motion equation of capital and thus also on the investment share in social product, that is:

$$\frac{\dot{A}(t)}{A(t)} = \frac{A_K}{A(t)}\dot{K}(t) = \frac{A_K}{A(t)}\left[sY(t) - \delta K(t)\right] \tag{15}$$

where A_K is the first derivative of $A(t)$ with respect to $K(t)$

- $A(t)$ grows so rapidly as to offset the capital productivity decrease, that is:

$$\frac{\partial Y(t)}{\partial A(t)}A_K + \frac{\partial^2 Y(t)}{\left[\partial K(t)\right]^2} \geq 0 \tag{16}$$

Now, if we assume that population grows over time in accordance with the logistic model and the concept of carrying capacity we previously proposed, then:

$$N(t) = \frac{C(t)\ /\ c(t)}{1 + qe^{-n_i t}} \tag{17}$$

Where q is the initial condition, which now assume the subsequent form:

$$q = \frac{\left[C(0)\ /\ c\ 0\ \right] - N(0)}{N(0)} \tag{18}$$

In accordance with equation *(17)*, the population growth rate is given by the following expression:

$$n(t) = n_i\left(1 - \frac{N(t)}{C(t)\,/\,c(t)}\right) = n_i\left(1 - \frac{c(t)}{(1-s)y(t)}\right) \tag{19}$$

where $y(t)$ is *per capita* output or the labour productivity.

Consequently, population growth can be greater than zero if, and only if:

$$\frac{(1-s)\,y(t)}{c(t)} > 1 \tag{20}$$

In this model, then, there are two possible kinds of accumulation: capital accumulation, depending on saving, and "worker accumulation", depending on the excess of potential *per capita* consumption over social subsistence. Worker accumulation – population growth, in other words – can be greater than zero if and only if the share of *per capita* product not intended for capital accumulation is greater than the social individual subsistence.

But what are the conditions under which this share of *per capita* product can exceed *per capita* subsistence?

Let us consider the output growth rate, calculated as the total differential of output divided by its level at the time t.

$$g_Y(t) = \frac{\dot{Y}(t)}{Y(t)} = \alpha\frac{\dot{K}(t)}{K(t)} + (1-\alpha)\frac{\dot{L}(t)}{L(t)} + (1-\alpha)\frac{A_K}{A(t)}\dot{K}(t) \tag{21}$$

Considering that:

$$\dot{K}(t) = g_K(t)K(t) \tag{22}$$

where:

$g_K(t)$ is the growth rate of $K(t)$

and performing the appropriate substitutions we have:

$$g_Y(t) = \left[\alpha + (1-\alpha)\frac{A_K}{A(t)}K(t)\right]g_K(t) + (1-\alpha)n(t) \tag{23}$$

Thus, $g_Y(t) > n(t)$ implies that:

$$\left[\alpha + (1-\alpha)\frac{A_K}{A(t)}K(t)\right] g_K(t) > \alpha n(t) \tag{24}$$

Dividing both equation members by α and remembering the exponents of the Cobb-Douglas are interpretable as the elasticities of the output to the inputs, we have:

$$\left[1 + \frac{Y_L(t)L(t)}{Y_K(t)K(t)}\frac{A_K}{A(t)}K(t)\right] g_K(t) > n(t) \tag{25}$$

where:

$Y_L(t)$ is the marginal product of the labour at time t.
$Y_K(t)$ is the marginal product of the capital at time t.

In accordance with *(19)*, $g_Y(t) > n(t)$ implies that

$$\left[1 + \frac{Y_L(t)L(t)}{Y_K(t)K(t)}\frac{A_K}{A(t)}K(t)\right] g_K(t) > n_i \frac{(1-s)y(t) - c(t)}{(1-s)y(t)} \tag{26}$$

This latter condition tells us that, at each point in time, the capital growth rate, plus the percentage increase in the ratio between labour share and capital share of output due to the capital growth rate itself, has to be greater than the product of the intrinsic population growth rate and the percentage of *per capita* output not destined to capital accumulation that exceeds individual subsistence.

Thus, the increase in the effectiveness of labour per unit of capital has to be greater than the decrease in capital productivity in the absence of technical change. This condition is all the truer insofar as technical change is the result of a planned activity in which firms invest and is biased toward labour saving without the interest rate falling as usually happens in capitalistic economic systems.

4. - Fertility Changes and Demographic Transitions

The behaviour of the demographic system in our model is totally parametric, because birthrate and death rate, as well as the growth rate which is their resultant, are dealt with, in analogy with pure ecological models, as biological constants. But in human populations they are a product of social structures as well as biology. That is why demographers deal with them as "behaviours", socially and culturally determined. The death rate is, for example, the result of standards of living and health care. Fertility, in turn, is the result of the family structure, the form of production organization and the sectorial composition of social output. Thus, demographic behaviours could be modelled as mathematical functions of social and economic variables. They can be also modelled as optimizing behaviour, as is the practice with the major economic models of endogenous fertility, but not necessarily. In particular, they could be modelled as functions of *per capita* income to show the phenomenon of demographic transitions, in other words the relative changes in birth and death rates that module the population growth rate during the different phases of economic development.

In all these cases, the human population time path is no longer governed by the difference between the actual population stock and the environmental carrying capacity for it. Population growth can also slow down against an increasing potential carrying capacity. In our model, continuing with a behavioural approach, this feature could be rudimentarily captured by putting *per capita* subsistence as an increasing function of *per capita* income or appropriately modelling the saving rate as a function of time or income. Of course, *per capita* subsistence (consumption) and the saving rate can also be modelled as optimizing behaviours of rational agents (households), as in the major endogenous fertility models (Barro and Becker, 1989; Benhabib and Nishimura, 1989, 1990).

With technical progress inducing constant or increasing returns on the capital, the Euler theorem no longer applies. So, if the population growth rate is other than zero (Bertola, 1993), distributive shares are not constant over time. In optimizing fertility models (Barro and Becker, 1989; Benhabib and Nishimura, 1990), this could induce households to change their fertility choices. In this case, of course, the relationship between population dynamics and economic growth could become more complex, depending on the shape of household utility functions and, in particular, on the structure of household intertemporal preferences.

5. - Conclusions

According to the model illustrated, with technical progress inducing constant or increasing returns on the capital and parametric or hysteretic individual behaviours, the carrying capacity for historically determined mankind can grow over time as economic output does. New goods and services available for new individuals are the result of capital accumulation endogenously producing technological progress and improving the efficiency of labour, along a growth path that can proceed without the brakes of decreasing returns. In this context, a positive population growth rate is the effect of a progressive shifting of the carrying capacity upwards, produced by capital accumulation itself. Under these conditions, an exponential population growth, as experienced over the last two centuries, can be interpreted as the apparent effect of the enlargement of the earth's carrying capacity for mankind produced by the economic growth, and not the exponential engine of a growing human pressure on the natural environment, as some ecologist literature assumes.

Acting so, humanity can progressively increase its *effective environment*, intercepting the flows of materials and energy previously used by other living species or geophysical and geochemical processes, to satisfy its growing social needs. Of course, in a finite world this is not possible for ever. Yet this process could probably still run on for some centuries more, creating the potential conditions to eliminate human misery and improve the living standards of all the human beings, until all the materials and energy of the planet have been utilised to satisfy human needs, or until new kinds of "bads", by-produced in traditional production activities, like pollution, increasingly offset the gains of economic growth. Even in this last case, however, it is possible to imagine production processes oriented to transform "bads" into goods with increasing returns. The real problem, therefore, will very probably be how the wealth produced is used in term of equity.

BIBLIOGRAPHY

ARROW K.J., «The Economic Implications of Learning by Doing», *Review of Economic Studies*, vol. 29, 1962, pages 155-173.

ARROW K.J. - BOLIN B. - COSTANZA R. - DASGUPTA P. - FOLKE C. - HOLLING C. S. - JANSSON B.O. - LEVIN S. - MALER K.G. - PERRINGS C. - THIRD D.P., «Economic Growth, Carrying Capacity and the Environment», *Science*, vol. 268, 1995, pages 520-521.

BARRO R.J. - BECKER G.S., «Fertility Choise in a Model of Economic Growth», *Econometrica*, vol. 57, no. 2, 1989, pages 481-501.

BARRO R.J. - SALA-I-MARTIN X., *Economic Growth*, New York, McGraw-Hill, Inc., 1995.

BECKER G.S. - GLAESER E.L. - MURPHY K. M., «Population and Economic Growth», *American Economic Review*, vol. 89, no. 2, 1999, pages 145-149.

BECKER G.S. - MURPHY K. M. - TAMURA R., «Human Capital, Fertility, and Economic Growth», *Journal of Political Economy*, vol. 98, no. 5, Part. 2, 1990, S12-S37.

BENHABIB J. - NISHIMURA K., «Endogenous Fluctuations in the Barro-Becker Theory of Fertility», in WENIG A. - ZIMMERMANN K.F. (eds.), *Demographic Change and Economic Development*, Berlin, Springer-Verlag, 1989.

-.-,-.-, «Endogenous Fertility and Growth», C.V. Starr, Center for Applied Economics, *Working Papers*, n. 90-20, 1990.

BERTOLA G., «Factor Shares and Savings in Endogenous Growth», *American Economic Review*, vol. 83, no. 5, 1993, pages 1184-1198.

CLARK W.C, *Mathematical Bioeconomics. The Optimal management of Renewable Resources*, New York, John Wiley & Sons, Inc., 1990.

COHEN J.E., *How Many People Can the Earth Support?*, New York, London, Norton & Co., 1995.

COSTANZA R., «What is Ecological Economics?», *Ecological Economics*, vol. 1, no. 1, 1989, pages 1-7.

EHRLICH P. - HOLDREN J., «The People Problem», *Saturday Review*, vol. 4, 1970, pages 42-43.

-.-,-.-, «Impact of Population Growth», *Science*, vol. 171, 1971, pages 1212-1217.

-.-,-.-, «Impact of Population Growth», in RIKER R.G. (ed.), *Population, Resources and the Environment*, Washington DC, US Government Printing Office, 1972, pages 365-377.

FOLEY D.K. - MICHL T.R., *Growth and Distribution*, Cambridge (Mass), London, Harvard University Press, 1999.

KALDOR N., «A Model of Economic Growth», *Economic Journal*, vol. 68, 1957, pages 591-624.

KELLEY A.C., «Population and Development: Controversy and Reconciliation», *Journal of Economic Education*, vol. 16, no. 3, 1985, pages 177-188.

KING R.G. - REBELO S.T, «Public Policy and Economic Growth: Developing Neoclassical Implications», *Journal of Economics*, vol. 98, no. 5, part II, 1990, pages S126-S150.

-.-,-.-, «Transitional Dynamics and Economic Growth in the Neoclassical Model», *American Economic Review*, vol. 83, no. 4, 1993, pages 908-931

KREMER M., «Population Growth and Technological Change: One Million B.C. to 1990», *Quarterly Journal of Economic Education*, vol. 108, no. 3, 1993, pages 681-716.

LOMBORG B., *The Skeptical Environmentalist*, Cambridge (UK), Cambridge University Press, 2001.

LOTKA A.J., *Analytical Theory of Biological Populations*, New York, London, Plenum Press, 1998.

MALTHUS T.R., *An Essay on the Principle of Population*, Baltimore (Md.), Pelican Books, 1970.

MCNAMARA R.S., *One Hundred Countries, Two Billion People: The Dimensions of Development*, London, Pall Mall Press, 1973.

MEADOWS D.H. - MEADOWS D.L. - RANDERS J., *Beyond the Limit. Global Collapse or a Sustainable Future*, London, Earthscan, 1992.

-.-,-.-,-.-, *The Limits to Growth: The 30-Year Update*, White River Junction (VT), Chelsea Green Publishing Co., 2004.

MEADOWS D.H. - MEADOWS D.L. - RANDERS J. - BEHRENS W., *Limits to Growth*, New York, Universe Books, 1972.

REBELO S., «Long-Run Policy Analysis and Long-Run Growth», *Journal of Political Economy*, vol. 99, no. 3, 1991, pages 500-521.

ROMER P.M., «Increasing Returns and Long-Run Growth», *Journal of Political Economy*, vol. 94, no. 5, 1986, pages 1002-1037.

-.-, «Endogenous Technological Change», *Journal of Political Economy*, vol. 98, no. 5, part II, 1990, pages S71-S102.

ROMER D., *Advanced Macroeconomics*, New York, McGraw-Hill Inc., 2001.

SCARANO G., «Capital Accumulation, Technological Progress and Environment», *International Journal of Global Environmental Issues*, vol. 8, no. 4, 2008.

SOLOW R.M., «A Contribution to the Theory of Economic Growth», *Quarterly Journal of Economics*, vol. 70, no. 1, 1956, pages 65-94.

-.-, «The Economics of Resources or the Resources of Economics», *American Economic Review*, vol. 64, no. 2, 1974, pages 1-14.

-.-, «Intergenerational Equity and Exhaustible Resources», *Review of Economic Studies*, vol. 41, 1974, pages 29-45.

SMIL V., «How Many People Can the Earth Feed?», *Population and Development Review*, vol. 20, no. 2, 1994, pages 255-292.

SMULDERS S., «Endogenous Growth Theory and the Environment», in VAN DEN BERGH J. C.J.M. (ed.), *Handbook of Environmental and Resource Economics*, Cheltenham, Northampton (Mass), Edward Elgar, 1999.

VERHLUST P.F., «Notice sur la loi que la population suit dans son accroissement», *Correspondance mathématique et physique*, vol. 10, 1838, pages 113-121.

The Post-Malthusian Moment: Some Responses to Population Explosion in Britain c. 1840

Patrice Bouche*
University of Lille

We deal with the "Post-Malthusian" stage of falling mortality and sustained fertility, from a history of ideas perspective. We argue that minor writings provide an insight into the various shades of contemporary responses to population explosion that paved the way for a subtler understanding of demographic trends. Population literature was not all either pro- or anti-Malthusian: one publication by physician Charles Loudon exemplifies a non-Malthusian panacea *meant to contain population growth. While the British government's response boiled down to pauper management, Loudon and others suggested that fostering the well-being of the masses might help control population growth.*
[JEL Classification: J13].

Keywords: history of ideas, Britain, 19th century, population literature, population explosion, child mortality, natural contraception, poor law reform, labour supply/labour glut, home colonisation, age of marriage, sexual morality, providentialism.

* < *patrice.bouche@univ-lille3.fr*>.

1. - Introduction

Our object is to summarise a selection of intellectual responses formulated at the time of the unfolding in Britain of what we now call the Post-Malthusian period of rapid population increase. By analysing, as it were, some insiders' views of the said stage of demographic evolution, our modest aim is to provide researchers in economic history with a different vantage point, a decentralised point of view from which to look at the range of possible causes and consequences, and indeed of possible construals of the whole phenomenon. We may well judge the proposals made in that period unscientific by modern standards. Written documents from the past may seem valuable to the economic historian only inasmuch as they provide factual indications of states of being relative to a given period. When studying historical trends, however, we will argue that one may turn to accounts and theories worked out at the time when these trends were first identified, if only because, although lacking hindsight, contemporaries did have an instinctive knowledge of some factors obtaining at the time which may elude the historian. Too many authors tried their hand at offering explanations for and remedies to the perceived "redundancy of population" in Great Britain in the early decades of the 19th century, for their writings to be rejected as irrelevant to the ongoing historical investigation into the interaction between demographics and economic progress.

In the first edition of his *Essay*, Malthus had set out to describe the apparently inescapable cycle of relative and localised demographic and economic growth spurts, followed by decline, which has since been called the "Malthusian Trap". Still, it is to be noted that Malthus's main aim in 1798 was to respond to revolutionary writers, and it was in so doing that he *happened* to choose a demographic objection as his line of argument, whereas Edmund Burke[1], for example, had chosen to speak from a constitutional ground. Malthus argued that an "ideal" society would fatally relapse into inequality and misery, because of the demographic pressure resulting from people being able to entertain encouraging prospects for themselves and their progeny. In the process, the clergyman stumbled into a time ripe for demographic disputes, as the decennial census instituted in the United Kingdom in 1801 proved, decade after decade, that population had indeed a tendency to increase. The population of England alone grew from 8.3 million in 1801 to 14.9 million in 1841[2], an arguably arresting 80% hike,

1. BURKE E. (1790).

2. Cf. Facsimiles of Census Returns at *www.histpop.org*

while the tremendous increase experienced in Ireland up to the Great Famine is well-known. This phenomenon led contemporary observers, in the 1830s and 1840s, to a reformulation of Malthus's Law of Population into a question about the collective destiny of a society actually experiencing population explosion.

To these observers, however, what made the population debate urgent was, rather than censuses, such trends as the concentration of masses of poor people in numerous new urban centres (Manchester, Leeds, Glasgow, etc.), and, even more pressingly, the increase in the number of paupers receiving relief funded by parish rates. Indeed, central to the population debate at the time was the fiscal cost of the proletarian poor. The increasing liability represented by the unemployed and unemployable poor on the parish rates levied on middle-class owners in England, had led to the well-known Poor Law Amendment Act of 1834. Under this act, a system of workhouses was to be established to replace traditional "outdoor relief" and make dependency on relief "less eligible" to the poor than the worst-paid job in a given area. After 1834, Parliament went on debating on the implementation of the act, which proved chaotic, and the book which we propose to deal with was written in an attempt to bring a contribution to the debate before new amendments were voted.

One Scottish physician, Charles Loudon, writing from Paris, published in 1842 a lengthy volume in French[3], *Solution du problème de la population et de la subsistance*, to urge that all mothers in Britain should breastfeed their babies consistently for a full three years, as this, according to the author, would delay the next conception, and thus, by spacing out pregnancies by four years – taking into account the then high child mortality levels – would allow for a sufficient decrease in the general rate of procreation.

Such a publication may be seen as quixotic and anecdotal. However, Loudon gave a very detailed, although somewhat desultory account of his personal understanding of the population question, from a spiritual as well as medical and economic point of view. In fact, the physician was not alone in his quest for social harmony: his wife, Margracia Loudon, also authored some now forgotten books, on the highly controversial topics of Corn Law Repeal and Universal Education[4]. Their works, and Charles's *Solution* in particular, are based on a providentialist world-view, and are, as such, striking examples, to the historian of ideas, of the non-dialectical discourses characteristic of individuals seeking reassurance in pe-

3. LOUDON C. (1842), Solution du problème de la population et de la subsistance [Solution of the population and sustenance problem], Hereafter referred to as Solution...

4. LOUDON MRS. [MARGRACIA] (1835) and (1845).

riods of intense change, such as the early 19th century was, as experienced in Britain. Thus, Charles was offering "triennial lactation" as a *panacea*, and without making clear how it should be enforced. He did nonetheless try to delineate a type of demographic regime which he called the "multiplicative state", that may offer a permanent escape from both Malthusian stagnation and population explosion. He also mentioned a number of contemporary writers on the subject, whose own analyses will give us a broader insight into the terms of the debate in that period.

2. - Coming to Terms with the Explosion of Population

The classification of medical endorsements of Malthusianism expounded by Hamlin and Gallagher-Kamper[5] seems to miss such stances as Charles Loudon's. Indeed, despite his philanthropic discourse, Loudon's cannot be labelled as mere "Descriptive Malthusianism", since he did propound a very particular response to population increase. But neither can Loudon be called a "Prescriptive" Malthusian according to the authors, since that would entail an endorsement of Malthus's recommendation of marriage disincentives and the abolition of the Poor Law, whereas Loudon firmly opposed late marriages and sexual abstinence, and was favourable at least to an employer-funded type of poor relief[6].

The whole Malthusian model from its origin has been the butt of abuse because of its avowed political and corollary class bias. Probably the most famous opponent of the Malthusian notion of an imbalance in population numbers about that time was the "Radical Tory" member of Parliament Michael Sadler, who had taken the doctrine to task in his six-volume treatise *The Law of Population* (1830). The geologist and economist George Poulett Scrope was another objector of the «iron necessity and unavoidable natural tendency to deterioration in the condition of the mass of mankind»[7]. Both these writers simply saw an increasing population as a potential source of increased aggregate wealth, provided the people were given the possibility to work themselves into prosperity.

Nevertheless, Loudon does not dwell on these debatable premises, and instead excuses Malthus for having been a "clergyman", rather than a physician[8], which

5. Hamlin C., Gallagher-Kamper K., (2000, pages 115-140, page 117).
6. Loudon C. (1842, page 286).
7. Scrope G.P. (1833, page 455).
8. Loudon C. (1842, page 208).

he thinks accounts for Malthus's inability to come up with an acceptable and above all efficient remedy to the problem that he identified. Loudon's advocacy of a medical response to the perceived uncontrolled increase in population, as well as being characteristic of the 1840s, when the problem posed by mushrooming urban centres began to be tackled in hygienist terms, quite conforms to our modern view of demographics. Where Loudon's considerations do fall short of our scientific expectations, however, is in his reaffirmation of a "providential" design relative to the progress of population. What Loudon meant by "providential" was a course *proposed and planned for* by God, rather than an actual order of things. Malthus's error, Loudon wrote, had consisted in his "mistaking the *possible* for the *natural* increase of man"[9]. In many such humanitarian, or indeed proto-socialist writings of the 1830s and 1840s, indeed, the perceived concomitance of unprecedented economic growth and of mass poverty was described as disharmony (*dissonance*[10]). In a reasoning characteristic of millenarian beliefs, Loudon was indeed distinguishing between a potential for harmony inscribed in (human) nature, and the "perverted" standards irrationally followed by men since time immemorial. This perception entailed, rather than a belief that mankind had fallen from some previous Edenic state, a notion that men had never allowed God's design to be fully realised, through prejudice and an "abuse of free-will".

Charles Loudon wrote in 1842 long developments on what were to him the main causes of present and future rapid population increase. He first dwelt on atrocities committed throughout history, in wars, religious rituals or ancient circus games, thus explaining in his own way how human immorality was responsible for holding population in check, although only partly so, as he added a remark also made by Malthus, on the rapidity with which population would pick up again after wars or epidemics. Loudon then hailed the end of barbarism, in war and as a substitute for government, and the progress of information and exchanges, as a result of technological improvement and territorial expansion. Moreover, he pointed out how, as a consequence of the current population levels, wars would henceforth only have a minor influence on population numbers[11], since wars could then arguably be seen as geographically limited events.

In other words, the advance of civilisation signalled the end of the prevalence of Malthusian "positive checks" on population growth. This, Loudon argued,

9. LOUDON C., (1842, page 209) «Confondant l'accroissement possible avec l'accroissement naturel de l'homme».
10. LOUDON C. (1836, page 208).
11. LOUDON C. (1842, page 59).

had opened the path for a continuing explosion of population, not only in Great Britain or the Western Hemisphere, but also in the whole world:

> we cannot consider the past circumstances of the world, and depend upon experience as upon a guide; I have tried to demonstrate, quite to the contrary, that we have a lot to fear from the rapid increase of population. Millions, or thousands of millions will henceforth be saved, who in the former situation of society would have inexorably perished, or would never have been born.[12]

The conditions for this unprecedented explosion must be expected to last, in view of a consequence of technological improvement emphasised by Loudon: information had been disseminated so widely thanks to the comparative ease with which books and, even more importantly, periodicals were now printed and distributed, that a reversion of world society to the barbarism of earlier periods was no longer possible.[13]

Loudon's warning about the future increase of population up to "*milliards*" may be said to have a less abstract ring to it than other 18th or early 19th century computations about geometrically increasing numbers arranged somewhat compulsively in tables. Loudon's view of mankind's reproductive powers is straightforward, and similar to Malthus's: men, and especially the poor, who make up the majority of the population, had always produced, on the whole, large numbers of children. Infant or child mortality may well remain in future a frequent occurrence: in fact, Loudon does not expect any significant improvement to this, but rather prefers to base his calculations on an average of about two surviving children out of four.

The permanence of this "check" notwithstanding, the decline of other positive checks will necessarily enable more individuals to live so that they reproduce. Loudon's observation is based on the notion, recurrent among early 19th century writers, that morality, humanity and accountable, rather than arbitrary governance, have progressed. We may see this manner of looking at the factors influ-

12. LOUDON C., (1842, page 83)«nous ne pouvons contempler l'état passé du monde, et en appeler à l'expérience comme notre guide; j'ai voulu prouver, au contraire, que nous avons beaucoup à craindre par rapport à l'accroissement rapide de la population. Des millions, des milliards seront désormais sauvés, qui dans l'ancienne situation de la société eussent infailliblement péri, ou n'eussent jamais vu le jour».

13. LOUDON C. (1842, page 75-76).

encing demographics as adding substance to the theoretical exponentiality of the well-publicised doubling of a given population every 25 years under favourable conditions, as observed in North America in the 18th century, which was an example put forward by Malthus as one of the main arguments for his theory.

One of Loudon's more notable remarks on the United States is about the fact that that prosperous country was already under the necessity of founding new colonies, such as Texas[14]. Rather than a sign of self-confidence, this may indeed have been interpreted as a sign of concern about the finiteness, albeit relative, of the country's resources. Then, Loudon goes against the grain of the age when he writes that a time will come when America "closes its ports to newcomers".

Emigration was obviously one of the most frequently advocated remedies for overpopulation, but a domestic alternative was also touted by philanthropists, by the name of "home colonisation". Loudon had previously been a supporter of such policy, as can be seen in his first attempt at publicising triennial lactation, a short pamphlet published in English in 1836. Strikingly enough, the full title of this pamphlet, *The Equilibrium of Population and Sustenance demonstrated; showing, on physiological and statistical grounds, the means of obviating the fears of the late Mr. Malthus and his followers*, indicated an anti-Malthusian orientation. Probably following on his wife's extensive essay in favour of a repeal of the Corn Laws, Charles was adding a proposal to Margracia's piecemeal construction of a more equitable economic system based on free trade. Yet, in a highly polarised debate, Charles's pamphlet was an ambiguous piece: triennial lactation was of course a contraception method, albeit the most "morally" acceptable and "healthiest" one, which clearly made him a supporter of birth control. Still, at the same time, the physician was of opinion with anti-Malthusian economist G. P. Scrope, one of his wife's main inspirations, that there was

> no error in Political Economy so much calculated to retard the progress of civilisation and welfare of the poor, as the idea that population is likely by small allotments of land to increase so much, that not only will the surface of the world be covered with a starving population, but the greatest misery will prevail amongst mankind.[15]

14. LOUDON C. (1842, page 50).
15. LOUDON C. (1836, page 5).

Loudon in 1836 referred, quite lightly we may say, to assertions found in such periodicals as the conservative *Quarterly Review* to the effect that "the resources of mankind for the production of food, in the Western world alone, are such as to meet every possible increase of population, for an indefinite number of ages to come."[16] In agreement with his wife[17], Loudon was thus proposing that the working people should be dealt out plots of land, as a kind of safety net, to work themselves out of need in times of scarce employment. However, another economist, Robert Torrens, had pointed out in 1835 that "home colonisation", if practised on land of poor quality, "instead of counteracting the decline of profits and wages, resulting from the state of foreign trade, [...] would render the rates of wages and profits lower than before".[18]

In his 1842 book, as we have shown, Loudon had stopped sounding confident about the tractability of the population problem. He quoted an anti-Malthusian writer, Archibald Alison, a lawyer and historian, and an exponent of what may be called the "Manifest Destiny" of the Anglo-Saxon race, who had indulged a couple of years before in calculating that Ireland might be made to yield potatoes for 40 million people, and England and Wales for 75 million, emphasising that even then,

> the density of the population in the first view would not exceed that on the margin of the Lake of Zurich, where the comfort and well-being of the peasantry *exceed that of any spot on the habitable globe,* although there is scarcely an *acre and a quarter* to each individual. [19]

But Loudon now rejected this prospect. For one thing, such intensive farming would be, as the modern term goes, unsustainable:

> in order to obtain such a result, it would be necessary not only to slaughter all draft cattle, but also all the animals used for human food; rivers would have to be emptied of fish.[20]

16. LOUDON C. (1836, pages 11-12).
17. LOUDON MRS. [MARGRACIA](1835, chap. XI, pages 175 ff).
18. TORRENS R. (1835, page 250).
19. ALISON A.(1840, pages 480-481).
20. LOUDON C.(1842, pages 11) «pour arriver à un tel résultat, il faudrait non seulement détruire les animaux de trait, mais encore tous ceux qui servent à l'alimentation de l'homme; il faudrait désempoissonner les rivières».

Secondly, Loudon considered that the subdivision of land into individual plots would result in a general impoverishment and the levelling of society, of which he conjured up a nightmarish vision, evidently inspired by the condition of the Irish peasantry at the time:

> No-one who really loves our mother country can accept to see England offer the strange sight of a succession of potato gardens, and our agricultural population forced into direst beggary, [...] no-one can desire to see all families, rich and poor, pent up in huts and cabins, driven into a state of vice and misery horrible to contemplate, even in imagination.[21]

In accordance with a socially conservative argument, most famously illustrated by Mandeville in the "Fable of the Bees", as well as by Malthus, Loudon deemed luxury and rank necessary to the economy, and even to the very preservation of "civilisation". He held primogeniture to be preferable to the French practice, since the Revolution, of sharing land equally among heirs[22].

Alison, and other writers, on the contrary, emphasised the positive effect on the common people of acquiring property, even of a modest value. Alison considered that what he called a "mercantile" (meaning a manufacture and commerce-driven) economy would not secure the prosperity of the working people. Rather, he looked forward to the diffusion of a social order comparable to that he had observed in Switzerland, Flanders, or even France, although in the latter country, he thought taxation too heavy. Property fostered prudence in the workers, as well as a capacity to afford, and a desire to procure a greater variety of articles of consumption. This type of prosperity, far from encouraging procreation, permitted the development of what Alison called "the limitations to the principle of population". It was however essential, for the people to develop prudence, that property and consumption be free from excessive taxation.

Historically, Alison added, wealthy civilisations had always declined into a state of "corruption", and been overrun by purer, nomadic peoples, before they

---

21. LOUDON C. (1842, pages 12) «Non! il n'est aucun de ceux qui aiment véritablement notre mère-patrie qui puisse vouloir que l'Angleterre offre l'étrange spectacle d'une série de jardins de pommes de terre, nos paysans voués à la mendicité la plus déplorable, [...] il n'est personne qui puisse désirer voir toutes les familles riches et pauvres renfermées dans des huttes ou des cabanes, réduites à un état de vice et de misère horrible à contempler, même en imagination».
22. LOUDON C. (1842, pages 273).

ever reached a state in which population outstripped subsistence[23]. This vision was of course reminiscent of that of the Roman Empire, and may seem hardly different from Malthus's pessimistic outlook. Where it did allow Alison to differ from Malthusianism, however, was in making the continuance of a state/civilisation conditional on its ability to prevent "corruption" from setting in, instead of the state having to act against population increase:

> if any state is ever to acquire immortality, it will be from the establishment of those institutions which, by securing in a durable manner the welfare of mankind, supersede the necessity of such violent changes in their number.[24]

This remark may sound rather tautological, unless one considers the optimal state of society to be one of simple but stable prosperity for the masses, with temperance and industriousness, rather than greed and opulence, being the main aims pursued by every individual. Such a society would be incorruptible, both in the moral and in the material senses of the term. This prospect, we may add, could be called the Victorian Project, that is, a collective aspiration, expressed throughout the literature of the period, for general self-reliance and sobriety among all classes.

3. - Towards a "Multiplicative" Society

Loudon subscribed to the Malthusian/Ricardian notion that "labour is dear when it is scarce". We shall nevertheless see later on that his proposal did not entail a drastic reduction of the labour supply. In any case, the physician's and indeed most of his contemporaries' economic understanding of the population problem can be summed up under two heads, namely, national food self-sufficiency (Corn Laws were still applying), and avoiding labour gluts. He hoped the workers may be placed in an advantageous bargaining position in relation to employers[25], which was a characteristic motif of "philanthropic" economic discourse.

However, Loudon did not expect or even wish the working people to control their numbers through sexual abstinence, which Malthus had recommended from 1803, even after declaring in the first edition of his *Essay* that "the passion between

23. ALISON A. (1840, page 470-471).
24. ALISON A. (1840, page 470-472).
25. LOUDON C., (1842, page 287).

the sexes" was to remain invariable. Based on the observation that there was in Britain "more than one instance of ten to twelve-year-old boys having positively cohabited with equally young girls"[26], Loudon was actually recommending that such situations should be institutionalised, and that boys and girls should become engaged between the ages of 7 and 14, and married before 21. This was to secure them from any immoral behaviour, and in particular to prevent girls from falling prey to seducers[27]. Moreover, he considered that the strict application of triennial lactation would result in too large a decrease of population if couples did not have children from an early age[28].

On the other hand, Loudon could not tolerate the idea of "non-conception"[29], although one Malthusian disciple, the master taylor Francis Place, had been so bold as to recommend its practice by the workers as early as 1822[30], through a book, but also "contraceptive handbills" for the information of the working people. The diffusion of contraceptive methods was quite out of the question at the time, given that the moralisation of the new urban crowds was a constant aim of the British middle classes in the 19th century, and that, probably even more potently, English working-class people themselves were quite hostile to the idea of practising contraception, contrary to what appears to have been the case in many areas of France.

Loudon's *panacea* offered the clear advantage of circumventing the thorny question of contraception, while proposing a "natural", indeed a "providential" method of conception avoidance. Yet, given that he had been residing in France for some time, a country which had already started, from the beginning of the 19th century, to experience a decrease in fertility, we may wonder why Loudon paid so little attention to the phenomenon.

Thomas Doubleday, one author whom Loudon debated with through their respective publications, by contrast, proposed the theory, apparently derived from the French socialist writer Charles Fourier, that men's fertility decreased as they became better-fed, and *vice versa*. The British workers' diet was compared unfavourably in particular with the French people's diet, which Doubleday said was

26. LOUDON C. (1842, pages 206) «plus d'un exemple de garçons de dix et de douze ans qui ont positivement vécu en concubinage avec des filles également jeunes».
27. LOUDON C. (1842, page 186).
28. LOUDON C.(1842, page 205).
29. LOUDON C.(1842, page 122).
30. PLACE F. (1822, chap. VI).

more varied and richer in animal products. The Malthusian principle that this theory refuted most frontally was the positive relationship between income *per capita* and population growth. Doubleday stated that

> whenever a species or genus is endangered, a corresponding effort is invariably made by nature for its preservation and continuance, by an increase of fecundity or fertility; and that this especially takes place whenever such danger arises from a diminution of proper nourishment or food, so that consequently the state of depletion, or the deplethoric state, is favourable to fertility, and that on the other hand, the plethoric state, or state of repletion, is unfavourable to fertility [...].[31]

The explosion of population, according to Doubleday, who was a disciple of the radical and violently anti-Malthusian writer William Cobbett, was caused by the fact that «Manifesting as [England] does all the signs of external wealth and power, [...] the condition of the majority of the English people has, for a series of years, been deteriorating and still continues to deteriorate».[32] We may argue that, although Doubleday's theory seems to point, at least metaphorically speaking, to the modern notion of demographic transition, Loudon's insistence on the care to be devoted to existing individuals, seems to be more to the point regarding the economic value of the individual.

However, Loudon could only explain away the higher rate of increase in "England and Ireland" than in France, by England's milder climate and island position, its higher medical proficiency, its wealth from colonies, more efficient agriculture and earlier marriages[33]. While some of these elements might have been accurate explanations, there remained the case of the Irish, who, as an allegedly exploited population, had demonstrated a tremendous growth rate since the late 18th century. Indeed, Archibald Alison had seen Ireland as the clearest case against the application of Malthusian preventive checks:

> The system of repressing the numbers of the poor by depriving them of relief, has there been tried to its *fullest extent;* for centuries, misery and want have stalked through the land; and the redundancy of the people, as well

31. DOUBLEDAY T. (1843, pages 5-6).
32. DOUBLEDAY T. (1843, pages 98-99).
33. LOUDON C. (1842, pages 267-268).

> as the density of the population, are in consequence now greater than in any country of the world.[34]

The problem posed by the high fertility rate observed in Britain in the early 19th century was obviously compounded by its limited area and the comparatively mediocre fertility of its land, which at the time was the subject of an intense and highly polarised debate between partisans and adversaries of free trade. Although his wife had actually published one of the earliest full-length popular economics books on the subject in 1835, *Philanthropic Economy*, in which she launched a relentless attack against protectionist landowners, Charles Loudon for his part declined to express an opinion on the Corn Laws[35]. At the same time, however, he made it clear that he considered that Britain could not feed more than one-third more people "with ease"[36]. He added that this limit might probably be reached very soon, namely, within 45 years from 1842[37]. What has since been termed replacement rates were so high, he said, as to nullify the effect of emigration: the masses leaving Europe «in one year or even one century were like a mere drop trickling from the pool of population»[38]. The continuous increase of the British population throughout the 19th century, in spite of the unabated flow of emigrants leaving the country during the same period, have since proved such a view to be correct.

Thus, although we may at first have seen Loudon's contribution to the Malthus debate as simplistic and panacean, we now perceive that his was not an overly optimistic view of the problem. When summarising Loudon's objections to both the Malthusian and anti-Malthusian parties, we find that, with emigration and home colonisation ineffective to quell population growth, Britain was labouring under several obstacles to a harmonious socio-economic development, meaning, in the physician's words, a situation of "equilibrium between population and subsistence"[39]. Again, Loudon does not seem to have laid as much hope as his wife on the prospect of the freeing of the corn trade, which in any case was not effective until 1846, and which was supposed to allow Britain to live more com-

---

34. ALISON A. (1840, page 214).
35. LOUDON C. (1842, page 287).
36. LOUDON C. (1842, page 289).
37. LOUDON C. (1842, page 11).
38. LOUDON C. (1842, page 49).
39. LOUDON C. (1842, pages 52).

pletely off its manufacturing production, in an international environment oddly envisaged as non-competitive.

Charles Loudon had been one of the medical inspectors who contributed to the 1833 Report on factory children. He was not an adversary of the "manufacturing system" *per se*, and had mostly recommended that children under 14 should not work more than 10 hours a day[40], as well as hygienic improvements to factory buildings. As a philanthropically-minded physician, Loudon did not consider that the condition of factory workers improved naturally with the growth of industry. Indeed, he pointed out how women in Manchester, as they were working from early till late, and coming home exhausted, were unable to breast-feed their children[41]. One of the main principles of harmonious demographic growth according to Loudon was to preserve those human beings who were already living, rather than aim for a "multiplicity of births"[42]. Prolonged breast-feeding would not only act as a natural contraceptive method. It would, perhaps more importantly, work as a cheap method for improving children's – and, ultimately, every individual's – health in the whole society. Here, Loudon was recommending, first, from a medical point of view, that quality be substituted for quantity.

Loudon, moreover, pointed out that devoting more time and care to each child made more sense from a macroeconomic point of view than allowing population numbers to balance out through child mortality[43]. The physician evaluated the net loss incurred by the country from child mortality as "at least 4 or 5 million sterling pounds"[44]. This was taking into consideration that about one third, out of one million children born annually in the United Kingdom, died before they could start to earn their living, and, as it were, make up for the money and time expended on their raising.

Loudon called the more balanced demographic regime that society ought to aim for, the "Multiplicative State", from the 18th century mercantilist economist James Steuart's remarks on the subject of population, which in fact anticipated the gist of Malthus's *Essay* by thirty years. Steuart divided

40. *Second Report of the Central Board of His Majesty's Commissioners for inquiring into the Employment of Children in Factories,* 1833, C3, page 24.

41. LOUDON C. (1842, page 144).

42. LOUDON C. (1842, page 188) «ce n'est point la multiplicité des naissances que nous devons avoir en vue, mais la conservation des êtres humains déjà existants».

43. LOUDON C. (1842, pages 276-277).

44. LOUDON C. (1842, page 328).

> propagation into two branches, to wit, multiplication, which goes on among those who can feed what they breed, and mere procreation, which takes place among those who cannot maintain their offspring.[45]

As we have seen, Loudon further defined the nefarious "Procreative State" as that in which women had no control over the number of children they produced, or indeed over the time when they fell pregnant, and too often had children from much older, or licentious men. The triennial lactation *panacea*, combined with early marriages of young men and women of equal age, would result in spaced out pregnancies, children not being left to fend for themselves before they were of working age, as well as older people being able to depend on a larger group of (potentially) employed adults in every extended family. The combination of high fertility and declining mortality characterising early 19th century England would thus (in time) give way to medium (though constant) fertility and low to medium mortality rates (given that the population would be healthier, but comparatively older). At least that is how we may interpret Loudon's explanation of his system:

> A multiplicative state may never have existed in the world, or perchance approximately : […] A multiplicative state will be composed, instead of a larger number of children, of a majority of adults. A multiplicative society is necessarily the providential course of our existence, because means of subsistence will precede households.[46]

Rather than reducing the labour supply, then, Loudon pointed the way forward as being a *more productive* instead of a procreative population, since "adults make up the real force and wealth of a country"[47]. Contrary to what many anti-Malthusian writers seemed to assume, Loudon said, large numbers of people did not automatically equal wealth, because children, even though they may have been employed from an early age, were not as productive as fully-grown – and

45. STEUVART J. (1805, page 208).

46. LOUDON C, (1842, page 244) «Un état multiplicatif n'a pas peut-être existé dans le monde, ou du moins approximativement :[…] Un état multiplicatif sera composé, au lieu d'un plus grand nombre d'enfants, d'une majorité d'adultes. Une société multiplicative est nécessairement le cours providentiel de notre existence, parce que les moyens de subsistance précéderont les ménages».

47. LOUDON C. (1842, page 286) «ces adultes constituent réellement la force et la richesse d'un pays».

healthy – adults. On the other hand, Loudon was quite aware that such a demographic regime would not solve definitively, or at all, the cyclical disproportion between labour supply and demand. Thus, he added yet another element to his system, by asserting the need for the labour market to be regulated as by an "association" or a "mutual insurance company", run by the "masses" under the supervision of certain "persons", so that every worker should know what vocation to pursue[48]. Although Loudon does not quote from Steuart on this topic, we may note the economist's remark to the same effect:

> if it be the duty of a statesman to keep all his people busy, he certainly should acquire the most exact knowledge possible of the numbers and propagation of those of every denomination, that he may prevent any class from rising above or sinking below the standard, which is best proportioned to the demand for their respective industry.[49]

The working of this mechanism, even though parallels may be made with proto- or modern socialist writers, does not seem to have been envisaged as heavily bureaucratic by Loudon. Besides, he argued that its cost had to be balanced against the losses constantly incurred under existing conditions:

> in a multiplicative society, the expense will be quite less than that made in the current procreative society, that is, because of the enormous mortality of children and adolescents before they reach their twelfth or fourteenth year.[50]

Thus, Loudon's *panacea* would not work out by itself, which doubtlessly is to us more rational. When describing all such attempts as Loudon's at responding to the perceived excessive population increase, we may in fact refer loosely to the modern term of "demographic engineering", in the sense that the bulk of the working population was conceived of as an adjustable quantity. The implementation of Loudon's proposal would have involved just as regimental a method as Malthus's recommendation of late marriages. Indeed, Loudon emphasised that

48. Loudon C. (1842, pages 327-328).
49. Steuart J. (1805, page 209).
50. Loudon C. (1842, page 327) «dans une société multiplicative la dépense sera bien au dessous de celle perdue dans la société procréative actuelle, je veux dire par la mortalité énorme d'enfants et d'adolescents avant qu'ils n'arrivent à leur douzième ou quatorzième année».

population should continue to increase excessively if the early marriages which he recommended failed to be combined with strict triennial lactation, or, conversely, that population might shrink just as excessively, should the effect of triennial lactation not be compensated by early marriages[51]. Loudon's perception of the thin limit between growth and decline, however, may have been quite lucid. On the other hand, Loudon was not wishing for such an ambitious goal as the British population becoming stationary. In fact this would have been a mixed blessing only, as it might have undermined Britain's ascendancy especially as compared with the fast-growing United States [52].

4. - Conclusion

Such incidental writers as Loudon may well be said to hold the mirror to subsequent historians, by not only providing interpretations of trends, but above all, by putting forward "remedies", that is, non-dialectic proposals as to how possibly damaging trends may be reversed. Indeed, their providentialism may be taken as a warning against the temptations of historical determinism, which lurk, in particular, behind such periodisation as the notion of "Industrial Revolution". What makes Loudon's contribution non-dialectic mainly is his vague suggestion that triennial lactation should be diffused through the "moral influence" of physicians or clergymen[53]. Notwithstanding, we hope to have shown that Loudon sensed that his *panacea* would only ever have a limited effect. Besides, his comparative avoidance of an overbearing tone, so common in the authors of books expounding "Principles", or "Laws", or "Solutions", and even the rather desultory structure of the volume, may be said to demonstrate Loudon's awareness of the multiplicity and interrelatedness of factors at play in demographic evolution.

---

51. LOUDON C. (1842, page 205).
52. LOUDON C. (1842, page 289).
53. LOUDON C. (1842, page 298).

BIBLIOGRAPHY

ALISON A., *The Principles of Population and their Connection with Human Happiness*, London, Cadell, vol. II, 1840.

BURKE E., *Reflections on the Revolution in France*, 1790.

DOUBLEDAY T., *The True Law of Population, Shewn to be Connected with the Food of the People*, London, Effingham Wilson, 2nd ed., (1841) 1843.

HAMLIN C. - GALLAGHER-KAMPER K., «Malthus and the Doctors: Political Economy, Medicine, and the State in England, Ireland, and Scotland, 1800-1840», in *Malthus, Medicine, and Morality: "Malthusianism" after 1798*, ed. Brian Dolan, Amsterdam, Rodopi, 2000, pages 115-140, page 117.

LOUDON C., *The Equilibrium of Population and Sustenance Demonstrated; Showing, on Physiological and Statistical Grounds, the Means of Obviating the Fears of the Late Mr. Malthus and his Followers*, Leamington Spa, no. 15, 1836.

-.-, *Solution du problème de la population et de la subsistance*, Paris, Galignani, 1842.

LOUDON MRS. [MARGRACIA], *Philanthropic Economy, or The Philosophy of Happiness, Practically Applied to the Social, Political, and Commercial Relations of Great Britain*, London, Churton, 1835.

-.-, *The Light of Mental Science, Being an Essay on Moral Training*, London, Smith, 1845.

PLACE F., *Illustration on Proofs of the Principles of Populations*, ch. VI, 1822.

SADLER M., *The Law of Population*, London, Murray, 1830.

SCROPE G.P., *Principles of Political Economy, Deduced from the Natural Laws of Social Welfare, and Applied to the Present State of Britain*, London, Longman, 1833.

Second Report of the Central Board of His Majesty's Commissioners for inquiring into the Employment of Children in Factories, C3, 1833, page 24.

STEUART J., *The Works, Political, Metaphysical, and Chronological, of the Late Sir James Steuart*, vol. 1, London, Cadell, 1805.

TORRENS R., *Colonization of South Australia*, London, Longman, 1835.

Index

GPSR Compliance
The European Union's (EU) General Product Safety Regulation (GPSR) is a set of rules that requires consumer products to be safe and our obligations to ensure this.

If you have any concerns about our products, you can contact us on

ProductSafety@springernature.com

In case Publisher is established outside the EU, the EU authorized representative is:

Springer Nature Customer Service Center GmbH
Europaplatz 3
69115 Heidelberg, Germany

www.ingramcontent.com/pod-product-compliance
Ingram Content Group UK Ltd.
Pitfield, Milton Keynes, MK11 3LW, UK
UKHW021045050925
462611UK00013B/1397
* 9 7 8 1 3 4 9 3 5 1 9 7 8 *